The Shoe in Sport

The Shoe in Sport

Supported by the Orthopedic/Traumatologic Society for Sports Medicine

Edited by

Dr. med. B. Segesser

Prof. Dr. med. W. Pförringer
In collaboration with Drs. E. Stüssi and
A. Stacoff

Translated by

Thomas J. DeKornfeld, M.D.

YEAR BOOK MEDICAL PUBLISHERS, INC.
CHICAGO • BOCA RATON

WOLFE PUBLISHING, LTD.
LONDON

Published in the United Kingdom by Wolfe Publishing, Ltd., 2–16 Torrington Place, London WC1E 7LT, England.

This book is an authorized translation from the original German edition published and copyrighted in 1987 by perimed-Fachbuch Verlagsgesellschaft mbH, Erlangen, West Germany. Title of the German edition: *Der Schuh im Sport*.

1 2 3 4 5 6 7 8 9 0 KC 93 92 91 90 89

Library of Congress Cataloging-in-Publication Data
Schuh im Sport. English.
    The Shoe in sport / edited by B. Segesser, W. Pförringer in collaboration with E. Stüssi and A. Stacoff; translated by Thomas J. DeKornfeld.
        p. cm.
    Translation of: Der Schuh im Sport.
    Bibliography: p.
    Includes index.
    ISBN 0-8151-7814-X
    1. Athletic shoes—Health aspects. 2. Foot—wounds and injuries—Prevention. I. Segesser, B.
II. Pförringer, W. III. Title.
RD757.S45S313 1989   89-5284
617'.585—dc19   CIP
United Kingdom ISBN: 0-7234-1514-5

Sponsoring Editor: Linda A. Pierpoint
Associate Managing Editor, Manuscript Services: Deborah Thorp
Production Project Manager: Carol A. Reynolds
Proofroom Manager: Shirley Taylor

CONTRIBUTORS

H. A. Bahlsen
Biomechanics Laboratory
University of Calgary
Calgary, Alberta, Canada

Dr. med. H.-W. Bär
Orthopedics-Sportsmedicine
Member of GOTS*
Murnau, West Germany

Dr. med. N.-L. Becker
Orthopedic Surgeon
Tübingen, West Germany

Prof. Dr. med. G. Biehl
Member of GOTS*
Chief, Division of Orthopedics
Köln, West Germany

Dr. F. Bodem
University Orthopedic Clinic
Mainz, West Germany

Dr. med. X. Bonefeld
Bergische University
Gesamthochschule Wuppertal
Wuppertal, West Germany

Prof. Dr. med. F. Brussatis
University Orthopedic Clinic
Mainz, West Germany

Prof. P. R. Cavanagh
Director, Center for Locomotion Studies
Pennsylvania State University
University Park, Pennsylvania

Dr. med. N. Czuik
Bergische University
Gesamthochschule Wuppertal
Wuppertal, West Germany

Dr. J. Denoth
Biomechanical Laboratory ETH
Zürich, Switzerland

Prof. Dr. med. W. Diebschlag
Institute for Work Physiology
Technical University
Munich, West Germany

Dr. med. T. Engels-Zewko
Stuttgart Sports Clinic
Stuttgart, West Germany

Dr. E. C. Frederick
President, Exeter Research Inc.
Brentwood, New Hampshire

Prof. Dr. med. D. Gebauer
State Orthopedic Clinic
Munich, West Germany

Dr. med. K. H. Graff
Division of Orthopedics
Alfried-Krupp Hospital
Essen, West Germany

Dr. W. Hauser
Member of GOTS*
Technical Surveillance Association
Munich, West Germany

F. Heidinger
Institute for Work-Physiology
Technical University
Munich, West Germany

Prof. Dr. med. H. Hess
President of GOTS*
Chief, Division of Orthopedics
St. Elisabeth Clinic
Saarlouis, West Germany

Dr. med. J. Holder
Maingau Hospital
Frankfurt/Main, West Germany

X. Kaelin
Biomechanical Laboratory ETH
Zürich, Switzerland

*Gesellschaft fur orthopädisch-traumatologische Sportmedizin (Society for Orthopedic/Traumatologic Sports Medicine).

Prof. Dr. med. H. Krahl
Member of GOTS*
Chief, Division of Orthopedics
Alfried-Krupp Hospital
Essen, West Germany

Assoc. Prof. Dr. med. K. Liebig
Chief of Orthopedics
University Clinic
Waldkrankenhaus St. Marien
Erlangen, West Germany

Dr. S. M. Lüthi
Biomechanical Laboratory ETH
Zürich, Switzerland

Dr. med. B. Marti
Institute for Social and Preventive
   Medicine
University of Bern
Bern, Switzerland

Dr. med. M. Masson
Chief, Orthopedic Division
St. Elisabeth Clinic
Saarlouis, West Germany

Dr. med. W. Menke
University Orthopedic Clinic
Mainz, West Germany

Dr. med W.-D. Montag
Orthopedic Surgeon
Member of GOTS*
Weilheim, West Germany

Prof. Dr. B. M. Nigg
Member of GOTS*
Biomechanics Laboratory
University of Calgary
Calgary, Alberta, Canada

Prof. Dr. M. Pfeiffer
Institute for the Athletic Sciences
University of Salzburg
Salzburg, Austria

Prof. Dr. med. W. Pförringer
Member of GOTS*
State Orthopedic Clinic
Munich, West Germany

Prof. Dr. med. B. Rosemeyer
Member of GOTS*
State Orthopedic Clinic
Physician-in-Chief
Munich, West Germany

Dr. med. J. Runzheimer
Specialist in Orthopedics and
   Sportsmedicine
Maingau Hospital
Frankfurt/Main, West Germany

P. Schaff
Technical Surveillance Association
Munich, West Germany

Dr. med. B. Segesser
Member of GOTS*
Rennbahn Clinic for Orthopedics and
   Sportsmedicine
Zürich, Switzerland

A. Stacoff
Biomechanical Laboratory ETH
Zürich, Switzerland

Prof. Dr. med. K. Steinbrück
Member of GOTS*
Physician-in-Chief
Stuttgart Sports Clinic
Stuttgart, West Germany

Dr. E. Stüssi
Member of GOTS*
Chief, Biomechanical Laboratory ETH
Zürich, Switzerland

Dr. med. A. Thiel
Member of GOTS*
Chief Orthopedic Division
Hellersen Hospital for Sports Injuries
Ludenscheid, West Germany

Dr. V. Tiegermann
Biomechanical Laboratory ETH
Zürich, Switzerland

Dr. med. W. Treibel
Munich, West Germany

Dr. A. Vogel
Ski Research Syndicate
Fachhochschule München
Munich, West Germany

Dr. med. R. Volkert
University Orthopedic Clinic
Mainz, West Germany

Dr. med. K. Wietfeld
Orthopedics, Sportsmedicine and
   Physical Therapy
Clinic am Burggraben
Bad Salzuflen, West Germany

Prof. Dr. D. Winklmair
Syndicate for Testing
   and Metrology
Fachhochschule München
Wörthsee, West Germany

As humans evolved, the shoe became the point of contact and buffer between man and the hard surface of the earth. This relationship has become extremely important in athletic performance. The call for improved performance significantly affected the entire world of athletes—both in the area of training and in the area of equipment technology. The shoe affects the athlete's performance and serves to support the foot as a tool, as a shock absorber, and as a launching pad.

Is there really a need for shoes? The examples of athletes like Zola Budd (Fig 1) and Abebe Bikila suggest that in a technologic environment the evolution of the athletic shoe parallels the decline of our organs of locomotion.

Giving serious consideration to our organs of locomotion opens up an enormous area of activity to the athletic shoe industry. It has to meet the needs of the championship athlete as well as those of the everyday athlete, in all areas of athletic activity. Thousands upon thousands are joining the ever-expanding rank of runners. Today we need athletic shoes for all age groups and for widely varying requirements.

The buyers of athletic shoes are always looking for the "ideal shoe" (Fig 2). They encounter a bewildering variety of options and are largely dependent for information on the more or less aggressive sales pitches that are directed at all athletes in all possible ways. The advertising campaigns increasingly include scientific findings that indicate that the manufacturers of athletic shoes rely not

FIG 1.

FIG 2.

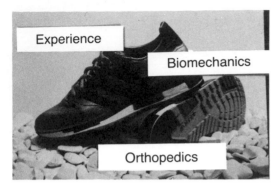

FIG 3.

only on past experience, but also on the results of sports-oriented scientific research in the development of their products (Fig 3).

This volume should assist in defining the role and the contributions of science in the further development of the athletic shoe and in recognizing the contributions made by the various research groups, who are all interested in the problems of the athletic shoe.

Less attention will be paid to the technical and material aspects of the running surface and the shoe, and more to the medical and orthopedic criteria for the athletic shoe. For this reason, the "shoe problem," as it exists in the various fields of athletic endeavor, will be studied with respect to the biomechanical, medical, and technical aspects of shoemaking. The findings should enable the interested reader to distinguish between hucksterism and humbug on the one side and the scientifically sound improvements in the athletic shoe on the other.

The undiminished interest in the problems of the athletic shoe is a clear indication for the appropriateness and timeliness of this volume. We are indebted to the authors of the various chapters for the opportunity to explore new, international areas of activity. We are particularly indebted to our two colleagues, Drs. Jenoure and Feinstein, whose hard work made the publication of this volume possible. We also wish to express our deep appreciation to Dr. Segesser's secretary, Ursula Wehrli, and to Messrs. Peter Michel and Alex Stacoff who helped in the shaping and revision of the manuscript.

Dr. med. B. Segesser
Prof. Dr. med. W. Pförringer

CONTENTS

PART 1 _____ The Running Shoe

1.

The Biomechanics of Running and Running Shoe Problems

P.R. Cavanagh*

From a historical perspective, running is the most important physical activity. It was a significant contributor to human evolution. As a form of athletic activity, the foot races were the cornerstone of the ancient games, and they were also the central theme of discussions when the revival of the Olympic Games was being considered in 1897. At the present time, running plays an important role in all programs to promote fitness and health in both the United States and Europe.

Interest in running continues to grow. The celebrated Boston Marathon never had more than 300 starters between the years 1897 and 1964. There was a dramatic increase in participants during the 1970s.

Even though this increase has not been sustained, it is estimated that between 20 and 35 million people engage regularly in some running activity in the United States. It is generally assumed that the victory of Frank Shorter in the marathon at the 1972 Munich Olympic Games was the catalyst for the increasing popularity of running sports in the United States.

The development of the science of sports biomechanics kept pace with the enormous increase in the popularity of running. Membership in the International Society of Biomechanics has increased steadily since its organization in 1968. This parallel development readily explains why sport biomechanics scientists turned their attention to the running shoe.

Early running shoes, like the ones from the United States illustrated in Figure 1–1, were little more than slightly modified regular footwear. The current situation is dramatically different. There are presently at least 200 different kinds of running shoes available, incorporating every conceivable innovation. Not all of these innovations are based on scientific studies. Many of them were the result of the practical experiences of coaches and shoe designers. It was only in the last decade that scientific investigations began to make an impact on the evolution of the running shoe.

*The author wishes to thank the PUMA Corp. for support of this study.

3

FIG 1–1.
Running shoes from 1912.

This chapter will present some of the results of the biomechanical experiments conducted on long distance running that were important in the design of the running shoe. A discussion of the kinematics of the foot and of the shoe are included, as well as of the experiments designed to determine the center of pressure path and the resulting forces under the shoe. The most recent studies on the measurement of pressure distribution under the human foot are also presented.

KINEMATICS

When we look at the foot of the runner at the moment of touchdown, it seems at times as though the foot moves backward relative to the running surface. Experiments have shown that this, in fact, is not the case. As shown in Figure 1–2, the average horizontal, forward direction heel velocity vector was approximately 1 m/second in a group of ten test subjects. None of the experimental subjects demonstrated either a zero forward velocity or a retrograde velocity vector at the moment of touchdown. These findings serve to explain why the running shoes wear out most rapidly in the region of first ground contact. The wear is caused by the large amount of friction movement between the shoe and the ground and not by the large vertical forces. Direct methods, e.g., force and pressure measurements, have shown that normally the first contact with the ground takes place at the lateral edge of the shoe.

The pattern of movements preceding ground contact was studied by Nigg et al.,[15] Bates et al.,[1] and Clarke et al.[7, 8] Since the leg maintains a fairly constant angle in relation to the frontal plane, there has to be pronation at the subtalar joint. The typical motion sequence is as follows: first there is contact between the ground and the lateral edge of the shoe, and then the movement at the subtalar joint brings the entire plantar surface of the shoe in contact with the ground. During this period, the leg maintains its position. Scientists,

physicians, and shoe manufacturers occasionally suggest that pronation is harmful to the runner. This is certainly not correct. A certain amount of pronation is essential, and it is only excessive pronation that may result in lower extremity injury. In these cases, particular attention must be devoted to the special requirements of the footwear used by these runners. There is a whole generation of running shoes on the market today equipped with antipronation devices that help to keep excessive pronation to a minimum.

Experiments in which Steinmann pins were placed into the lower extremity to accurately measure joint displacement have demonstrated that even significant changes in the movements of the subtalar joint had little effect on the movement in the patellofemoral joint.[13]

The movements of the shoe during the terminal phase of ground contact have received little attention to date, since it is assumed that the shoe is not moving at all at that point in time. Depending on the amount of

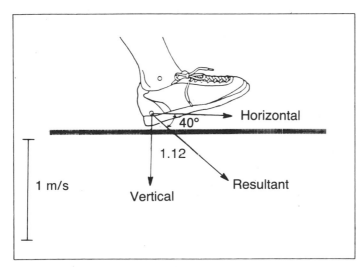

FIG 1–2.
Velocity components on ground contact.

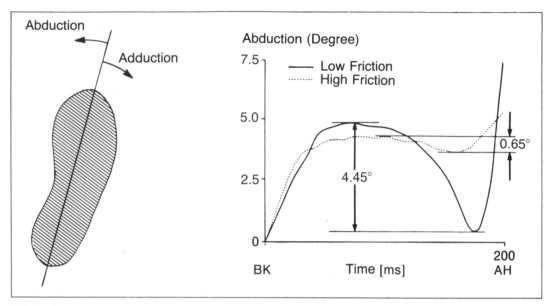

FIG 1–3.
Rotational tendency on ground contact. BK=ground contact; AH=lift off.

friction between the shoe and the ground, there can be up to a 5-degree abduction of the foot that can be seen just before the foot is lifted off the ground (Fig 1–3). There is a rotational momentum even if the friction is great enough to prevent most of the abduction. In such a case, the runner will have the tendency to rotate the upper part of the shoe in relation to the sole.[12]

THE GROUND REACTION FORCES

A force platform permits the determination of the center of pressure path underneath the shoe. Even though these values are of a somewhat general nature, they do permit a classification of the running style of an individual. Figure 1–4 shows three ground reaction force curves obtained from three different runners all

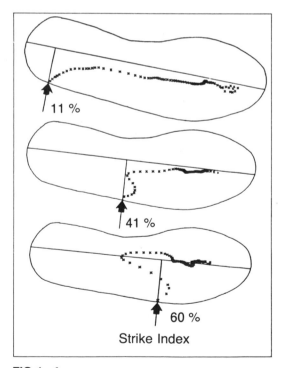

FIG 1–4.
Center of pressure patterns: Three runners with matched running speeds.

running at the same speed. We have developed a "strike index" according to which a value of zero is assigned to an initial contact with the back end of the heel and value of 100 to initial contact with the most anterior part of the shoe. The three runners from Figure 1−4 can be characterized as heel strikers, midfoot strikers and forefoot strikers. The different types of running naturally place different requirements on the running shoes. This becomes even more obvious when we examine the pressure values and the force values.

The typical forces generated under a running shoe, at a speed of 3.5 m/sec, are shown in Figure 1−5.[4] In the case of the heel striker, the ground reaction force curve shows an initial peak, followed by a secondary, more slowly rising peak. It should be noted that the first peak is absent in the midfoot runner. Nigg et al.[15] have characterized the first peak as a passive one and the second peak as an active one.

The values in Figure 1−5 have no dimensions since they were obtained by using the body weight of the subject as the divisor. It can be seen that forces equivalent to at least three times the body weight are generated under the foot. Running style−dependent variations can be observed relative to the anteriorforce components. In the heel runner, there is a single peak of about half the body weight during the braking phase. In contrast, there are two peaks in the midfoot and forefoot runners. Occasionally, double peaks can also be seen in a hindfoot striker.

When high-speed motion pictures

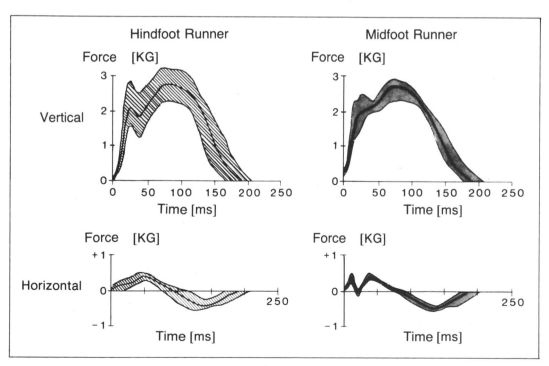

FIG 1−5.
Ground reaction forces.

taken in the sagittal plane of a mid-foot or forefoot striker are analyzed, it often appears that, in a level run, the heel does not touch the ground at all. Thus the entire ground contact phase is under the control of the posterior muscles of the leg.

The center of pressure path and the ground reaction forces can be melded into a single display, as shown in Figure 1–6. In this representation, one must imagine that one sees the foot of the runner from below and from the side while the runner moves from left to right. The line below the shoe represents the magnitude and direction of the force vector. Its point of origin is the central point of the pressure. Considerable variations can be observed when the same shoe is worn by different runners.

When detailed studies are performed on individual athletes, it is well to remember that very different load patterns may appear below the runner's left and right foot. Two examples are shown in Figures 1–7 and 1–8. Both were obtained from runners who participated in the 10,000 m race at the Los Angeles Olympics. The data were obtained at racing speeds, i.e., at approximately 6 m/second.

In athlete A, the peak values are of approximately the same magnitude, but there is a difference in the center of pressure path. The point of initial contact is somewhat more posterior in the left foot. This difference is also manifested by the appearance of a typical first, heel-striking peak in the left foot tracing.

Athlete B (see Fig 1–8) manifests the most pronounced asymmetry that we have ever seen. Even though the values for the center of pressure paths and strike indices were similar on both sides, the values for the vertical and anteroposterior force components showed a noticeable difference. During the first 50 msec after ground contact, the force under the right shoe was more than 700 newtons greater than that under the left foot at a similar time. Similarly the braking force under the right shoe was 350 newtons greater. These differences point out the need for the development of different shoes for the two feet.

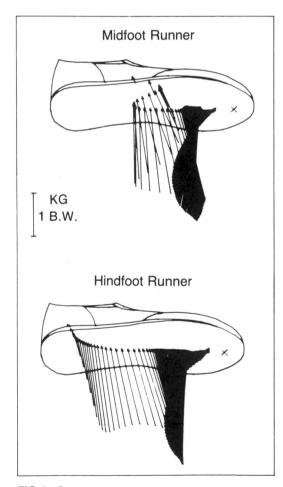

FIG 1–6.
Force vector courses.

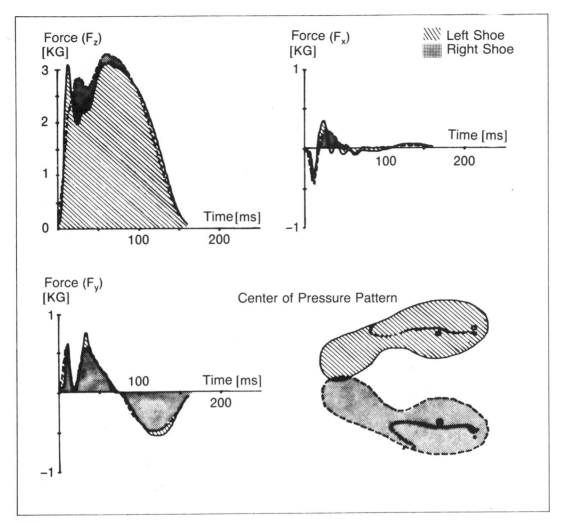

FIG 1−7.
Olympic 10,000-m runner (Runner A).

PRESSURE MEASUREMENT

During the past 10 years, considerable interest has developed in measuring the distribution of pressures under the foot. Significant contributions to this subject were made by Chodera[6] in Czechoslovakia, Duckworth et al.[9] in England, and Müller-Limmroth et al.[14] and Hennig and Nicol[11] in Germany. Cavanagh et al. [2, 3] developed a pressure-measuring plate consisting of a thousand pressure-sensitive elements that can display the data obtained in the form of a three-dimensional graphic grid.

During ground contact, normally, more than 300 of these elements are activated, and the complete distribution of pressure can be displayed graphically and continuously by a computer. Figure 1−9 graphically illustrates the late support phase of running barefoot, with the force contact area located approximately in the middle of the forefoot. It is evident

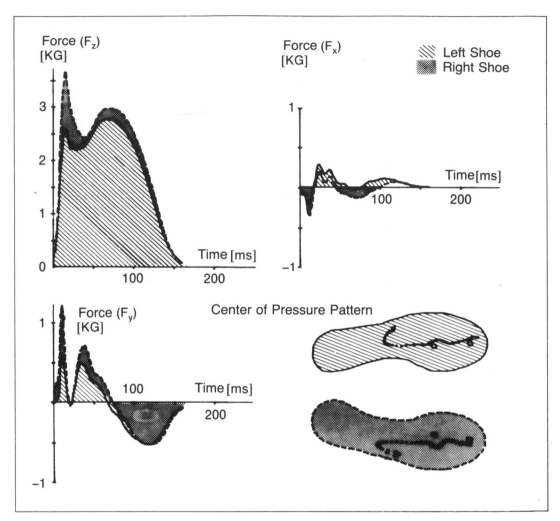

FIG 1–8.
Olympic 10,000-m runner (Runner B).

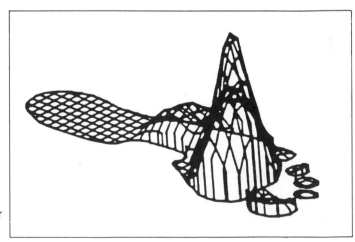

FIG 1–9.
Pressure diagram 106 msec after
ground contact.

that such a pictorial display allows more deference to the loading history of the anatomical structures than a diagram of the center of pressure pattern.

A series of such pictorial displays permits the evolution and study of a pressure distribution pattern (Fig 1–10,A). In this experimental subject (Athlete B from Fig 1–8) after contact had been made by the forefoot, there was a brief ground contact by the heel, with a value of approximately 700 kPa. The pressure under the foot decreases slowly, and during the remainder of the contact phase, there are pressure peaks under the first and second metatarsal heads. If a computer-controlled motion picture camera is used, an animated series can be obtained.

To this point in the article, the function of the lower extremity has been emphasized in considering the biomechanical differences measured and the ensuing requirements of the running shoe. Actually, the structure of the foot is just as important as its

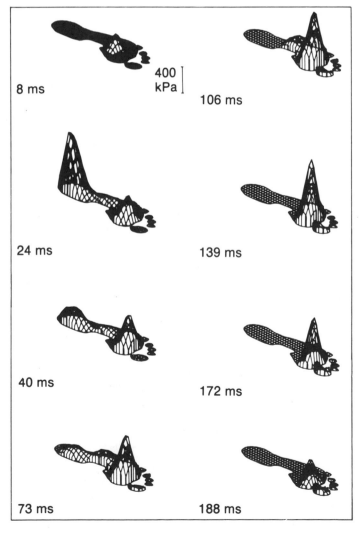

8 ms

400 kPa

106 ms

24 ms

139 ms

40 ms

172 ms

73 ms

188 ms

FIG 1–10.
Pressure diagrams over time.

function and affects the latter in a variety of ways. The three feet shown in Figure 1–11 are very different structurally. They show a continuum from pes cavus to pes planus. From a functional point of view, this continuum may be described as going from the rigid to the hypermobile. The pressure distribution in these three feet shows that, at a speed of 3.3 m/sec, there is indeed a difference in ground-foot interaction among the three types of feet.

Figure 1–12 shows the peak values of pressure in all areas of the foot independent of the time of contact. In the pes cavus foot, high pressure is seen at the heel and none at the midfoot. In contrast, the normal foot and the pes planus show high values in the midfoot and peak values in the area of the forefoot. The pressures under the three types of feet were also compared during slow walking, at which time the foot is under considerably decreased load. In the pes cavus, the peak values were lower, but there were no changes in the no-load areas. These measurements substantiate earlier observations, i.e., that the pes cavus is rigid and does not absorb shocks well, while the pes planus can alter its structure to cushion the reaction forces. Obviously, these two individuals required different types of running shoes.

CLOSING REMARKS

Finally, there is another consideration that belongs primarily to the

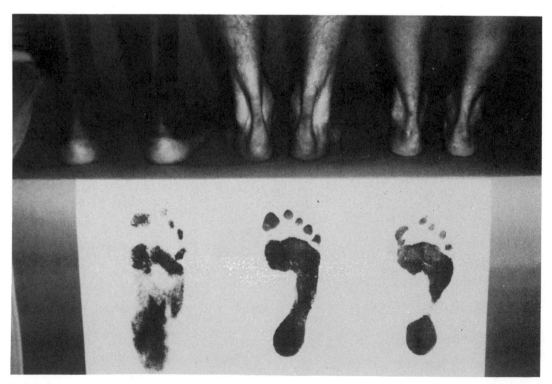

FIG 1–11.
The different foot structures in pes planus, normal foot, and pes cavus (from *left* to *right*).

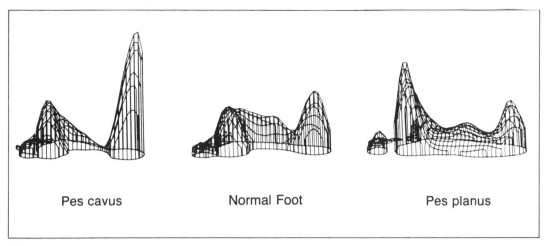

FIG 1–12.
Pressure peaks from running in three types of feet.

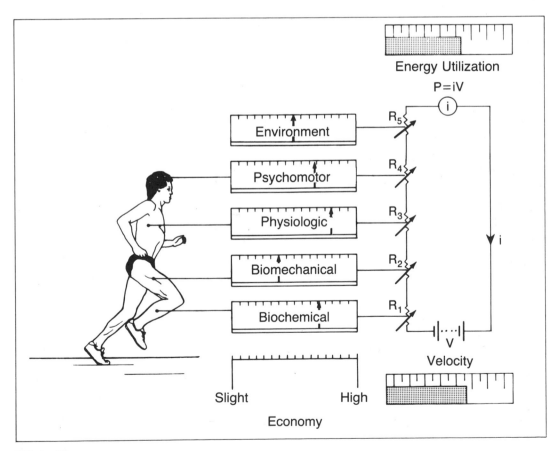

FIG 1–13.
Factors affecting the economy of running.

area of material study rather than to biomechanics. The ability of various materials to absorb shock has been studied continuously with test equipment that can simulate the effects of running a distance of 300 km. The changes that occur in the ability of the shoe to protect the runner's feet are considerable and alarming when one considers that some runners may use the same shoes over a distance of 2,000 km. To develop materials with better aging properties must become a primary goal of the shoe industry.

From the point of view of performance, it must be of the greatest interest to determine if a shoe contributes to the physiologic economy of running and therefore to the enhancement of competitive distance running. As shown in Fig 1–13, the economy of running is affected by a variety of factors including physiologic, psychologic, biomechanical, and extrinsic factors. One of the most interesting biomechanical considerations is the possibility that the shoe may store energy, which it can then return to the runner.[10]

SUMMARY

This chapter briefly summarizes some of the basic biomechanical concepts that are of importance in the design of shoes. An increase in interest in biomechanical investigation and the support given by the shoe industry to such studies have affected the development of this science in a most positive way. Unfortunately, commercial interest can sometimes result in less freedom of exchange of scientific information. Meetings such as that which generated this volume of papers help to overcome such barriers.

Acknowledgement

The author wishes to express his appreciation to his colleagues at Pennsylvania State University who have contributed to this study in many ways.

REFERENCES

1. *Bates, B., L.R. Osternig, B. Mason, S.L. James:* Lower extremity function during the support phase of running. In: Biomechanics VI-B, pp. 30–39. *Asmussen, E., K. Jorgensen* (eds.). University Park Press, Baltimore 1978
2. *Cavanagh, P.R., M. Ae:* A technique for the display of pressure distribution data beneath the foot. J. Biomech. 13 (1980), 69–75
3. *Cavanagh, P.R., E.M. Hennig:* A new device for the measurement of pressure distribution on a rigid surface. Med. Sci. Sport, Exer. 14 (1982), 153
4. *Cavanagh, P.R., M.A. Lafortune:* Ground reaction forces in distance running. J. Biomech. 13 (1980), 397–406
5. *Cavanagh, P.R., M.M. Rodgers:* Pressure distribution under the human foot. Proceedings of the 1984 European Society of Biomechanics Meeting, Davos (in press)
6. *Chodera, J.:* Pedobarograph— Apparatus for visual display of pressures between contacting surfaces of irregular shape. Czechoslovak patent No. 104 514 30d, 1960
7. *Clarke, T.E., E.C. Frederick, C. Hamill:* The study of rearfoot movement in running. In: Sport shoes and playing surfaces, pp. 1–23. *Freder-*

ick, E.C. (ed.). Human Kinetics Publishers, Champaign, Ill. 1984

8. *Clarke, T.E., M.A. Lafortune, K.W. Williams, P.R. Cavanagh:* The relationship between center of pressure location and rearfoot movement in distance running. Med. Sci. Sport Exer. 12 (1980), 92

9. *Duckworth, T., R.P. Betts, C.I. Franks, J. Burke:* The measurement of pressures underneath the foot. Foot and Ankle 3, 3 (1982), 130–141

10. *Frederick, E.C.:* Measuring the effects of shoes and surfaces on the economy of locomotion. In: Biomechanical aspects of sport shoes and playing surfaces, pp. 93–106. *Nigg, B.M., B.A. Kerr* (eds.). The University of Calgary, Calgary, AL 1984

11. *Hennig, E.M., K. Nicol:* Registration methods for time-dependent pressure distribution measurements with mats working as capacitors. In: Biomechanics VI-A, pp. 361–367. *Asmussen, E., K. Jorgensen* (eds.). University Park Press, Baltimore 1978

12. *Holden, J.P., P.R. Cavanagh, K.R. Williams, K.M. Bednarski:* Foot angles during walking and running. In: Biomechanics IX. Human Kinetics Publishers, Champaign, Ill. (in press)

13. *Lafortune, M.A., P.R. Cavanagh:* "Screw Home" mechanism of the knee during walking. Program of 4th Meeting of the European Society of Biomechanics (1984), 132

14. *Müller-Limmroth, W., H.R. Beierlein, W. Diebschlag:* Die Druckverteilung unter der menschlichen Fußsohle. Qualitative und quantitative Meßergebnisse. Z. Orthop. 115 (1977), 929–936

15. *Nigg, B.M., J. Denoth, B. Kerr, S. Luethi, D. Smith, A. Stacoff:* Load, sport shoes, and playing surfaces. In: Sport shoes and playing surfaces, pp. 1–23. *Frederick, E.C.* (ed.). Human Kinetics Publishers, Champaign, Ill. 1984

2

N.-L. Becker

Specific Running Injuries and Complaints Related to Excessive Loads— Medical Criteria of the Running Shoe

As a piece of athletic equipment the shoe must perform a number of tasks. It must support, guide, and protect the foot from shocks and from deleterious external factors. It should also support the entire locomotor effort involved in running, without negatively affecting the natural functions of the foot. Athletes must be able to run, jump, stop, accelerate, turn, change direction rapidly, slide, brace themselves, and recover their balance. The forces generated during the locomotor process are channeled through the shoe into the running surface. These demands cannot be met fully by an athletic shoe. This results in compromises that create footwear problems for the athlete in general and for the runner in particular.

Dazzled by fancy names, the buyers believe that they can match the athletic performance of the champion who wears "that shoe," or after whom the shoe is named. The choice is not made easier by the plethora of promises and a roster of specific advantages, most of which the merchant cannot even explain. The modern materials used in the manufacture of shoes adapt to the foot only after several hours of wear. If the shoes do not fit then, it is too late to take them back. The runners can get valuable tips from inspecting their old, worn out shoes. Normal wear should encourage the athlete to buy the same type of shoe again. If the shoe did not fit properly, the foot and occasionally the entire athlete may have been injured. If the foot of the athlete was strong enough to mold the shoe to individual requirements, the shoe was probably destroyed (Fig 2–1).

CUSHIONING THE IMPACT

According to the different running styles, we can distinguish hindfoot runners from midfoot and forefoot runners. The hindfoot runner keeps his or her knee straight while the heel makes the initial contact and decreases the impact by a rotary twist of the foot. The midfoot and forefoot runner keeps his or her knee and hip slightly flexed and thus absorbs the shock of contact in a more elastic fashion. The technical finesse of the midfoot and forefoot runner avoids the passive force peaks that characterize the heel and hindfoot runners. This is why the technically accomplished runner avoids heel contact and places his foot on the ground at the ball of the foot, with a slapping motion followed by a forward sliding motion of the foot over the ground. The good sprinter practically never touches the ground with his heel.

Nevertheless, the impact of ground

contact must be minimized. This is accomplished, regardless of the type of contact, through a twisting of the foot, i.e., pronation. The heel assumes a moderate X position, the navicular bone is depressed, and the leg is rotated inward (Fig 2–2). This damping rotatory motion is controlled by the tightening of the ligaments and muscles, principally of the tibialis anterior and posterior muscles. The degree of pronation depends on the weight of the athlete, his or her technical competence as a runner, and the contours of the running surface. The pronatory motion is the most important component of the normal cushioning process, but it can be substantially modified by the running shoe.

In contrast to barefoot running, this important, cushioning pronatory movement is markedly emphasized when the athlete runs in shoes, since the normal tilting motion across the outer edge of the heel is made impossible by the slightly extended sole. The hindfoot is flexed into a marked valgus position by the lever action of the sole, and the foot slides into the inner leather lining of the shoe, where it comes to a sudden stop. The leather lining is consequently distorted (Fig 2–3).

This relationship can be recognized by the Achilles tendon β-angle, i.e., the angle between the calcaneus and the Achilles tendon. In barefoot running, the angle changes only slightly per unit of time, while, when the athlete runs in shoes, the angle velocity is considerably accelerated, leading to a sudden asymmetrical pull on the Achilles tendon, mostly in a medial direction (Fig 2–4).

FIG 2–1.
Shoe destroyed by the individual shape of the foot.

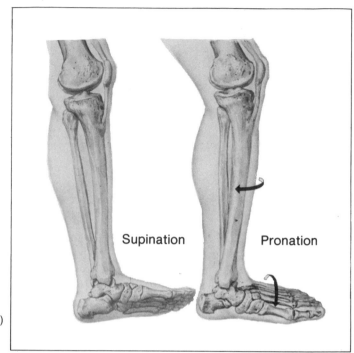

FIG 2–2.
Cushioning through pronation. (From Brody, D.M.: Running injuries. Clinical Symposia (Ciba) Vol. 32, No. 4 (1980). Used by permission.)

TOE MOBILITY

The precondition for a trouble free "take off" is the free and unfettered mobility of the toes in every direction, forward, sideward, and upward. Problems occur only if the big toe is forced into a valgus position inside the shoe and loses its load-bearing ability. This leads to an increased load being placed on the second and third toes, which were not designed for this task. The anterior brace points are thus displaced, resulting in the instability of the forefoot and in the possibility of developing a splayfoot, a hallux valgus with corn formation, and toenail distortion. The cause for this change is frequently a last that is too small and an inner sole that is rounded too much anteriorly; this ignores the differences between foot types and does not follow the "Golden Pattern [Golden Mean]" proposed by the German Orthopedic Society in 1951.

INJURIES

Running injuries can occur anywhere and are generally considered to be surgical problems. During a fall, extensive abrasions may occur, particularly in the area of the trochanter. Lacerations caused by spikes are most common in the Achilles tendon area.

FIG 2–3.
Distorted heel cover.

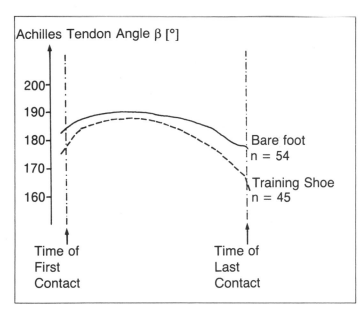

Achilles Tendon Angle β [°]

Time of First Contact

Time of Last Contact

Bare foot n = 54

Training Shoe n = 45

FIG 2–4.
Changes in the Achilles tendon angle. (From Nigg, B.M., S. Luethi: Bewegungsanglysen beim Laufschuh. Sportwissenschaft 3 (1980), 309–320. Used by permission.)

Dislocations of the ankle occur when a person is running on uneven surfaces. Spontaneous rupture of the Achilles tendon may occur, and blister formation is a frequent injury (Fig 2–5).

Improper placement of the foot and the resulting incorrect load distribution and deficient shock attenuation can lead to a series of complaints in the area of the leg, the hip, and the spinal column. When a runner complains about unusual problems in the lower extremity, it is not sufficient to examine the feet. The entire locomotor apparatus must be studied, and the signs and symptoms of all possible injuries must be investigated.

Chondropathy and chondromalacia (Fig 2–6) are often encountered in runners. The patella is often forcibly displaced laterally during flexion of the knee due to the natural anatomical structure of the patella. This is particularly common if there is a pre-

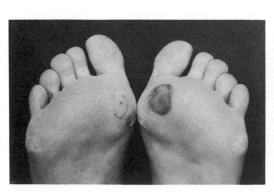

FIG 2–5.
Hemorrhagic blister.

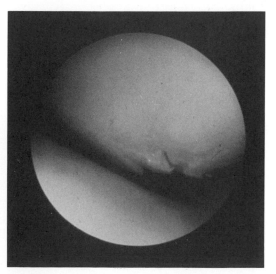

FIG 2–6.
Chondromalacia.

existing dysplasia, as a result of a muscular imbalance. Heel runners are most frequently affected, since in them the quadriceps is relaxed at the moment of impact, at which time it must contract rapidly and pull the patella laterally. At the same time, the leg rotates internally to cushion the impact. The runner who has a patella alta is even more anatomically disadvantaged. A patient who presents with knee problems is typically the beginning runner or the athlete who has recently increased his running distances. Clinically, we find a retropatellar rub, a significant retropatellar compression type pain when the patella is stretched against resistance. Pain is also produced by extending the knee from a 30-degree flexion.

In beginning runners and in runners with genua vara, we encounter the iliotibial band syndrome on the lateral aspect of the knee joint (Fig 2–7). When during the run the knee is flexed and extended, the iliotibial tract jumps back and forth across the femoral condyle, producing the abrasive effects leading to the syndrome. Pain on pressure over the lateral condyle is the basis for the clinical diagnosis. Excessive pronation during cushioning aggravates this syndrome. In addition to anti-inflammatory therapy, it is well to remember the shoe. If the shoe is worn out or defective, it may contribute to the iliotibial band syndrome. An orthopedic arch support or new shoes must be provided. In the differential diagnosis, a popliteus muscle tendinitis must be considered. This condition may also be due to excessive pronation and increased internal rotation of the leg. It is encountered particularly after running on a declining surface, as for instance running downhill. Under these conditions, the popliteus muscle endeavors to prevent the forward dis-

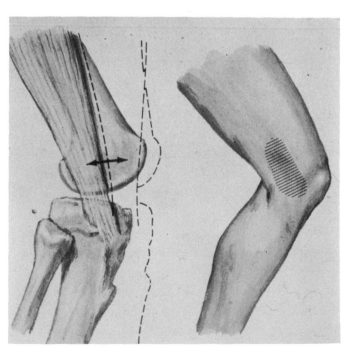

FIG 2–7.
The iliotibial band syndrome. (From Brody D.M.: Running injuries. Clinical Symposia (ciba) Vol. 32, No. 4 [1980]. Used by permission.)

placement of the femoral condyle on the tibial plateau. On clinical examination, point tenderness is found over the tendinous insertion of the popliteus muscle, just proximal to the lateral ligament. The mistaken diagnosis of lateral meniscus tear is made frequently and must be excluded by differential diagnosis.

Irritation and inflammation of the patellar tendon and necrosis at the insertion of the patellar ligament suggest an increased load and torsion of this ligament. This occurs with patellar chondropathy, particularly when excessive pronation during the cushioning process leads to increased internal rotation of the leg.

Pain along the tibial edge is a sign of increased load on the lower leg and is seen primarily in runners who are in poor physical condition, in beginning runners, and in persons who run on hard surfaces. This excessive load syndrome is aggravated by poor shoes that permit hyperpronation and that do not sufficiently cushion the impact. Poor running posture with increased external rotation of the hip and extreme lateral heel contact with the ground can also lead to excessive load injuries in the lower leg. The tibialis posterior muscle is frequently affected, since it is passively stretched when the foot is pronated and the lower leg is internally rotated. This leads to irritation at the site of origin at the interosseous membrane and the posterior aspect of the tibia and fibula. This in turn leads first to a tendinitis and secondarily to an osseous metaplasia at the site of origin of the tibialis posterior muscle and to ensuing periosteal irritation. Typically, the pain begins at the medial side of the tibial edge at the end of the run. If

running continues, dull lower leg pain is experienced during the run as well.

In extreme cases, stress fractures of the tibia can occur. In the early stages, these are frequently missed on standard x-ray films but show a marked increase in density on the scintigram (Fig 2–8, A–C). Therapy would remain incomplete if the runner were not provided with better footwear or an arch support to prevent the pathologic hyperpronation.

Pain in the anterolateral aspect of the tibia, radiating distally into the foot is pathognomonic of the compartment syndrome and is due to an overload on the tibialis anterior muscle. This entity is caused by excessive pronation due to changing the style of running from hindfoot to forefoot, running on an uneven surface, running in the mountains, increasing the training requirements, or running in shoes having too soft a sole.

In addition to stretching exercises and strengthening the tibialis anterior muscle, it is most important to provide a good shoe that can cushion the impact.

The ankle can also be affected by excessive pronation, particularly in the presence of loose ligaments. There will be pain over the lateral malleolus as a consequence of a pathologic, excessive pressure. An orthopedic inner sole and good circumferential support for the heel should maintain the calcaneus in a neutral position.

The most frequent pathology among runners is Achilles tendinitis. In acute cases, there are inflammatory changes in the tendon sheath. In chronic inflammation, mucoid degeneration and longitudinal tears in the

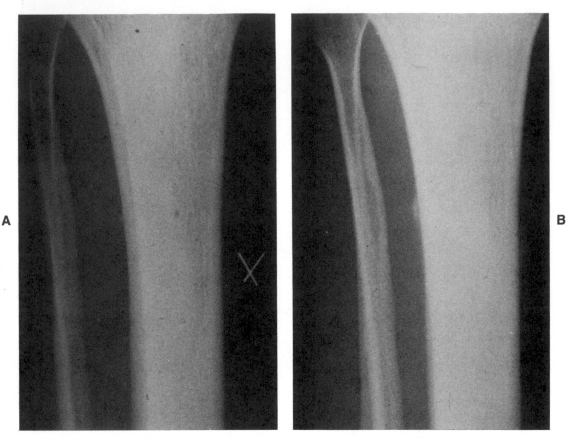

FIG 2–8.
Stress fracture of the tibia. **A,** on presentation; **B,** 4 weeks later; **C,** scintigraphic image.

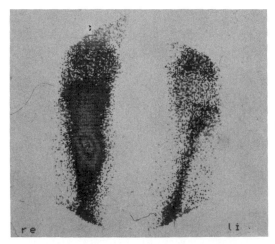

tendon may lead to the development of painful knot formation in the tendon itself. This pathology may have a variety of causes. Running on rigid soles, extensive running in mountainous terrain, improper heel wedge, a heel counter that is too soft, or a distorted heel counter lead to an asymmetrical pull on the Achilles tendon and to repeated inflammatory reactions. Anatomical factors that may lead to the development of this condition include the pes cavus and hindfoot and forefoot varus that cause the foot to be in supination at the time of impact. This leads to a hyperpronatory compensation and a torsion of the Achilles tendon. The runners frequently complain of pain that is present early during the run, disappears later during the run, but reappears again at the end of the run or the following morning. In acute cases, there may be a pressure-sensitive area at the insertion of the Achilles tendon, primarily on the medial side. Occasionally this is accompanied by crepitation, swelling, and painful knot formation. These patients must have rest, anti-inflammatory therapy, preferably without steroids, shoes with a flexible sole, a molded Achilles tendon protector, and a solid heel counter. An elevation of the sole by 1.5 cm is permissible for a short period but must be accompanied by stretching exercises of the lower leg muscles. If there is excessive pronation, an orthopedic insert must be incorporated or a different type of shoe must be used.

Excessive load is manifested in the foot by irritation of the plantar fascia and the development of calcaneal spurs. Pain is described in a characteristic location on arising in the morning or at the beginning of the run. During the run, the pain may disappear. A pes cavus or excessive pronation may contribute to this condition. In the differential diagnosis, the tarsal tunnel syndrome and an irritation of the medial branch of the tibial nerve must be considered.

Pain in the hip may appear during or after the run. Its cause is frequently a difference in the length of the two legs, which leads to an irritation of the trochanteric bursa. Bursitis in the area of the ischial tuberosity occurs in sprinters when training is accelerated. This must be differentiated from an insertion tendinitis of the shortened ischiocrural musculature, which is a frequent finding among runners. Differential diagnostic considerations must include anatomical variations, e.g., lumbosacral vertebral anomalies, degenerative changes in the spinal column with irritation of the sciatic nerve, and bursitis in the area of the piriformis muscle.

THE EFFECTS OF THE RUNNING SHOE ON THE PHYSIOLOGY OF THE FOOT

The running shoe affects the physiology of the foot and thus participates significantly in the development of almost all disease states. The goal of shoe design is to affect the pronation and to decrease the vertical peak forces. Attenuating elements of varying hardness in the heel area should be able to modify the rebound elasticity according to the weight of the runner and the characteristics of the running surface. Wedge-shaped nubs allow a dissipation of energy by structural distortion. Special synthetic substances having significant rebound potential can absorb peak forces when inserted into the shoe as wedges. Structurally incorporated air cushions are well recognized. These may be in the area of the heel or under the entire sole and absorb the distortion energy during the initial contact with the ground. The cushion stores this energy and returns it to the runner at the time of push-off in the form of recoil energy without loss of elasticity or material fatigue.

Excessive pronation can be affected by a strong heel counter. Short, vertical stabilizers are usually combined with an orthopedic insert and can absorb the hyperpronatory motion. A median wedge made of some hard substance can block the excessive pronation. If we assume that during contact and rocking the heel behaves like a golf ball rolling down an inclined plane, then the rounded-off heel of this shoe should be cut away and the radius of the heel of the shoe fitted to the radius of the heel.

How difficult it is to affect the physiology of the foot can be seen in the complex compound soles and in the multiple wedges of varying hardness that appear to be built more for an ailing foot than for a healthy one.

One tries to adapt the shoe more and more to the human foot by changing the form of the last. The so-called straight last is being increasingly abandoned in favor of the curved last, which favors the runner who runs more in a supinatory direction. This curved last, however, is not an innovation but only an adaptation to the foot. If a line is drawn through the principal points of the curved last, this form of last resembles the Golden Mean except that the heel and joint portions are kept smaller.

Not every foot that deviates from the norm requires orthopedic correction. A 50-year-old runner, who, in addition to his daily run, runs the marathon every 14 days, wears regular shoes without any problems. A substantial hallux valgus deformity makes it possible for him to wear mass-produced footwear (Fig 2–9). Small pieces of linen are placed between the toes. Even though the foot looks abnormal, it performs well, since the severe deformities are well compensated for.

FIG 2–9.
This man also runs the marathon.

THE ATHLETIC SHOE

Problems of excessive load on the lower extremity in runners, and particularly in beginning runners, can usually be cleared up by careful study of and meticulous attention to the running shoe. By solving the shoe problem, the complaints frequently disappear with astonishing speed. The athletic shoe is a central problem in all forms of athletics in which a shoe is worn, and particularly in those activities where the shoe is the only piece of athletic equipment. The athletic shoe must be appropriate to the sport in which it is used, but must be even more appropriate to the foot, since athletic activity is likely to lead to excessive load on a foot weakened and distorted by civilization and underutilization.

To avoid the problems of excessive stress related to footwear, all athletes should consider the following points when buying athletic shoes:

1. They should stand and walk around in the fully laced shoe.
2. The big toe and the little toe must not be constrained.
   There should be no unpleasant pressure on the medial aspect

of the toenail of the big toe. It
should be possible to curl the
toes.

3. The lacing should be variable.
4. When the first contact is made
   with the heel, the foot should
   not deviate medially.
5. When contact is first made
   with the heel, there should be
   neither unpleasant pressure
   nor pull on the Achilles tendon.

BIBLIOGRAPHY

1. Adidas, 8522 Herzogenaurach:
   Laufen 83, Produktinformation
2. *Becker, N., H. Mau:* Der Sportschuh
   (The athletic shoe). In: Stellenwert
   der Sportmedizin in Medizin und
   Sportwissenschaft, S. 321–327. *Je-
   schke, D.* (Hrsg.). Springer, Berlin–
   Heidelberg–New York–Tokyo 1984
3. *Brody, D.M.:* Running injuries. Clinical Symposia (ciba) Vol. 32, No. 4
   (1980)
4. *Bühler, E., H. Gall, H. Drexel:* Untersuchung der Bodenkräfte in Abhän-
   gigkeit von der Aktivität einiger
   Beinmuskeln während der Stand-
   beinphase des menschlichen Ganges.
   Z. Orthop. 121 (1983), 37–43
5. *Diepschlag, W.:* Die Druckverteilung
   an der Fußsohle des Menschen im
   Stehen und Gehen, barfuß und im
   Schuh. Z. Orthop. 120 (1982), 814–
   820
6. *Hort, W.:* Der Sportschuh auf moder-
   nen Kunststoffbelägen. Ortop. Praxis
   11 (1978), 825–827
7. *Marquardt, W.:* Orthopädische
   Schuhe und Einlagen. Orthopädie 8
   (1979), 310–326
8. *Nigg, B.M.:* Biomechanische
   Überlegungen zur Belastung des Bewegungsapparates. 3. Heidelberger
   Orthopädie-Symposium 1979, S. 44–
   54: Thieme, Stuttgart 1980
9. *Nigg, B.M., J. Denoth, P.A.
   Neukomm:* Load on the human
   body. Biomechanics VII (1979), 88–
   105
10. *Nigg, B.M., S. Luethi:* Bewegungsan-
    alysen beim Laufschuh. Sportwis-
    senschaft 3 (1980), 309–320
11. *Nigg, B.M., B. Segesser:* Biomecha-
    nische Aspekte zu Sportschuhkor-
    rekturen. Orthop. Praxis 11 (1978),
    831–833
12. Nike International, 6108 Weiterstadt,
    Produktinformation
13. Nike Research News Letter, Vol. 1,
    No. 3, Summer 1982
14. Puma Dassler, 8522 Herzogenaurach,
    Produktinformation
15. *Schmollinsky, G.:* Leichtathletik.
    Sportverlag, Berlin 1980
16. *Segesser, B., B.M. Nigg:* Insertion-
    stendinosen am Schienbein, Achillo-
    dynie und Überlastungsfolgen am
    Fuß—Ätiologie, Biomechanik, thera-
    peutische Möglichkeiten. Orthopädie
    9 (1980), 207–214
17. *Segesser, B., A. Stacoff:* Verletzung-
    sprophylaxe durch geeignetes
    Sportschuhwerk. AST 7 (1981), 308–
    315
18. *Witt, A.N., H. Rettig, K.F. Schlegel,
    M. Hackenbroch, W. Hupfauer:* Or-
    thopädie in Praxis und Klinik, Bd. I:
    Allgemeine Orthopädie. Thieme,
    Stuttgart–New York 1980

3 The Running Shoe: Dilemmas and Dichotomies in Design

E.C. Frederick

Over the last two decades, the running shoe has undergone an accelerated evolution. The simple, uniform designs of the 1960s have given way to today's complex, highly specialized products. Consider the proliferation of models of shoes. Twenty years ago runners could choose between track spikes and a single "running shoe" for road and cross-country racing and training. Now literally hundreds of models are available to satisfy the most esoteric needs. One can find special shoes for heavy runners or for light runners, for marathons, for cross-country, for heel strikers or midfoot strikers, and so on.

Because of the specificity and sophistication of today's designs, both consumers and shoemakers have been heard to wonder if there is anything left to design. Have we provided for all the needs of the majority of runners, or are there still possibilities for significant improvement? It can be argued that the pace of technical innovation has slowed considerably in recent years. Some would take this as proof that all the significant improvements have been made. I would argue that this apparent slowing of innovation is really just a consequence of the increased complexity and sophistication of our understanding of the biomechanical needs for which the running shoe must provide.

An interesting thread runs through our current thinking about the functions we should require sport shoes to perform. Many of the needs we are uncovering and refining turn out to be mutually exclusive. Indeed, design dilemmas and dichotomies present a greater challenge to today's sport designers and researchers. For example, how can we achieve stability and good cushioning when soft materials promote instability? How can we make shoes both flexible as well as stable when firm, stable cushioning systems are inflexible? Equally challenging dichotomies exist between weight and cushioning or support; efficiency and weight; midsole durability and cushioning; and traction and outsole durability. One challenge of the 1980s for biomechanists and shoe designers alike is to overcome the contradictions presented by these dilemmas and dichotomies.

What follows is the summary of some of the key demands that must be addressed in the design of running shoes and an elaboration of some of the dilemmas and dichotomies that arise when one attempts to provide solutions to these demands.

DEMANDS

Attenuation

Few conclusions can be drawn from the last 10 years of research on cushioning requirements in running other than the observation that it is a complex problem. If we define cushioning as the attenuation of peak forces, and further define *good* cushioning as the attenuation of those forces to levels that can be tolerated by the musculoskeletal system, we have only raised more questions that cannot be answered.

What forces must cushioning systems attenuate? Surely not all forces are to be lessened. After all, some, such as propulsive forces, are important to performance. What are the tolerable magnitudes of those forces? This is a complex issue that involves, among other things, a knowledge of the response of various musculoskeletal structures to repeated stress and detailed information on the magnitude of the forces in question. Little of this type of information exists.

On the surface, it seems as though we have made no progress in our research on cushioning. While it is true that we have few answers, we have advanced our definition of the problem considerably in the last decade.

Using force platforms, Cavanagh and LaFortune,[9] Frederick et al.,[19] and Nigg et al.[24, 25, 26] have determined that during running the magnitude of vertical force between the ground and the foot is of the order of two to three times the runner's body weight. Two force peaks typically occur: an impact peak rising in the first 20 to 30 msec after footstrike, and a propulsive or active peak occurring roughly 100 msec after footstrike has struck.

When one recalls that both feet strike the ground some 1,500 times per mile, it seems reasonable that repeated loading of a magnitude of two to three times body weight might produce negative biologic effects if it is not attenuated. Radin et al.[28] and Voloshin and Wosk[30] have shown, for example, that a lack of sufficient shock attenuation is linked to degenerative changes in joints and to low back pain. It is presumed that many of the chronic musculoskeletal disorders that athletes present are at least exacerbated by repeated impact loadings.[3, 24−26]

About 80% of runners land heel first and exhibit the typical two-peaked vertical ground reaction force curve.[9, 23] The two peaks in force are localized in different regions of the shoe.[5] The impact peak occurs when the center of pressure is in the center of the heel of the shoe, and the active peak when the center of pressure is under the ball of the foot. Most experiments on impact shock concentrate on the heel cushioning because forefoot propulsive force is a requirement of movement and not really an impact.

These observations provided a rationale for Cavanagh and co-workers[6−8, 18] at Pennsylvania State University to develop an impact tester.

This device drops a weighted shaft a distance of 5 cm onto the surface of the heel or forefoot of the sock liner in the shoes. The shaft is instrumented to provide a record of either acceleration or force (which in turn is converted to acceleration).

Although confusing results have been reported from studies comparing material tests of running shoes with measurements of vertical ground reaction forces, while the subject is wearing the same shoes,[3, 10, 22] some important conclusions have emerged from this work. Clarke et al[10] have shown that materials can be too soft, causing them to maximally compress (bottom out) resulting in a loss of cushioning. We have also shown in our laboratory that excessively hard models can cause an increase in shock to the leg.

Clarke et al.[11] have suggested that the unexpected lack of correlation between the material test results performed on the shoe alone and the actual force-platform data collected with subjects running in the shoes is perhaps due to the fact that the body is adjusting its kinematics in response to the perceived hardness of the shoe. This adaptation changes the ground reaction force pattern that is recorded and so hides any shock absorbing by the shoe. The observation that runners respond to the physical characteristics of the shoe underlines the importance of accurately measuring the physical characteristics and controlling initial conditions in experiments where physical characteristics and the response of subjects are compared.

Kaelin et al.[22] controlled the initial conditions of landing in a comparison of a physical impact test and the vertical force response of human subjects to shoes of various hardnesses. Though they controlled any adaptation by specifying initial conditions, they still found discrepancies between the physical test results and the ground reaction force values that they ascribed to the geometry of the shoe sole. Clearly, both adaptation and sole geometry interact with sole hardness to influence the impact the body experiences.

From these assorted findings, we can draw a few preliminary conclusions about cushioning. It is important to understand that they will certainly be revised and refined as our understanding of the problem progresses.

1. There is probably an optimum hardness range for cushioning systems. They can be too soft, allowing "bottoming out," and they can be too hard, causing increased shock to the leg.[25]

2. The construction of the shoe, i.e., geometry and materials and techniques used to put it together, is also important. For example, a stiff innersole board cemented to the top of a soft foam midsole can give it the functional hardness of a much firmer material, and excessive flare on the lateral side of the heel can introduce leverage effects that exacerbate the impact shock.[22]

3. The range of demands (uphill vs. downhill, soft vs. hard surfaces, and heavy vs. light runners)[14] placed on the cushioning provided by an individual shoe generally overlap the design and manufacturing tolerance currently used in the industry, i.e., no one shoe can satisfy all needs, and too great a range in material properties ex-

ists within a number of examples of an individual model. In the future, we need more focus on quality control of materials and on individualizing design to overcome this problem.

4. Cushioning durability is another important demand. The cushioning provided by the shoe sole should be the same after 1,000 km of running as it is when the shoe is new. Most materials currently in use cannot meet that criterion.[1, 7]

Flexibility of the Sole

The need for flexibility of the sole has never been proved scientifically, but it is certainly a feature of design that most runners list as a strong preference. Observation of high-speed film of various runners indicates that the shoe is required to bend at a point just behind the metatarsal heads to an angle of about 30 degrees. It is reasonable to speculate that the additional torque required to bend a stiff shoe through this arc might well contribute to local muscle fatigue and perhaps to injury. Although no studies have been published to confirm this relationship, many physicians and therapists cite inflexible shoes as a cause of shin splints—a common inflammation of the muscles and associated tendons of the front of the shank. These observations and good sense tell us that flexibility should be one of the qualities we demand of running shoe design.

Weight

That shoes should be light weight also makes good sense, and it has been shown that weight has a signifi-

cant effect on performance as well. Frederick[16] has shown that carrying 100 g of excess weight on each foot while running at a range of speeds increases energy expenditure by 1%. This may not seem like a significant effect, but it can add 1 to 2 minutes to the time required to run a competitive marathon.

Hardness of the Sole

Curiously enough sole hardness also has a significant effect on the energy demands of running. Frederick et al.[17] showed that soft shoes significantly lower the energy required to run at a pace of 3.8 m/second. In addition, Frederick[15] has shown that this softness effect can cancel out at least a portion of the cost of carrying extra weight. For example, subjects wearing soft-soled shoes used 2.8% less energy while running at a marathon pace despite the fact that the soft shoe weighed an average of 33 g per pair more than the firmer-soled model used for comparison.[20] These studies indicate that running shoes used primarily for competition should not only be lightweight but relatively soft as well.

Control of Pronation

Yet another quality of running shoes is their stability or, more precisely, their ability to control pronation. A number of authors have implicated overpronation in the etiology of a number of sport injuries.[13] It is generally considered desirable to be able to control the amount of pronation that occurs in individuals who display an excess of this movement. The design of running shoes can have a great influence on how much control is provided. Clarke et al.[12] have shown that the angle of flare of the sole and sole hardness have a significant influence on the maximum pronation that occurs while the athlete is running. Flares up to 30 degrees appear to reduce pronation, and increasing midsole and heel wedge hardness over a durometric range of 25 Shore A to 45 Shore A causes a decrease in maximum pronation.

Research from our laboratory has shown that the design of the last with which the shoe is constructed can also have a significant effect on pronation.[2] Straighter lasts with more medial support and a wider base in the heel significantly reduce maximum pronation.

Bates et al.[4] and Stacoff and Kaelin[29] have shown that increased heel height decreases maximum pronation. Clarke et al.[12] were not able to confirm such an effect within the range of heel heights and lifts that one would normally encounter in a running shoe. They were, however, able to show that heel height reduced the maximum velocity of pronation that occurs during the early part of foot contact.

Other qualities that are also important in shoe design but that have not been so thoroughly studied are

- Outsole durability.[27]
- Traction.[15]
- Breathability of the upper.[7]

DICHOTOMIES AND DILEMMAS

Many of the desirable qualities of running shoes summarized in the previous section have the peculiar property of being mutually exclusive. In our efforts to find the perfect shoe design, we are challenged by the need to meet all demands despite such contradictions. Several examples of contradictions in the design of running shoes are

- Features that promote stability and weight.
- Soles that provide good traction are often not durable.
- Taking weight out usually reduces cushioning and stability.
- Added cushioning increases instability.
- Firmer midsoles are more stable but promote inflexibility.

The last two examples present a particular challenge to the shoe designer. We will consider these examples in more detail and discuss how they might be resolved.

Providing cushioning conflicts with the need for stability and flexibility. The relationship between sole hardness and maximum pronation is shown in Figure 3–1. Decreasing the hardness of the sole increases pronation. Nigg et al.[25] have suggested that, from the point of view of cushioning, the optimum hardness for running shoe soles is in the range of 35 to 45 Shore A. Yet if pronation control were our sole objective, we would likely choose a firmer sole material. This dilemma confronts us with an uncomfortable choice between poor cushioning and inadequate stability. The way out is to look to thicker rather than softer soling materials for our cushioning. Figure 3–2 is a schematic representation of what we cur-

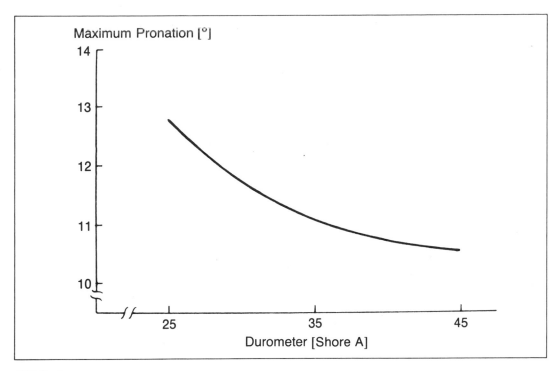

FIG 3–1.
The relationship between sole hardness and maximum pronation. Very soft soles have an accentuated effect on pronation.

rently know about the relationship between cushioning and stability when we use soling materials of various hardnesses and thicknesses. A quick glance at this figure reveals an optimum solution, i.e., an ideal combination of thickness and hardness when our objective is to minimize pronation and maximize cushioning.

The data of cushioning vs. hardness are from Nigg et al.[25] The data on the relationship between heel height and stability are from Stacoff and Kaelin[29] and Clarke et al.[12] The data on thickness vs. softness are from Frederick et al.[17] Because these data are from different sources and the measurement techniques and the construction of the shoes used for the experiments may differ somewhat, we have to be cautious about too

precise an interpretation of the results. It is likely, however, that the general nature of the interactions between these four variables will remain intact, even if the exact thickness and hardness of the optimal solution vary.

Before we are tempted to gloat over such a simple solution to such a difficult dilemma, let me point out that the optimum solution we have chosen will result in a decrease in flexibility of the sole. The two major factors that influence the flexibility of a piece of foam like the polymeric foams used in running shoe soles are hardness and thickness. Hardness is linearly related to flexibility, with harder materials being less flexible. Resistance to bending in a uniform structure equals a constant times the

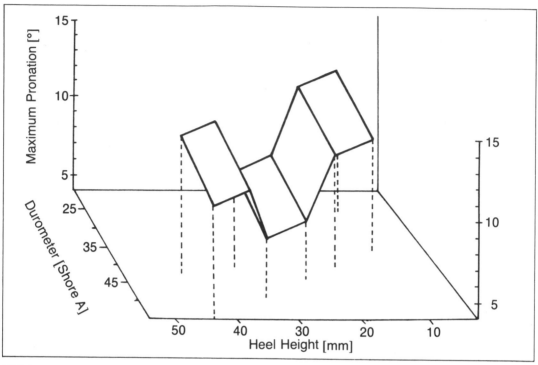

FIG 3–2.

Schematic representation of the influence of heel height and hardness (durometer) on maximum pronation. Using the findings of Nigg et al.,[25] we defined the range of acceptable cushioning as an initial condition. Nigg et al.[25] have shown that 35 to 45 Shore A durometer in a normal sole thickness is optimum. We included in the plot only those combinations of hardness and heel height that would produce an impact attenuation equivalent to that produced by Nigg's 35- to 45-Shore A shoes of normal thickness.[17] Any combination of heel height and hardness shown provides optimal cushioning. Further, the relationship between these various combinations and maximum pronation was predicted by Clarke et al.[12] and Kaelin et al.[22] The plot reveals that optimum cushioning and hindfoot control are found when heel heights of 25 to 35 mm and durometric measurements of 40 to 55 Shore A are properly combined.

width of the structure times the square of its thickness, i.e., the dimension in line with the load.[21] Figure 3–3 shows a schematic representation of how thickness and hardness influence flexibility. It is not difficult to see that our optimum solution to the cushioning vs. stability dichotomy is not a good solution to maximize flexibility. For maximum flexibility, soles should be as soft and, in particular, as thin as possible.

The easiest way out of this dilemma is to take advantage of a property of structures that are being bent. As we can see in Figure 3–4, a block of foam that is being bent is under compressive strain along its top half and under tensile strain on its bottom half. Reducing either the compressive modulus of the top half or the tensile modulus of the bottom half would make the block more flexible. Slicing the bottom half of the block at the point of bending would solve the tensile strain problem. The compressive strain problem can be helped by using a bar of softer material in the top half of the block, just behind the spot where the metatarsal heads will rest. This is where the greatest bending stress occurs.

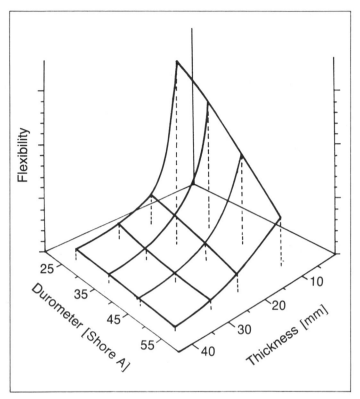

FIG 3–3.
Schematic representation of the interaction of thickness, hardness (durometer), and flexibility. Note the relatively greater significance of sole thickness.

CONCLUSIONS

These two examples and the other dichotomies and dilemmas that were mentioned prove that many challenges and opportunities for innovation still await the shoe designer and his colleagues in biomechanics. As far as this scientist can see, the design of running shoes will continue to improve in visually subtle but functionally dramatic ways as we conquer the contradictions in design that challenge us and as we peel back the many layers of complexity that shroud our understanding of the biomechanical and physiologic needs of runners.

Acknowledgments

The original English text of this chapter was kindly provided by the author.

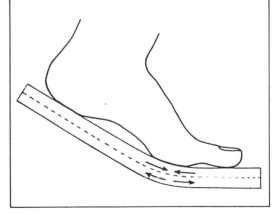

FIG 3–4.
Diagram of a bending block of foam. Note that bottom layers are in tension and top layers are in compression. Reducing the modulus of either tension or compression of the bottom or top would decrease the resistance to bending.

REFERENCES

1. Anon. The compaction problem in running shoes. Nike Research Newsletter 1, 4 (1982), 1
2. Anon. Rearfoot control, cushioning and shoe design. Nike Research Newsletter 2, 1 (1983), 2
3. *Bates, B.T., S.L. James, L.R. Osternig, J.A. Sawhill, J. Hamill:* Effects of running shoes on ground reaction forces. In: Biomechanics VII. *Morecki, A., K. Fidelus* (eds.). University Park Press, Baltimore 1982
4. *Bates, B.T., L.R. Osternig, B. Mason, S.L. James:* Lower extremity function during the support phase of running, pp. 31–39. In: Biomechanics VI. *Asmussen, E., K. Jorgensen* (eds.). University Park Press, Baltimore 1978
5. *Cavanagh, P.R.:* A technique for averaging center of pressure paths from a force platform. J. Biomech. 11 (1978), 487–491
6. *Cavanagh, P.R.:* Testing procedure. Runner's World 10 (1978), 70–80
7. *Cavanagh, P.R.:* The running shoe book. Anderson World, Mountain View, CA 1980
8. *Cavanagh, P.R., R.N. Hinrich, K.R. Williams:* Testing procedure for the runner's world shoe survey. Runner's World 10 (1980), 38–49
9. *Cavanagh, P.R., M.A. La Fortune:* Ground reaction forces in distance running. J. Biomech. 13 (1980), 397–406
10. *Clarke, T.E., E.C. Frederick, L.B. Cooper:* Effects of shoe cushioning upon ground reaction forces in running. Int. J. Sports Med. 4 (1983), 247–251
11. *Clarke, T.E., E.C. Frederick, L.B. Cooper:* Biomechanical measurement of running shoe cushioning properties. In: Biomechanical aspects of sport shoes and playing surfaces, pp. 25–33. Nigg, B.M., B.A. Kerr (eds.). University of Calgary, Canada 1983
12. *Clarke, T.E., E.C. Frederick, C.L. Hamill:* The effect of shoe design on rearfoot control in running. Med. Sci. Sport Exer. 15, (1983), 376–381
13. *Clarke, T.E., E.C. Frederick, C.L. Hamill:* The study of rearfoot movement in running. In: Sport shoes and playing surfaces, pp. 166–189. Frederick, E.C. (ed.). Human Kinetics Publishers, Champaign, Ill. 1984
14. *Frederick, E.C.:* Body size and biomechanical consequences. In: Sports medicine, sports science: Bridging the Gap, pp. 47–57. *Cantu, R.C., W.J. Gillespie* (eds.). Collamore Press, Lexington, MA 1982
15. *Frederick, E.C.:* Physiologic and ergonomic factors in running shoe design. Applied Ergonomics 15 (1984), 281–287
16. *Frederick, E.C.:* The energy cost of load carriage on the feet during running. In: Biomechanics IX, pp. 295–300. *Winter, D.A., R.P. Wells, K.C. Hayes, A.E. Patla* (eds.). Human Kinetics, Champaign, Ill. 1985
17. *Frederick, E.C., T.E. Clarke, C.L. Hamill:* The effect of shoe design on shock attenuation. In: Sport shoes and playing surfaces, pp. 190–198. *Frederick, E.C.* (eds.). Human Kinetics Publishers, Champaign, Ill. 1984
18. *Frederick, E.C., T.E. Clarke, J.L. Larsen, L.B. Cooper:* The effects of shoe cushioning on the oxygen demands of running. In: Biomechanical aspects of sport shoes and playing surfaces, pp. 107–114, Nigg, B.M., B.A. Kerr (eds.). University of Calgary, Canada 1983
19. *Frederick, E.C., J.L. Hagy, R.A. Mann:* The prediction of vertical impact force during running. J. Biomech. 14 (1981), 498
20. *Frederick, E.C., E.T. Howley, S.K. Powers:* Lower O_2 cost while running in air cushion type shoe. Med. Sci. Sport Exer. 12, 2 (1980), 81
21. *Hildebrand, M.:* Analysis of verte-

brate structure, pp. 444–445. John Wiley & Sons, New York 1974

22. *Kaelin, X., J. Denoth, A. Stacoff, E. Stuessi:* Cushioning during running—material tests contra subject tests. In: Biomechanics: Current interdisciplinary research, pp. 651–656. *Perren, S., E. Schneider* (eds.). Martinus Nijhoff Publishers, Dordrecht 1985

23. *Kerr, B.A., L. Beauchamp, V. Fisher, R. Neil:* Footstrike patterns in distance running. In: Biomechanical aspects of sport shoes and playing surfaces, pp. 135–142. *Nigg, B.M., B.A. Kerr* (eds.). University of Calgary, Canada 1983

24. *Nigg, B.M., J. Denoth, B. Kerr, S. Luethi, D. Smith, A. Stacoff:* Load, sport shoes and playing surfaces. In: Sport shoes and playing surfaces, pp. 1–23. *Frederick, E.C.* (ed.). Human Kinetics Publishers, Champaign, Ill. 1984

25. *Nigg, B.M., J. Denoth, S. Luethi, A. Stacoff:* Methodological aspects of sport shoe and sport floor analysis. In: Biomechanics VIII-B, pp. 1041–1052. *Matsui, H., K. Kobayashi* (eds.). Human Kinetics Publishers, Champaign, Ill. 1983

26. *Nigg, B.M., J. Denoth, P.A. Neukomm:* Quantifying the load on the human body. In: Biomechanics VII, pp. 88–105, *Morecki, A., K. Fidelus* (eds.). University Park Press, Baltimore 1982

27. *Perkins, P.J., R.E. Whittaker:* Improving the wear performance of sports footwear. In: Biomechanical aspects of sport shoes and playing surfaces, pp. 177–184, *Nigg, B.M., B.A. Kerr* (eds.). University of Calgary, Canada 1983

28. *Radin, E.L., R.B. Orr, J.L. Kelman, I.L. Paul, R.M. Rose:* Effects of prolonged walking on concrete on the knees of sheep. J. Biomech. 15 (1982), 487–492

29. *Stacoff, A., X. Kaelin:* Pronation and sportshoe design. In: Biomechanical aspects of sport shoes and playing surfaces, pp. 143–151. *Nigg, B.M., B.A. Kerr* (eds.). University of Calgary, Canada 1983

30. *Voloshin, A., J. Wosk:* An in vivo study of low back pains and shock absorption in the human locomotor system. J. Biomech. 15 (1982), 21–27

PART 2 ——————— The Tennis Shoe

4 _____ The Tennis Shoe— Biomechanical Design Criteria

B.M. Nigg

S.M. Lüthi

H.A. Bahlsen*

During the last few decades, tennis has experienced an explosive growth. During the first half of this century, tennis was a recreational activity for the well-to-do. At the present time, it is available to all and also has a strong competitive component. In earlier years, tennis was played almost exclusively on grass or on the so-called clay courts. Today tennis is played on sand (clay), synthetic sand, grass, carpet, synthetic surfaces, mats, asphalt, and a variety of other surfaces. The previously strictly seasonal sport became a year-round activity. Its growth in some ways paralleled the growth of running (jogging).

It seems appropriate to devote considerable attention to the footwear used in this activity. Biomechanical analysis permits the study of two specific aspects of this footwear: (1) protection of the locomotor system from overloads and (2) performance. A search of the literature on biomechanics reveals that in recent years a veritable flood of papers has been published on the running shoe[2–5, 8, 11–15] but that there have been practically no publications about the tennis shoe. During the past decade, certain criteria have crystallized as far as the running shoe is concerned. One speaks of cushioning in the region of the heel, of pronation and excessive pronation during the support phase, and of supination during the takeoff phase.[9] Such attention has been devoted to the tennis shoe only recently.[1, 6, 16]

The purpose of this chapter is to establish and justify pertinent criteria for the design of tennis shoes. We will limit our attention to the problem of load and load reduction. An attempt to establish design criteria for the tennis shoe to reduce the load on the human locomotor system can be approached from a variety of directions. We see possibilities in the following:

- A study of the different movements that occur during tennis.
- A study of the discomfort and injuries caused by tennis.

*This work was supported by Adidas, Nike, AHFMR (Alberta Heritage Foundation for Medical Research), and NSERC (National Science and Engineering Research Council of Canada). The authors wish to express their appreciation for this support.

• A theoretical analysis (modeling) of the forces acting on and in the loco-motor system.

The first step is a discussion of the movements and of the complaints. The analysis of the external and internal loads will not be a part of this discussion.

MOVEMENTS IN TENNIS

The movements in running are cyclical. In contrast, the movements in tennis encompass a variety of movement patterns and are not cyclical. This may be one of the reasons why so much less has been published on the biomechanical aspects of tennis than on running (jogging). To quantify the various "movement patterns," a study was performed on 30 average and 4 advanced tennis players. In the average players, 300 strikes were analyzed during routine play. In the advanced players, an intensive, four-pronged study was performed. The specific activities that were studied were baseline play, attack at the net, volley, and smash. All parts of this study were performed "under pressure," i.e., the ball was played to the experimental subjects in such a way that they were just able to reach it. Three hundred strikes were evaluated for each type of activity. The same assessment techniques were used in both groups. Each strike received a five-part assessment:

1. Movement just prior to strike (walking, running, hopping)
2. Direction of strike (forward, backward, lateral)
3. Part of foot making contact (heel, ball of the foot)
4. Rotation of foot during strike (internal, external)
5. Direction after strike (forward, lateral)

All movements were performed on a hard surface (plastic-coated asphalt). The average players were also tested on two additional surfaces—clay and plastic.

The results of this study can be summarized as follows:

1. There is a difference between the movements performed by the average player and the player who trains or performs under pressure. In the average player, walking is the predominant form of movement, followed by running (forward), and sideslipping. The distribution is quite different in the trained athlete playing under pressure. Running and sideslipping are more frequent and appear at about the same rate as walking (Table 4–1).

The tennis shoe that has to meet the requirements of both the average player and the trained athlete, playing under pressure, must meet the known criteria for walking and running. It must also meet the additional requirements for lateral movements. The frequency of the various movements showed no significant difference relative to the playing surface among the average players. Sliding occurred on clay (sandy surface) only and was not observed on the other playing surfaces.

2. The region of the foot that touches the ground first is of interest with respect to the tennis shoe just as

TABLE 4–1.

Summary of the Frequency (in Percent) of the Different Types of Motion

Group	Motion				
	Walking	Running	Hopping	Jumping	Other
Under Pressure					
Baseline	28.2	33.9	32.9	2.6	2.4
Attack	30.6	47.1	19.8	0.5	2.0
Volley	33.6	19.9	27.1	4.6	14.9
Smash	33.5	18.3	36.2	11.5	0.5
Routine	73.5	15.2	8.8	1.8	0.7

it is with the running shoe. The findings for both the average player and for the player under pressure are shown in Table 4–2. The average player makes contact most frequently with the heel. Contact with the ball of the foot occurs only about half as often. In "pressure" players contact is made most frequently with the ball of the foot. It is also noted that contact with the inner or outer edge occurs with some frequency. These results indicate that the tennis shoe must be designed for landings on the heel, on the ball of the foot, and also on the inner and outer edges.

3. The most frequent direction of movement of the average player is forward. This occurs in more than 60% of all strikes. For the "pressure" player lateral movement becomes more frequent (Table 4–3). In baseline play and the volley, lateral movements occur about as frequently as forward movements. Lateral movements are frequently combined with landing on the forefoot. This emphasizes the importance of the relationship of lateral movements and load problems in tennis. In this respect, tennis is clearly different from running (jogging).

TENNIS INJURIES

The two studies that we have performed can give us information concerning the etiology of discomfort, pain, and injury in tennis. The first study was retrospective; 1,018 tennis players were asked to complete a questionnaire covering two to three seasons (1 season = 6 months).[10] Each participant was counted as one

TABLE 4–2.

Summary of the Frequency (in Percent) of Initial Ground Contact for Different Regions of the Foot

Group	Part of Foot				
	Heel	Ball	Outer Edge	Inner Edge	Other
Under pressure					
Baseline	27.1	54.6	5.0	3.8	9.3
Attack	26.4	53.5	4.6	1.5	14.0
Volley	24.0	54.3	2.3	2.9	16.5
Smash	25.5	56.3	3.3	2.0	12.9
Routine	58.2	27.2	0.7	1.2	12.7

TABLE 4–3.

Summary of the Frequency (in Percent) of the Different Directions of Motion

	Direction of Motion				
Group	Forward	Backward	Lateral	Vertical	Other
Under Pressure					
Baseline	46.3	10.3	38.9	1.1	3.4
Attack	48.6	26.1	22.1	1.9	1.3
Volley	32.4	12.1	40.4	4.1	11.0
Smash	35.0	21.0	36.6	3.6	3.8
Routine	61.1	8.7	16.1	0.7	13.4

case for each season. Most of the injuries focused on the back, the knee, and the ankle.

One of the interesting findings concerns the effect of playing surface on the frequency of injuries. When those injuries that could not have had any relationship to playing surface were eliminated, it became evident that there was a significant relationship between the type of playing surface and the frequency of complaints (Fig 4–1).

The two surfaces that permit some sliding, sand and synthetic sand, show significantly fewer problems than those surfaces that permit no sliding. Even though these findings relate to the playing surface, it seems reasonable to consider in this context friction and tennis shoe design as well.

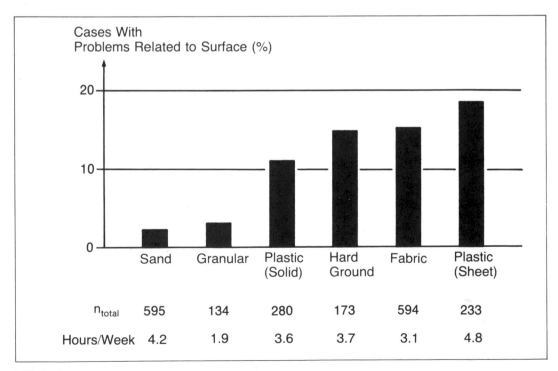

FIG 4–1.
Percent incidence of surface-related injuries for the different surfaces.

In a second study, the effect of the tennis shoe on the frequency of problems was investigated.[7, 9] Two hundred healthy subjects were examined anthropometrically, biomechanically, and medically at the onset of the study. Subsequently, half the subjects were given a soft tennis shoe, and the other half were provided with a stiff shoe. Both of these shoes were commercially available at the time. The subjects then played tennis, at least twice each week, for 2 months. If any problem occurred, they had to see a physician, who completed a questionnaire and made a diagnosis. The following were the most significant findings in this prospective study:

1. Of all participants, 39.8% complained of some injury that was examined and diagnosed by a physician. Most of these complaints involved the feet.

2. There was a difference between the two groups in the frequency of problems. The soft shoe group had an incidence of 32.1%, and the hard shoe group one of 47.1%. A breakdown of the injuries on the basis of location revealed that in the soft shoe group most of the problems were in the region of the arch of the foot. In the hard shoe group, the toes, ankles, and knees were primarily affected. This indicates that the shoe affects not only the frequency of occurrence but also the location of the injuries.

3. A biomechanical motion analysis revealed differences between the two groups, particularly in the lateral movements.[6] For the sake of clarity, it must be reemphasized that these movements occurred at the onset of the study. The variable that gave the most interesting results was the angle between the Achilles tendon and the heel counter. This angle will be referred to as the Achilles tendon angle. Changes in the magnitude of the angle are related to pronatory and supinatory movements of the foot (Fig 4–2). Subjects wearing the soft shoe showed, on the average, more supination than the subjects with the harder shoe. This was an expected result (Table 4–4). The interesting results of this study emerge only when the data are analyzed according to injuries with respect to type of shoe.

The "soft-shoe" subjects with injuries showed, on the average, more supination than the subjects in the same group who had no problems. In the "hard-shoe" group, the results were just the opposite. Subjects with complaints supinated less. These results suggest that there is an ideal range of supination as far as lateral movement is concerned.

CRITERIA FOR TENNIS SHOE CONSTRUCTION

The most important results of the two biomechanical studies can be summarized as follows:

1. Running (heel-toe) is a very frequent movement in tennis. The findings of the biomechanical studies on running shoes should be applied accordingly. This pertains particularly to heel cushioning in the lateral region of the hindfoot and to pronation.

2. Landing on the forefoot is very common in good players. Attenuation

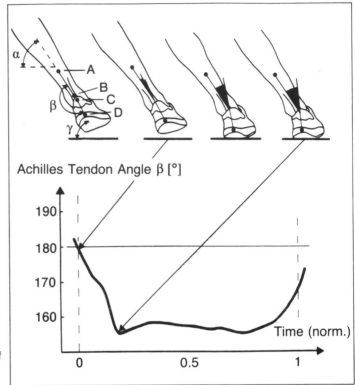

FIG 4–2.
Example of the temporal course of the Achilles tendon angle during lateral motion.

in the forefoot region is a new concept that must be investigated. Information about this problem area is scanty, since this aspect is of no importance in the running shoe (heel running).

3. The frictional relationships between shoe and ground are obviously important. The results of the retrospective study showed the dominant

TABLE 4–4.

Supination in Relationship to Type of Shoe and Injuries*

Shoe	Injuries	Supination (Degrees)	n
Soft	Without	21.1 (5.4)	93
	With	23.0 (4.2)	46
Stiff	Without	15.0 (6.3)	71
	With	11.6 (4.4)	69

*From *Luethi SM:* Biomechanical analysis of pain in tennis, Ph.D. thesis. University of Calgary, Canada, 1983. Used by permission.

influence of the playing surface. The frictional characteristics can be influenced by the shoe. Two aspects must be kept in mind: translation and rotation. As far as translation is concerned, the frictional characteristics are important primarily on surfaces that permit sliding. They are less important on surfaces where sliding is not possible. As far as rotation (resistance to rotation) is concerned, the frictional relationships are important on all surfaces. The range of the frictional coefficients (for translation) and of the momentum of rotation (resistance to rotation) for six different playing surfaces and ten different tennis and other shoes is shown in Figure 4–3.

The diagram shows two interesting phenomena: (1) Not all surfaces

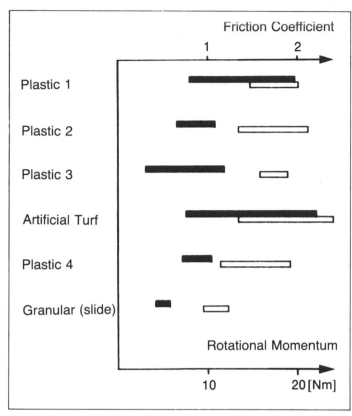

FIG 4−3.
The range of the friction coefficient (*solid line*) from a material testing study and of the maximal rotational momentum (*hollow lines*) from a study on experimental subjects wearing ten different tennis and "all-around" shoes.

react equally to the shoes. Artificial surface 3, for example, has a wide variety of results for the translational friction coefficient. The shoe is obviously important. The same surface shows only a narrow range for rotational resistance. On artificial surface 4, the results are reversed. (2) Translational and rotational friction can be quite different. The first three artificial surfaces show little difference for rotational friction but obvious differences in translational friction.

4. Lateral movements and supination during such lateral movement and changes in the direction of the movement are obviously all important when considering the load, the injuries, and their relationship to the tennis shoe. There seems to be an ideal range of motion. Both too little and too much supinatory movement have negative biomechanical effects. Too little affects the joints and too much the ligaments.

This chapter points out the important features of the tennis shoe from a biomechanical point of view (overloading the locomotor system). The significance of individual features is summarized in a somewhat speculative fashion. Since general information in this area is still relatively meager, it is likely that further studies will mandate revisions of the current thinking. The items in Table 4−5 should therefore be regarded only as a starting point for further discussions.

TABLE 4–5.

Summary of the Important Criteria
for the Design of Tennis Shoes
from a Biomechanical Perspective

Perspective	Significance
Supination	Very important
Cushioning—heel	Important
Cushioning—ball	Important
Rotational friction	Important
Translational friction	Important only on sand, granular surface, etc.

REFERENCES

1. *Bahlsen, H.A., B.M. Nigg:* Selection of a lateral test movement for tennis. In: Biomechanical aspects of sport shoes and playing surfaces, pp. 169–176. *Nigg, B.M., B.A. Kerr* (eds.). University Printing, Calgary 1983

2. *Cavanagh, P.R.:* The running shoe book. Mountain View, California 1981

3. *Clarke, T.E., E.C. Frederick, C. Hamill:* The study of rearfoot movement in running. In: Sport shoes and playing surfaces, pp. 166–189. *Frederick, E.C.* (ed.). Human Kinetics Publishers, Champaign, Ill. 1984

4. *Frederick, E.C.:* Measuring the effects of shoes and surfaces on the economy of locomotion. In: Biomechanical aspects of sport shoes and playing surfaces, pp. 93–106. *Nigg, B.M., B.A. Kerr* (eds.). University Printing, Calgary 1983

5. *Frederick, E.C., J.L. Hagy, R.A. Mann:* The prediction of vertical impact force during running. J. Biomech. 14 (1981), 498

6. *Luethi, S.M.:* Biomechanical analysis of pain in tennis. Ph.D. thesis. University of Calgary, Canada 1983

7. *Luethi, S.M., E.C. Frederick, M.A. Hawes, B.M. Nigg:* The influence of shoe construction on lower extremity kinematics and load during lateral movement in tennis. Int. J. Sport Biomech. 3 (1986), 166–174

8. *MacLellan, G.E., B. Vyvyan:* Management of pain beneath the heel and achilles tendinitis with viscoelastic heel inserts. B. J. Sports Med. 15 (1981), 117–121

9. *Nigg, B.M.:* Biomechanics of running shoes. Human Kinetics Publishers, Champaign, Ill. 1986

10. *Nigg, B.M., J. Denoth:* Sportplatzbeläge. Juris, Zürich 1980

11. *Nigg, B.M., G. Eberle, D. Frey, S.M. Luethi, B. Segesser, B. Weber:* Gait analysis and sport shoe construction. In: Biomechanics VI-A, pp. 303–309. *Assmussen, E.P., K. Joergeusen* (eds.). University Park Press, Baltimore 1978

12. *Nigg, B.M., S.M. Luethi:* Bewegungsanalysen beim Laufschuh. Sportwissenschaft 3 (1980), 309–320

13. *Segesser, B.:* Verletzungsprophylaxe durch geeignetes Sportschuhwerk. In: Die Belastungstoleranz des Bewegungsapparates, S. 194–203. *Cotta, H., H. Krahl, K. Steinbrück* (eds.). Thieme, Stuttgart 1980

14. *Segesser, B., B.M. Nigg:* Insertionstendinosen am Schienbein, Achillodynie und Überlastungsfolgen am Fuß—Ätiologie, Biomechanik, therapeutische Möglichkeiten. Orthopädie 9 (1980), 207–217

15. *Stacoff, A., X. Kaelin:* Pronation and sport shoe design. In: Biomechanical aspects of sport shoes and playing surfaces, pp. 143–151. *Nigg, B.M., B.A. Kerr* (eds.). University Printing, Calgary 1983

16. *Tiegermann, V.:* Reaction forces and EMG activity in fast sidewards movements. In: Biomechanical aspects of sport shoes and playing surfaces, pp. 83–90. *Nigg, B.M., B.A. Kerr* (eds.). University Printing, Calgary 1983

5   Tennis Injuries and Excessive Load Problems— Medical Criteria of the Tennis Shoe

G. Biehl

The explosive development and spread of tennis during the past two decades has, naturally, created considerable problems for sports medicine and traumatology. There is not only the trained athlete, who swings a racket on a daily basis, both outdoors and on the indoor courts, but there are also the large masses of leisure time and weekend tennis players, whose posture and locomotor apparatus is suddenly exposed to new and therefore unphysiologic loads. These mass participants frequently select their racket with great care but pay little or no attention to the selection of the best possible footwear.

The lower extremity, on which players, depending on training or talent, dance or stumble around on the tennis court, is a complex structure consisting of 26 bones and at least twice as many muscles and tendons. As long as this complex structure is not exposed to excessive loads, it will give its owner no headaches, i.e., sore feet. Unfortunately, tennis makes it very difficult for the feet to get through their motions without some problems. Contrary to popular belief, it is not the tennis elbow or the tennis shoulder that brings the player to the attention of the physician; 76% of all tennis injuries are located in the lower extremity (Fig 5–1).

ACUTE INJURIES

Muscle Injuries

The most common muscular injuries suffered by tennis players are strains, although occasionally true muscle tears may occur. The most common site for these muscular strains is among the innermost fibers of the median gastrocnemius muscle, and these strains can develop into true tears. These injuries occur when the toes on the affected side have to bear the entire weight of the player at a time when the calf muscles are con-

47

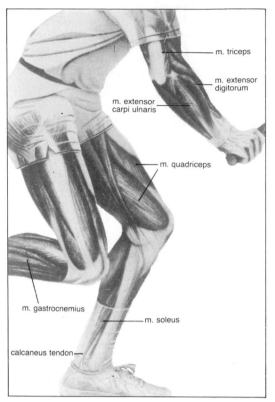

m. triceps

m. extensor digitorum

m. extensor carpi ulnaris

m. quadriceps

m. gastrocnemius

m. soleus

calcaneus tendon—

FIG 5–1.
The muscles typically used in tennis.

tracted, the knee is flexed, and the foot is in maximal plantar flexion. This injury is so characteristic of tennis that it is known as the "tennis leg." The player experiences a sudden sharp pain in the calf and may actually fall down. If the defect is minor, pain may not appear for 24 or 48 hours. Loss of function, limping, swelling of the calf, considerable tenderness to pressure, and the typical discoloration of a hematoma are the classic symptoms that make the diagnosis easy.

The median head of the gastrocnemius muscle is the most frequently affected component of the triceps surae muscle, since this is the only portion of the muscle that proceeds

medially. All the other flexors proceed laterally to the lateral condyle (lateral head of the gastrocnemius muscle) or to the head of the fibula (soleus muscle). The medial muscle belly of the gastrocnemius muscle has a different rotational function at the knee than the other calf muscles, and in this function, it has no synergistic muscles. This leads to contractural conflicts between the components of this three-headed muscle group that may lead to muscular tears once the limits of elasticity are exceeded. As far as therapy for the gastrocnemius tear or for the tangential separation at the level of the musculotendinous junction is concerned, the general principles of athletic injury management prevail. The decision whether to treat surgically or conservatively depends on individual findings.

Rupture of the Achilles Tendon

The same is true for the true rupture of the Achilles tendon. This injury is not rare in tennis and is manifested acoustically, particularly indoors, as the cracking of a whip. Achilles tendon ruptures occur more frequently indoors than out-of-doors and most commonly affect the players in the older age groups, who may have advanced degenerative changes.

Ankle Sprains

Other than the abovementioned strains, tears, and Achilles tendon ruptures, the most common acute tennis injury is an ankle sprain. It can be assumed that fully one third of the acute tennis injuries will be sprained ankles. The sprain frequently masks a true ligamentous tear, particularly of the fibular ligaments. This occurrence must be looked for and identified by radiography or by arthrography. As for etiology of this injury, the most commonly mentioned events are "turning an ankle," landing at an angle after a jump, slipping on the wet ground, or stepping on a ball (Fig 5–2). Particularly dangerous are the cinder courses that have been too heavily sprinkled in the summer, or that were not given enough time to dry out after a thunderstorm. In the fall, the presence of wet leaves on the playing surface is a source of real danger. Indoors this injury primarily affects the untrained player or the player who tries to play beyond his capacity. In these players, the coordination of the body, but particularly the coordination of the legs, becomes uncontrolled and dysrhythmic due to fatigue.

Therapy

First aid at the site of the injury consists of the application of an ice bag or of a cooling or elastic bandage. This must be followed by a diagnostic workup in the hospital or office to determine the extent of injury accurately and to initiate the surgical repair of a ruptured ligament. Surgical repair of a ruptured ligament permits the precise reconstruction of the injured part and prevents the later development of an unstable joint. The immediate removal of blood clots prevents later damage to cartilage, and visual inspection of the articulating surfaces will allow discovery of internal joint trauma.

It is of interest that recently the shoe industry has made a contribution to postoperative care by developing a special shoe with high lateral bars. These permit some flexion and extension of the joint but prevent supination. This concept is important when the prevention of the dreaded "immobilization complications" is considered. This partial mobility of the ankle keeps the calf muscles active, helps to prevent circulatory complications and swelling through the activity of the muscle pump, and presumably improves the generally poor nutrition of the articulating cartilage. Tennis players who have suffered such injury, or who are con-

FIG 5–2.
Torsion occurs usually as a result of slippage.

fronted with a recurring fibular ligament instability, may benefit from wearing such special shoes. These special shoes may actually be boots with malleolar pads and adjustable upper shanks. A slight elevation of the lateral edge of the shoe may be of considerable assistance.

CHRONIC OVERLOAD SYNDROMES

The Tennis Heel

The numerous overload syndromes and chronic irritative conditions in the calf and foot region in tennis players are much more significant than the acute injuries. The most important chronic condition is the so-called tennis heel, a condition that must be carefully examined and not taken at face value. Similarly, the condition of achillodynia is much too complex to permit an etiologic therapy or even a specific preventive regimen. Achilles tendon complaints may be due to Haglund exostoses or to dorsal calcaneus spurs. Usually these bony changes cannot be demonstrated, and yet tennis players complain bitterly about pain in the area of the Achilles tendon.

What is usually found is the so-called paratenonitis achillea, i.e., a chronic inflammation of the connective tissue sheath surrounding the Achilles tendon. This represents one of the most common overload syndromes encountered in sports medicine. We see this clinical picture both in the occasional tennis player whose tendon sheath is exposed to sudden, unexpected, and excessive loads and in the championship class player whose Achilles tendon is exposed to extreme loads.

Particular problems are presented by the different types of floors encountered in the indoor courts and by the very different types of surfaces and consistencies found in the outdoor playing areas. It can be taken for granted that the hard surfaces of the indoor courts, even the carpeted ones, are more unfavorable for the Achilles tendon and its sheath than the cinder courts or the granular artificial surface courts.

The pushoff forces in running are approximately 300 kPa, and the phase of acceleration is substantially shortened on artificial surfaces. Since the athlete touches the ground during running and jumping primarily with his toes, the entire work of jumping and shock attenuation must be borne by the triceps surae muscle and must be transmitted via the Achilles tendon and its sheath. Given a certain predisposition, these increased demands will inevitably lead to a state of chronic irritation. The complaints typically originate about three fingerbreadths above the insertion of the Achilles tendon. Complaints are predominant in the early training phases but may increase over a period of maximal training or competing. The para-achillary grooves are obliterated, and the para-achillary tissues are edematous and tender. Occasionally a mild crepitation is palpable or audible. At times there is some heat and reddening of the skin in this area.

Therapy

Therapy must begin with a complete prohibition of athletic activity. Local and systemic anti-inflammatory therapy, physical therapy, and elastic bandages that limit motion and keep the foot in a slightly extended position are all very beneficial. The most important item, however, is the procurement of a good tennis shoe that securely cushions the heel and the insertion of the Achilles tendon. In addition, the shoe should decrease the load by a slight elevation of the heel and should also have a good cushioning sole.

It should be mentioned that in cases that do not respond to conservative therapy surgical removal of the affected Achilles tendon sheath has given good results. In these cases it is very important to provide optimal footwear prior to resuming athletic activity so that the already weakened and previously affected Achilles tendon is properly protected. In true calcaneal spurring, the affected area must be well protected and cushioned with a soft insert. To do this successfully, the tennis shoe must be large enough to accommodate the individually designed insert. The shoe must also be high enough in the back to provide a solid support for the heel and to keep the insert from being displaced.

Plantar Aponeuritis

One of the very unpleasant manifestations of strain in tennis players is the so-called plantar aponeuritis. This is a painful hardening of the tendinous plate of the sole. The etiology of this condition is a combination of severe overexertion and a preexisting pedal anomaly, e.g., splayfoot. What is needed is an anatomically correct shoe that not only provides a soft base for the foot, but also corrects and supports it. Very painful tightening of the plantar aponeurosis can be encountered in the area of the midfoot as well. This is usually accompanied by cramping of the small muscles that support the transverse arch. In these cases, it is also important to make the necessary anatomical adaptation by inserting appropriate wedges.

The Tennis Toe

We must not ignore the extreme tip of the foot of a tennis player, i.e., the toes. Every tennis player who has claw toes or hammer toes is going to have a difficult time in selecting appropriate footwear. It is mandatory that the manufacturer of the athletic

FIG 5–3.
During service, the player rocks on the tips of the toes.

shoes provide increased toe space and/or incorporate padding at the potential pressure points. The greatest attention must be devoted to the prevention of the back-to-front displacement of the foot. It is this problem that is responsible for the development of the tennis toe, a condition well known to all tennis players. Every player who uses his height when serving and thus stands on his toes, or the player who frequently plays in midcourt and thus "glides" into the ball, is very familiar with this problem of toe mobility (Fig 5–3).

The toes need some free space. At the same time, the sole must provide a rotational and braking function in all directions. A rocker device has proved very helpful in this connection.

SUMMARY

The problem areas relative to the tennis leg and tennis foot are as follows: the Achilles tendon and the heel area, the ligaments of the ankle, the plantar aponeurosis, the plantar arch, and finally the toes that are exposed to the inevitable forward sliding motion, inseparable from tennis.

This places the following requirements on the manufacturer of tennis shoes: the athletic shoe industry must take into account the many and varying playing surfaces used both in summer and winter. The players are entitled to expect both a solid grip from the sole of the shoe, as well as a certain ability to slide and glide. It is important, particularly on the harder playing surfaces of the indoor courts, that sufficient cushioning be provided by the shoe, not only for the Achilles tendon and the foot, but also for the knee, hip, and spinal column. Soft padding is of critical importance in the area of the Achilles tendon and of the dorsal aspect of the foot. Good rocking in the area of the ball of the foot is equally important. The toes need room to move, and assistance in rocking makes good sense, as already mentioned above. To have an optimally designed footbed is extremely important in players with poor arch structure and midfoot complaints. If the ankle is chronically unstable, the heel counter must be strengthened laterally and malleolar padding must be provided.

Even though the athletic shoe industry has reached a remarkably high standard, there is still room for an improved exchange of information between the orthopedic surgeon, the active athlete, and the athletic shoe manufacturer. Improvements in the present standards can only be achieved when the practical experience of the player with foot problems and the biomechanical knowledge of the orthopedic surgeon can be transmitted to the manufacturer of athletic footwear. Accomplishing this goal will provide athletes with greater enjoyment in their activities, the physician with a happier patient, and the manufacturer with a satisfied customer.

6   Rapid Sideward Movements in Tennis

A. Stüssi

A. Stacoff

V. Tiegermann

In tennis, great strain is placed on the lower extremities, particularly during rapid sideward movements and changes in direction.[2, 6] The same is true for other sports where the same type of mobility is required. These include volleyball, basketball, and handball. It is important, therefore, to give careful consideration to the various types of motion involved in rapid sideward movement to find a way to reduce this strain.

The goals of this chapter are (1) to discuss from a biomechanical perspective the strain placed on the lower extremities during various movements and (2) to present the findings of two studies on rapid lateral movements (the effects of shoe shaft height on supination, and the effects on the ankle of friction between shoe and ground).

BIOMECHANICAL CONSIDERATIONS OF RAPID SIDEWARD MOVEMENTS

It is generally assumed that the heaviest strains in tennis are generated during the braking and/or rotatory movements when the foot is fixed in relation to the ground. In this situation, the foot is placed into an unphysiologic position that can lead to structural distortion if the strain is heavy enough. In rapid sideward movements, there are at least three ways in which a change in direction (braking and starting in the opposite direction) can take place when viewed from the perspective of functional anatomy (Fig 6–1):

1. With a forward lunge, the foot is positioned in the direction of motion.

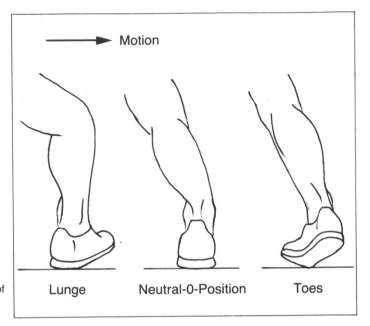

FIG 6−1.
Three possible landing positions of the foot in braking a rapid lateral move.

Lunge   Neutral-0-Position   Toes

2. The foot lands on the heel or forefoot in an approximately neutral-0-position, perpendicular to the direction of motion and of the tibia.
3. The foot lands on the lateral edge at the level of the ball of the foot, with the tibia in internal rotation (tiptoe position).

Forward Lunge

By virtue of the forward lunge, the axis of the ankle and the axis of the knee are perpendicular to the direction of motion. This provides the kinetic chain (thigh-leg-foot) with the optimal opportunity to capture the motion at the knee or ankle and thus prevent a lateral strain on the foot.

Neutral-0-Landing

In this position, the locomotor apparatus can capture a certain percentage of the motion in the subtalar joint and combine this with corrective motion in the ankle joint. The compensatory motion is necessary since the axis of the subtalar joint is not in an anteroposterior (AP) position. The muscles (peroneal group) and the lateral ligaments are exposed to considerable strain. This strain is aggravated by the fact that in this position the trochlea of the talus is not fully locked into the malleolar fork. The remaining braking motion is accomplished by bending the knee and the ankle joint at a 90-degree angle to the direction of the motion.

Tibia Internally Rotated —Tiptoe Position

The foot lands in an extended position on the lateral edge of the ball of the foot with the tibia in slight internal rotation. This leads to maximal instability in the ankle joint (the trochlea of the talus is the smallest). Due to the great distance between the blocked ball of the foot and the axis of the tibia, momentary forces may be generated that can adversely affect the entire supination line.

The three possible braking movements can occur in all athletes in a variety of combinations. What then can the athletic shoe do to improve the situations listed in the preceding items 2 and 3? The following possibilities exist: (1) The lateral ligaments and thus the peroneal muscles can be supported by appropriate shoe modifications (e.g., a high shaft), or (2) the major torsion effects can be avoided by allowing the shoe to glide over the ground. These options were investigated in the two studies discussed in the next two sections.

EFFECT OF THE HEIGHT OF THE SHAFT ON THE SUPINATORY MOTION IN RAPID LATERAL MOVEMENTS

The Problem

Shoes with three different shaft heights (prototypes) were used to investigate the lateral stability of the foot. To do the studies motion pictures were taken from the back at 200 frames per second.[4] The athletes were asked to change their seat rapidly between two chairs placed side by side, with a space between them and to do this without crossing their legs. Movies were taken of the third, fourth, and fifth lateral changes of position.

Experimental Design

The stability of the ankle was determined from the motion pictures by measuring the three angles (α, β, and γ) during the breaking phase, as described by Nigg et al.[2] The Achilles tendon angle β (Fig 6−2) was used as the criterion for lateral stability. Measurement errors due to the mobility of the skin were ignored as insignificant. The study population consisted of 15 male athletes (5 tennis players, 4 volleyball players, 3 handball players, 2 basketball players, and 1 netball player).

Six different prototype shoes were available for the study. They differed

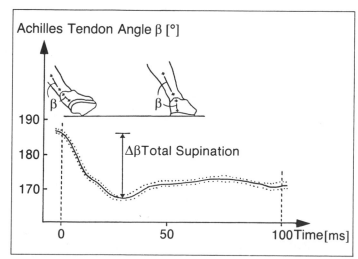

FIG 6−2.
Position and course of the Achilles tendon angle β. (Adapted from Nigg, B.M., S.M. Luethi: Bewegungsanalysen beim Laufschuh, Sportwissenschaft 3 (1980), 309−320.)

from each other by the height of the shaft and the construction of the sole (Table 6–1). Three shoes were provided with edging, as is frequently used in indoor shoes. The other three shoes had a conventional sole construction, as is commonly seen in tennis shoes and running shoes. The "low" shoes corresponded to normal running or tennis shoes. The "intermediate" shoes corresponded to basketball shoes, as far as the height of the shaft was concerned. The last two shoes had the shaft height of boxing shoes.

Purpose

The purpose of the study was to determine whether a design with an edging, and/or the height of the shaft had any effect on the lateral stability. To evaluate the results, a statistical trend test and a rank-sum test were used. The rank ordering was always done for all six shoes within the same test subject.

Results

The results are summarized in Figure 6–3.

1. In all braking maneuvers, the lower leg angle is very constant, i.e., in all subjects and with all 6 shoes, the angle was approximately 57 degrees at the time of contact with the surface and changed to approximately 59 degrees at the end of the 100-msec study period. This means that the experimental subjects all held their lower leg in about the same position during this braking maneuver, so that the starting point for the stability measurements remained approximately the same.

2. The Achilles tendon angle β showed no significant differences between the shoes with or without edging, at the time of maximal flexion (supination after approximately 50 msec). This means that the edging did not affect the lateral stability in any measurable way.

3. A significant difference could be demonstrated between the shoe with low shaft and the shoes with intermediate and high shaft. There was no difference between the shoe with intermediate shaft and the shoe with high shaft. This means that the high shaft has no additional effect on the stability of the shoes tested.

It is noteworthy that the interindividual scatter is substantially greater than the intraindividual scatter. This means that each person has his or her individual, characteristic supination range, which can, however, be affected by the height of the shaft.

It could be demonstrated that appropriate measures of design (height

TABLE 6–1.

Test Shoes (No. 1–6)

	Low: Shaft Height 10.5 cm	Medium: Shaft Height 14.5 cm	High: Shaft Height 23 cm
Without edging	1	3	5
With edging	2	4	6

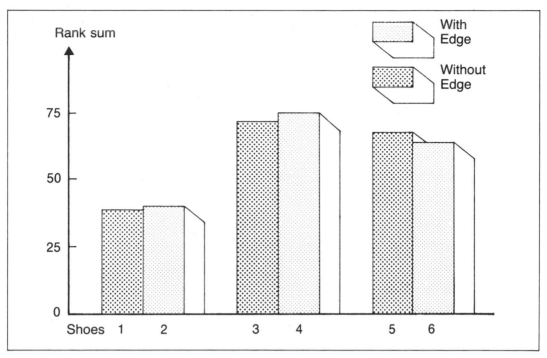

FIG 6–3.
Rank sums of the different shoe types relative to supination.

of shaft) could reduce the strain on the lateral ligaments and the peroneal musculature, i.e., shoes with high shafts can provide mechanical support for these structures. This does not mean, however, that a shoe with a high shaft can protect from distortion in every case.

THE EFFECTS OF SHOE-GROUND INTERACTION ON ANKLE STRAIN

The Problem

Like the last study, this investigation also dealt with the strain generated by rapid sideward movement.[6] The task set for the participants in this study (five experienced, male tennis players) was to transfer tennis balls from one container, at hip level, to another container 3 m away. The second container was placed so that the brake maneuver had to take place over a force plate (Kistler model) (Fig 6–4).

Methodology

In addition to measuring the forces and the contact coordinates, we also measured muscular activity in the peroneus longus (pronation) and soleus (supination) muscles to obtain an estimate of the muscle forces generated. By measuring the force generated by the braking maneuver and by the muscular activity, we could estimate the strain put on the ankle. In the experiment, we used a regular tennis shoe (Stan Smith Adidas). One half of the Kistler plate

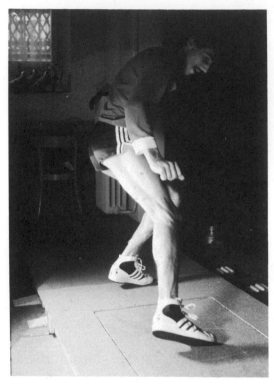

FIG 6–4.
Setup for measuring the load on the ankle on different floor coverings.

was covered with fabric, the other half was covered with sand.

Objective

The purpose of this study was to determine whether differing sliding potentials of the shoe could produce differing amounts of strain on the lateral ligaments and on the peroneal musculature.

Results

1. Measurement of force (Fig 6–5): Use of the four-dimensional vector diagram[5] in which the force vectors are shown at the point of contact, at a rate of 5 msec, demonstrated the difference in the braking maneuver on a fabric surface as compared to a sandy surface. On the fabric, the point of contact remains practically in one place, i.e., there is no slippage. On a sandy surface, the slippage is shown by a displacement of the point of contact to the right. The size of the force generated, represented by the length of the force vectors, clearly

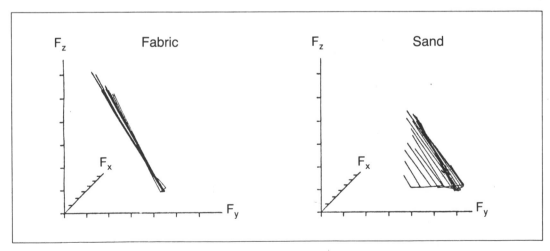

FIG 6–5.
Vectors of the braking force on sand and on fabric.

shows that more force was generated on the fabric than on the sandy surface. The figures show that the strain on the locomotor system is considerably greater on fabric than on the sandy surface. Measuring the friction coefficient for both surfaces reveals that the sandy surface has a friction coefficient of approximately 0.5 (static friction up to 0.6), while the fabric surface had a value of 1.0

The slide on the sandy surface results in a longer braking phase and thus generated less force. From the point of view of strain, it seems that a sliding friction of 0.5 is preferable to one of 1.0. If the friction coefficient is too small, it can lead to danger, since excessive slipperiness can lead to a fall and thus to injuries.

2. Electromyogram (EMG) and force: The results shown in Figure 6–6 are based on the same type of breaking maneuver as shown in Figure 6–5. The EMG activity of the soleus and peroneus muscles is shown, and the force generated is shown as a function of time. On the left is the result of a braking maneuver on a fabric surface, and on the right, the same on a sandy surface. As could have been expected on the basis of the vector diagram, the strain on the ankle (rotational momentum) that has to be captured by the musculature is smaller on the sandy surface (see the raw EMG, but also the integrated EMG tracing).

In both cases, a preliminary response can be seen that indicates an anticipatory response to the coming strain. The point where the motion comes to a stop is clearly different on the fabric surface and the sandy surface. This shows that during the braking maneuver on the sandy surface the muscle strain is less, and therefore the strain on the ankle is less as well. On takeoff, the activity of the soleus muscle is the same on both surfaces. Apparently the takeoff maneuver took place in the area of static friction of the sandy surface so that the same amount of force could be generated on this surface as on the fabric one.

It can be concluded from both studies (force and EMG) that the strain on the locomotor system is lower on a sandy surface than on a fabric surface. Too little friction between the shoe and the ground can also be dangerous for the athlete (slipping and falling). From the point of view of performance (championship athletes), a somewhat greater friction coefficient is desirable, since this would permit a more rapid response. The athlete could reach a desired point on the court more rapidly and thus be stationary when returning the ball.

For this reason, an optimal point must be found between the ability of the ankle to withstand strain (muscle training) and all likely playing conditions (friction coefficient between shoe and ground). It seems that by wearing a more stable shoe (i.e., one with a higher shaft) greater strain can be tolerated, and thus a friction coefficient closer to 1.0 becomes acceptable. Beginners and poorly trained tennis players should play with a type of shoe that allows some sliding even on a fabric surface.

These findings were substantiated by the studies of Spiess and Hasenfratz[3] who found in an investigation

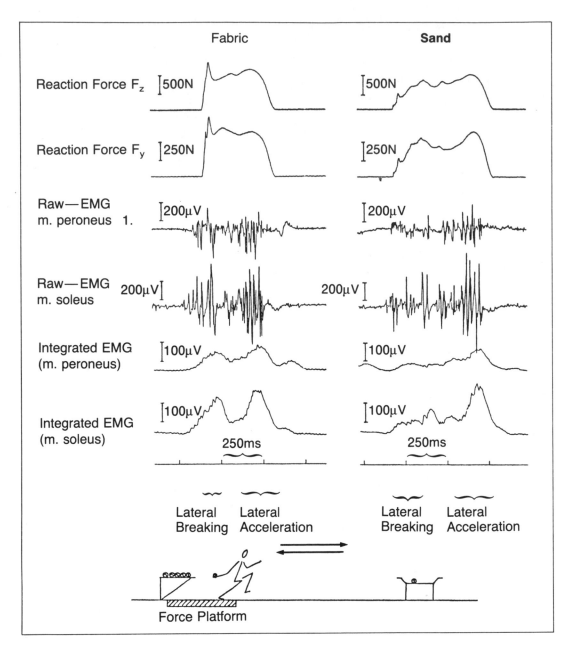

FIG 6–6.
EMG and force curves in lateral braking on sand and on fabric (for explanation see text).

of 2,481 injuries suffered by tennis players that most of the injuries and complaints involved the lower extremities (ankles and knees) and the back (Fig 6–7). It seems also that in tennis the principal strain on the lower extremity is generated by sudden changes in direction, by the braking maneuver, and, most acutely, by a lateral slip. This is no different from other sports, particularly indoor athletic activities. The most frequent in-

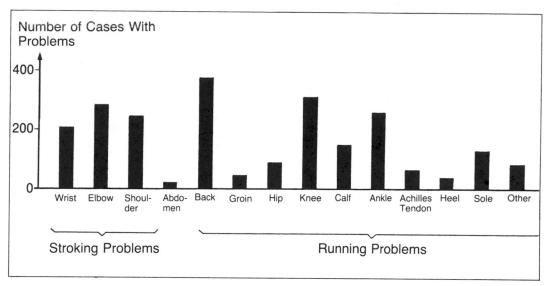

FIG 6–7.
Injury and complaint statistics from a study of 2,481 tennis players. (From Spiess, U., U. Hasenfratz: Beschwerden und Verletzungen beim Tennisspiel. Diplomarbeit in Biomechanik, T & S ETH-Zürich 1980. Used by permission.)

juries were sprains of the ankle, particularly of the lateral ligaments.

SUMMARY

A frequent cause of injury in tennis and in other indoor sports is the fixation of the feet during rapid changes in direction. If one disregards standing rotation, there are different braking maneuvers that, from a biomechanical point of view, carry different risks of injury:

Forward lunge	Small risk
Neutral-0-position	Intermediate risk
Internal rotation (tiptoe)	High risk

The results of two studies on rapid sideward movements show the effect of the height of the shaft of the shoe on stability and also the effects of the shoe-ground interaction on the strain placed on the locomotor apparatus, particularly on the ankle joints.

In view of the given functional anatomical conditions, it seems reasonable to construct a tennis shoe such that it both protects and supports the lateral ligaments and the peroneal muscles, and that it also has a sole designed and adapted to the different playing surfaces so that it permits some sliding. In this way, the risks of blocking the foot could be minimized when tennis is being played on a fabric surface.

REFERENCES

1. *Nigg, B.M., S.M. Luethi:* Bewegungsanalysen beim Laufschuh, Sportwissenschaft 3 (1980), 309–320
2. *Nigg, B.M., S.M. Luethi, A. Bahlsen:* Influence of shoe construction on the supination during sidewards movements in tennis. In: Biomechanics: Current interdisciplinary research. *Perren, S.M., E. Schneider* (eds.). Martinus Nijhoff, Dordrecht 1985

3. *Spiess, U., U. Hasenfratz:* Beschwerden und Verletzungen beim Tennisspiel. Diplomarbeit in Biomechanik, T&S ETH-Zürich 1980

4. *Stacoff, A., E. Stuessi, D. Sonderegger:* Lateral stability of sportshoes. In: Biomechanics IX. *Winter, D.A.* (ed.). Human Kinetics, Champaign, Ill. 1983

5. *Stuessi, E.:* Vierdimensionale Vektordarstellung der Bodenkräfte beim Gehen. Med. Orthop. Technik 6 (1977), 176−178

6. *Tiegermann, V.:* Belastung des Bewegungsapparates und deren Quantifizierung mit Hilfe der Elektromyographie. Inauguraldissertation an der ETH Zürich 1984

PART 3 — The Court Shoe

7   Indoor Athletic Playing Surfaces— Floor vs. Shoe

J. Denoth*

Every athletic discipline has its own athletic shoe. There are court shoes for handball, basketball, volleyball, soccer, and other sports. There are special shoes for track and tennis for both indoor and outdoor facilities. There is also a wide variety of jogging shoes, and golf shoes. This wide variety reflects the current status of the shoe business. Whether these differences in shoes derive from the traditions of the individual athletic disciplines or whether they originate with the shoe industry is immaterial. The important question is why and how do these shoes differ from each other?

At a time when athletics generally were being studied scientifically, it was inevitable that the athletic shoe also would become a subject for scientific investigation. The objectives in mind are performance and the load on the locomotor system. These are both of great importance, as much for the championship class competitor as for the masses who participate in athletics. The situation is quite similar in regard to the athletic playing surfaces.

For athletes there is a substantial difference between shoes and playing surfaces, as far as their options are concerned. Anybody can buy any athletic shoe, preferably one that has the most to offer. The playing surface is a given, frequently selected by a committee, which represents public and not athletic interests. The athletic building is usually a public edifice, the athletic shoe is private property. The athletic building and the playing surface must satisfy general criteria; the athletic shoe serves individual requirements. Both the playing surface and the shoe are assigned important roles during athletic activities. Both performance and the load on the locomotor system are important considerations.[1,2] What role can or should the shoe play? What are the requirements of an "ideal" playing surface?

The purpose of this chapter is twofold: to demonstrate the effects the playing surface has on the cushioning and stabilizing properties of the running shoe and to discuss a possible "division of responsibilities" between the athletic shoe and the playing surface.

BASIC CONSIDERATIONS

The "ground-athlete" interaction can take many forms. The ground— its color, configuration, or composi-

*This study was supported by the Schweitzerischer Nationalfond.

tion—can influence the psyche of the athlete. Behavior, particularly mobility, can be affected by it. It is primarily the mechanical interaction that is of interest. In mechanics, this is described as force and as momentum. The forces that affect the athlete during running, jumping, landing, and standing are the force of gravity and the ground reaction force.

It is advantageous to divide the ground reaction force into a horizontal and a vertical component. The vertical component is a "reaction force," since the ground represents a fixed and inescapable component. The horizontal component is primarily a friction force. According to Coulomb's law of friction, the sliding friction force depends on (or the static friction force is limited by) the normal force (vertical component) and the sliding friction coefficient (the static friction coefficient).

The ground reaction force depends heavily on the movements executed by the athlete. In active motion,[2] as for instance in running or in jumping to block a shot in volleyball, the hardness of the ground (or of the sole) has little effect on the size of the normal force. The reason for this is that, in general, the acceleration pathway cannot be increased significantly. In landing, or generally in the placement of the foot or another body part (passive), the hardness of the ground (and of the sole) exerts a major influence on the braking path and thus on the ground reaction force. Since the braking path can be easily doubled in length, it is possible to decrease the load correspondingly.

These general considerations indicate that hardness and the static and sliding friction coefficients are relevant in characterizing the athletic shoe and the playing surfaces.

CHARACTERISTICS OF THE GROUND AND THE SHOE

Hardness

The hardness of a material is a measure of the material's ability to withstand distortion. The distortion can be static or dynamic. As mentioned above, at the time of landing, it is the dynamic hardness of the ground or of the shoe that matters. Hardness has the following characteristic: if the hardness of the ground and of the shoe are known, the hardness of the shoe-ground combination can be calculated.

Distortion can also mean compressability of material or flexibility of material. Both forms of deformation may occur on indoor playing surfaces and are referred to as point elasticity and area elasticity (Fig 7–1). Area-elastic floors are more difficult to measure and are more complicated by comparison. This is because in addition to the flexion-resistant hardness of the floor, the mass of the floor that is brought into motion plays a significant role.[2] Many area-elastic floors have a large mass that has to be moved, and therefore such floors seem extremely hard on landing.

The order of magnitude of hardness of point-elastic and area-elastic floors and soles as of 1980 is illustrated in Figure 7–2. The indoor playing surfaces were several

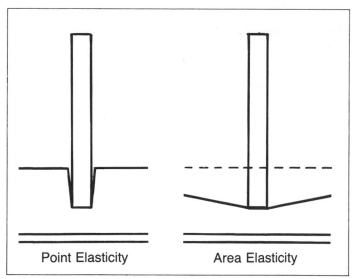

Point Elasticity   Area Elasticity

FIG 7–1.
Differential distortion characteristics of point-elastic and area-elastic court playing surface.

times as hard as the athletic shoes studied.

The Friction Coefficients

The friction coefficients, by definition, depend on the ground and on the shoe. There are no general rules of thumb for calculating the friction coefficients, e.g., if the coefficient between surfaces a/b and b/c are known, the friction coefficient a/c can be calculated. Several static friction coefficients are shown in Table 7–1. Static and sliding friction coefficients can be significantly altered by moisture or by different floor treatments.

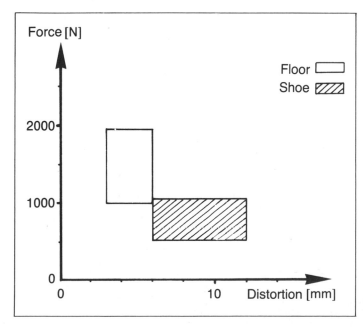

FIG 7–2.
Force-distortion characteristics of 12 point-elastic court surfaces in comparison with a series of athletic shoes.

TABLE 7–1.

Friction Coefficients of Several Shoe-Ground Combinations

Shoe/Sole	Floor/Surface					
	Varofloor (Felt)	Stuapren (Granular)	Nipolam 220 (PVC)*	Fairtop	Sand	Asphalt
All-around shoe (Rubber, low profile)	1.15–1.25	1.05–1.15	1.0–1.1	1.0–1.1	0.5–0.6	0.7–0.8
Jogging Shoe (Rubber, high profile)	1.05–1.15	0.95–1.05	0.8–0.9	0.85–0.95	0.4–0.6	0.7–0.8
Indoor tennis shoe (Rubber/cloth, no profile)	0.6–0.7	0.8–0.9	0.4–0.5	0.55–0.65	0.4–0.5	0.75–0.85

*PVC = polyvinyl chloride.

DISCUSSION

The properties of cushioning and stability required of the athletic shoe are usually measured in combination with a very hard, level playing surface. Can these properties be influenced by the playing surface? In principle, the answer is yes.

The impact force (passive phase of the ground reaction force) can, in theory, be decreased by the indoor playing surface, since the braking path is greater than on a very hard surface, such as asphalt (Fig 7–3). This means that cushioning is improved. If one examines the hardness of the different point-elastic floors and of the athletic shoes (see Fig 7–2), it appears that the chances for improvement with the existing indoor playing surfaces are modest, since the indoor playing surfaces are much too hard in comparison with the athletic shoe.

An indoor playing surface is level when free of load. The levelness of the floor is affected when the floor

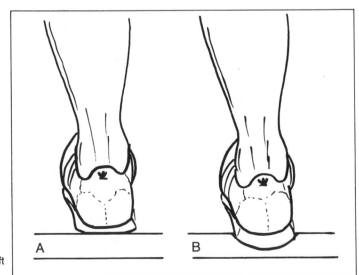

FIG 7–3.
The effect of the hardness of the floor during foot-ground contact (cushioning). **A,** hard floor; **B,** soft floor.

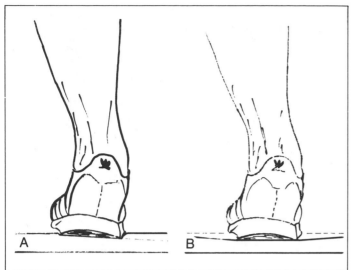

FIG 7–4.
The effects of the hardness of the floor on the stability of the athletic shoe. **A,** point-elastic floor, **B,** area-elastic floor.

"gives" under the impact of the support or takeoff phase. The levelness is maintained in area-elastic floors (Fig 7–4,A); in point-elastic floors it can be affected only negatively (Fig 7–4,B). The softer the indoor playing surface, the greater this effect. This means that stability cannot be improved by the playing surface.

The area-elastic floor has no negative effect on the stability of an athletic shoe, regardless of how hard it may be. On this basis, the ideal athletic playing surface would be soft and area-elastic. The athletic shoe could be hard, which would further improve its stabilizing function.

The athletic shoe must protect the body, particularly the lower extremities and the back, from shocks and guard the joints of the foot against extremes of motion. The playing surface must, more generally, protect the entire locomotor system from strains, even during falls. In this context, even a hard floor can be soft in comparison with the contacting head or knee.

CONCLUSION

In comparison with the athletic shoe, indoor playing surfaces are usually so hard that cushioning by the athletic shoe cannot be separated from the cushioning produced by the combination of shoe/playing surface. The same is true for stability, i.e., the stability of the athletic shoe can barely be distinguished from the stability of the combination of shoe/playing surface.

Division of the responsibilities between the shoe and the floor would be a valuable solution for the athlete. The floor would be responsible for the cushioning and the shoe for the stability.

REFERENCES

1. *Nigg, B.M.:* Biomechanics of running shoes, Human Kinetics Publishers, Champaign, Ill. 1986
2. *Nigg, B.M., J. Denoth:* Sportplatzbeläge. Juris, Zürich 1980

8

Typical Injuries and Overload Problems in Indoor Athletic Events— Implications for the Court Shoe

B. Segesser

There are several criteria that determine the requirements of a good athletic shoe:

1. By its design and the comfort it provides, the shoe must be attuned to the athlete and be adaptable to individual behavior patterns.
2. It must enable peak performances in each athletic discipline by supporting the movement pattern characteristic to each athletic activity.
3. As much as possible, it should guard against false moves and thus contribute to the prevention of injuries and overload problems.

In the formulation of a list of requirements for the ideal athletic shoe, medical science can make its contribution by an analysis of the sport-specific injuries.

THE INJURIES CHARACTERISTIC OF INDIVIDUAL ATHLETIC DISCIPLINES AND THEIR MECHANISM

Indoor athletic activities, such as handball, volleyball, and basketball, combine straight running with the movements typical of tennis. The lateral movements and the backward and forward and rotational movements are complemented by jumps (Fig 8–1). The biomechanical properties of the playing surface can accentuate these demands quite significantly. The effects of the opponent and the additional burden on the visual-motor reflexes occasioned by the demands of the athletic equipment are additional factors in the incidence

FIG 8–1.
In numerous court athletic events, there are lateral movements, rotational movements, and jumping loads, in addition to forward and backward movements.

of injuries. As far as the rate of injuries is concerned, in Switzerland these athletic activities are high on the "hit parade" of the sports that may result in injuries, right behind soccer and skiing. One third to one quarter of all injuries affect the ankle, and more than 60% of all injuries involve the ankle and knee. These are all injuries that could be influenced by more secure foot placement and better motion control, i.e., by a more appropriate shoe and playing surface (Fig 8–2).

In tennis, the sandy or composite granular playing surface allows a relatively free rotation and translation. In indoor athletic activities, the relatively firm blocking of rotatory and sideward momentum leads to a substantially increased stress on the fibular ligaments. A simultaneous buckling across the lateral edge of the shoe can also adversely affect the individual components of the fibular ligamentous chain dependent on the angulation of the ankle joint (Fig 8–3). A majority of the fibular ligament injuries are ignored, and this leads later to a post-traumatic insta-

FIG 8–2.
Marked lateral load in handball.

FIG 8–3.
Buckling over the lateral edge of the shoe leads to injuries of the fibular ligamentous chain.

bility of the ankle that must be compensated for by muscular activity.

The mobility of the ankle and subtalar joints makes a jump possible, with the assistance of a partially stiff takeoff lever. During landing from this jump, the forces generated are captured, more or less, by the previously contracted musculature. Depending on the condition of the ligaments and muscles, this movement may or may not be stabilized. The passive cushioning contributions of the shoe and foot are not adequate.

The extent of the range of motion of the foot during depression of the hindfoot and simultaneous pronation of the foot depends on the load on the compensatory muscle groups and the extent to which the forces generated can be passed on to the more proximal skeletal components. The position of the foot during takeoff and landing determines the torsion movement of the calf and thus, eventually, the valgus-directed motion of the knee joint. The extent to which the extensor mechanism of the knee joint and, particularly, the insertion of the patellar tendon and of the patella itself are placed under stress also depends largely on the action of the foot (Fig 8–4). The shoe can affect the typical overload problems of the knee joint seen in volleyball and handball, namely insertion tendinitis of the patellar tendon, the medial shelf syndrome, and chondromalacia of the patella.

THE CRITERIA OF THE ATHLETIC SHOE

The criteria that the court shoe has to meet are derived directly from the characteristic injuries and overload complaints. Particular attention must be paid to the forward and sideward movements of the foot. It appears that basketball players prefer higher shoes, while volleyball players prefer a low shoe. In Switzerland, handball players preferred a high shoe at one time, and a special shoe was designed for them. This actually led to a decrease in the incidence of fibular ligamentous injuries. Studies with slow-motion photography have shown that this shoe model did not significantly reduce the stresses of the supinatory movement (Fig 8–5). The conclusion that can be drawn is that the currently available, high-shaft indoor athletic shoes cannot adequately prevent injuries.

Lateral movement can be improved significantly through a control of the foot in the shoe by improving the stability of the heel, and also by better lateral strapping of the shaft. It must also be remembered that the partial blockade of the athletic shoe on the playing surface and the ensuing lateral movement of the foot in the shoe rapidly lead to a widening (spreading) of the shoe and a further loss of stability (see Fig 8–3).

Sideward movement cannot be captured by the upper of the shoe. By a lateral extension of the heel and sole of the mass-produced shoe, an attempt can be made, in the presence of ligamentous instability, to prevent the buckling motion over the lateral edge of the foot. A similar corrective action in the athletic shoe may lead to an increased leverage of the shoe in the face of an extended sideward movement and to an accentuation of the buckling potential whenever the

FIG 8–4.
Load on the knee when the foot is
fixed on the floor.

foot is partially blocked by the playing surface.

Since all indoor athletic activities include running as a major component, the court shoe must incorporate the desirable elements of a good running shoe.

ADDITIONAL SAFEGUARDS

Injuries and overload complaints could be largely prevented during indoor athletic activities by a good court shoe, which, unfortunately, does not exist at the present time. As shown by several studies, even the best passive stabilization—whether tape, bandage, or shoe—is insufficient if there is only inadequate active muscular stabilization. In view of this, and to provide the best active prophylaxis against injury, the greatest attention must be paid to proper training of the involved muscle groups. Improving the athletic shoe is insufficient by itself.

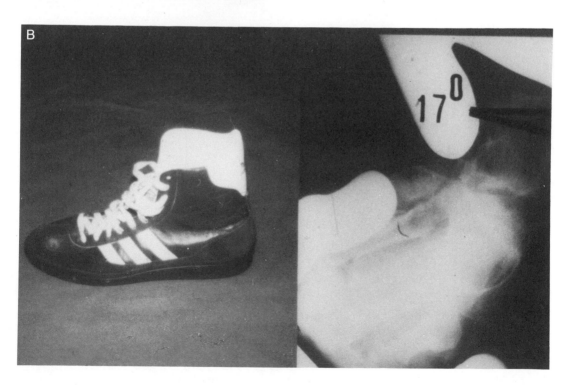

FIG 8–5.
A and **B**, as can be seen from these illustrations, lateral stability is not appreciably improved by this high-shaft shoe.

CONCLUSIONS

The large number of knee and ankle injuries suggests that, from the medical point of view, there is a need for shoes with better lateral stability and better control of the foot blocked by the playing surface. A shoe with an intermediate shaft height can provide improved lateral stability. The currently available court shoes can meet the prophylactic orthopedic requirements only partially. Improvements should be made in all areas (i.e., lateral stability, ground contact, cushioning).

9 Technological and Biomechanical Criteria of the Court Shoe

A. Stacoff

X. Kaelin

Matters of importance to the athlete and to the athlete's health include not only purely medical aspects and matters pertaining to the strain generated by the playing surface, but also the sequence of movements of the individual body parts of the athlete. The sequence of movements of the foot, however, is influenced in turn by the shoe, its geometry and its composition.

In contrast to the running shoe, the court shoe has received relatively little attention and was developed primarily on the basis of the manufacturer's experience. The relationship between the geometry of the shoe and the anatomy of the foot is of obvious importance to the manufacturer, and yet this relationship has been somewhat neglected.

The purpose of this chapter is to consider some of the fundamentals of the court shoe. This will be done from the point of view of biomechanics and should allow us to arrive at some general conclusions concerning the requirements of a court shoe.

THE FUNDAMENTALS

In listing the athletic activities in which the court shoe is used, we must mention first of all those activities that are limited almost exclusively to indoor athletic facilities (volleyball, basketball, etc.) or for which training and conditioning is performed mostly indoors (training and conditioning for track, etc.). In addition to these well-known athletic activities, we must also consider those usually offered within the framework of an athletic association. These latter may be quite varied and include activities such as gymnastics.

Shoes are available on the open market for these numerous indoor athletic activities. They can be designated as specialty shoes or as training shoes. They are supplied with the assumption that the latter are designed primarily for the average person who partakes of athletics, who may use the shoe in a variety of activities. The specialty shoe is designed with the competitive athlete in mind and is constructed to meet the specific requirements of the individual athletic activity.

It is true, however, that, in this case, theory and practice are not the same. On the one hand, many everyday athletes use specialty shoes, and on the other hand, many championship athletes are perfectly comfortable in training shoes. Both types of shoe are used commonly as street shoes. This means that the properties of these shoes (from a technical perspective) cannot live up to the specific, athletic specialty-limited requirements that the athlete may desire.

The question is, how can this odd development be possible? Is it possible to describe accurately the specific requirements of any given type of shoe? This would be desirable from the manufacturer's point of view. Unfortunately, there are no good studies of the frequency of certain types of movements, or of the relationship of these movements to injuries and overload complaints. At the present time, there is no basic, theoretical concept that encompasses these relationships.

Basically, all important athletic movements can be divided into three principal groups (Table 9–1). Walking was intentionally omitted. The advantage of such a simplified classification of movements is that it permits a comparison of the various athletic activities (no claim for completeness is made). A review of the literature reveals that the individual forms of movement have been studied with varying intensity. Running was studied extensively, although not necessarily in the context of indoor athletic activities. In recent years, much attention has been devoted to sideward running. With some exceptions, jumping, both on takeoff and on landing, is still an unknown quantity. So is the rotational movement. For this reason, it was impossible to present a comprehensive review of the forms of movement relative to the court shoe.

METHODOLOGY

This investigation selected lateral running and landing after jumps as its principal target from among the forms of movement listed in Table 9–1. Existing motion-picture film was used to determine the position of the feet at given points in time during the motion sequence. A dissected foot was placed into a rough approximation of the position and was then photographed. This was followed by

TABLE 9–1.

A Simplification of Different Forms of Motion

Principal Form	Motions Involved	Relevant References
Running	Forward	Cavanagh,[1] Clarke et al.,[2] Frederick,[3] Kaelin, et al.,[5] Nigg et al.[8]
	Sideward	Luethi,[6] Nigg et al.,[8] Stacoff et al.,[12] Tiegermann[14]
Jumping	Takeoff	—
	Landing	Valiant and Cavanagh[15]
Turning	Inward	Nigg and Denoth,[7] Stucke et al.[13]
	Outward	

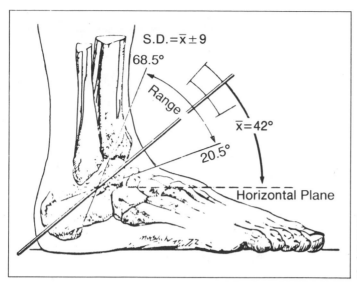

FIG 9–1.
Position of the subtalar joint (STJ) axis. (Adapted from Inman, V.T. The joints of the ankle. Williams & Wilkins, Baltimore 1976.)

an assessment of the lever action of the forces acting on the human foot, with and without shoes.

The direction of the axis of the subtalar joint (STJ) served as the basis for this representation.[4] This axis crosses the human foot (Fig 9–1) at an angle, and this makes an elucidation of the movement process difficult.

In this study, the foot was placed so that it was viewed from a posteroanterior direction along the longitudinal direction of the STJ axis (Fig 9–2). This permits a display of the order of magnitude of the various lever relationships.

DISCUSSION

Landing After Jumps

Landing after a jump can be divided into landing on the forefoot and landing with the foot in a horizontal position. It is assumed (although not statistically proved) that landing with the foot in the horizontal position occurs less frequently then landing on the forefoot. It is nevertheless of considerable interest since the vertical forces in this type

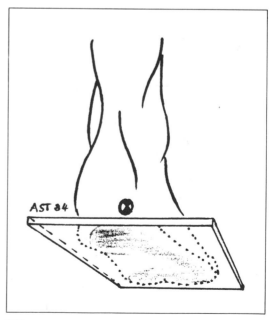

FIG 9–2.
Representation of a foot oriented along the subtalar joint (STJ) axis.

of landing may be up to six times the body weight.[15] This is roughly twice as much as could be expected in running. The recoil force appears after approximately 20 msec. The athlete may have acquired this landing technique as a matter of habit, or he may be distracted by the environment and "forget" therefore to tense the calf muscles. This is particularly true during play, where the attention is focused on the game. The tension of the muscles is neglected particularly later in the game, when concentration decreases and fatigue increases.

As far as the construction of athletic shoes is concerned, this means that the shoes must be provided with soles having the most effective cushioning materials and properties. Among the court shoes, the basketball shoe has the most elevated heel (Fig

9–3). In theory, this provides twice as much material that can be distorted on landing, when compared to the flatter shoes (e.g., the volleyball shoe).

Since not all materials used in soles can absorb the impact equally well and in the same way, it is important that the most suitable material be selected for the sole. This statement is supported by the observation that volleyball players regularly select shoes with thick soles during the training period. This suggests that these players know (although, maybe they don't know) that the shoe must have additional material to provide good cushioning. In competitive games, these athletes switch to lower shoes because they wish to feel that they are "closer" to the ground and to save about 50 g in weight.

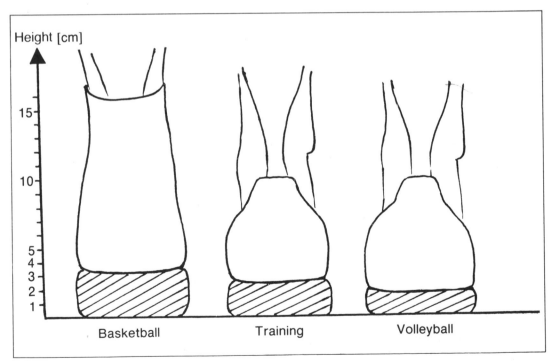

FIG 9–3.
Court shoes and the thickness of their sole. Measured in the shoe.

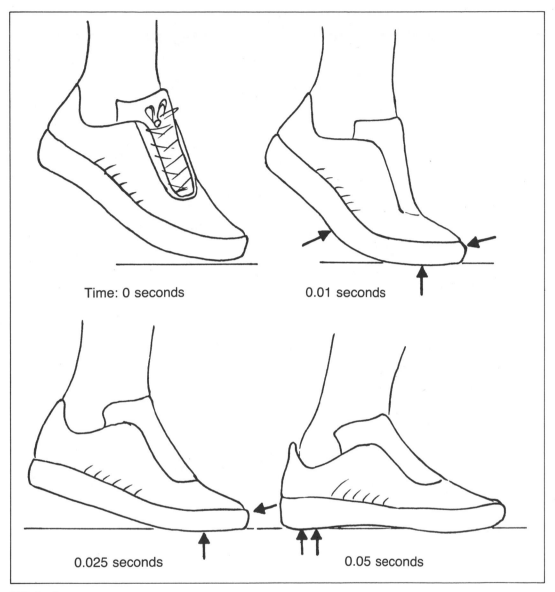

Time: 0 seconds

0.01 seconds

0.025 seconds

0.05 seconds

FIG 9–4.
Time sequence of landing on the forefoot. The distortion of the sole is indicated by the arrows.

As mentioned above, landing on the forefoot is probably the most frequent form of landing. Inspection of the films reveals that the sole can be distorted in several places (Fig 9–4). The reactive forces act relatively distant from the ankle joint, and thus the foot is "levered" into dorsal flexion and pronation. The heel makes contact after about 50 msec. This time lapse allows the previously stimulated calf muscles (triceps surae, tibialis posterior, etc.) enough time to "put the brakes on" this movement (Fig 9–5). In this type of landing, the reaction forces are smaller than in the flat-footed landing. Nigg and Denoth[7] report a force 3.5 times the body weight and Valiant and Cavanagh[15] one of 4.3 times the body weight. The implications for the manufacturer are the same as for the flat landing: good cushioning must be provided.

The pronatory movement raises another shoe problem that must be addressed, i.e., the lateral stability of the shoe.

It can be seen frequently during a game that the forefoot landing occurs with internal rotation of the tibia and adduction of the foot (Fig 9–6,A). This movement sequence has multiple causes, i.e., loose lateral liga-

ments, fatigue, or muscular imbalance.[11] The foot position brings the force impact point of the vertical reaction force closer to the STJ axis. If then the construction of the sole is such as to further shift the force impact point medially, a supinatory movement will ensue, which increases the risk of injury (Fig 9–6,B). For this reason, the shoes should be constructed so that the lever arm is shifted laterally, without, however, the introduction of a hard edge to the sole of the shoe.

Opponents and teammates frequently make a contribution to serious fibular ligament injuries. During the landing, it is possible to land on the foot of another player. This can generate a force on the sole of the foot that impacts on the medial side, provides a rotatory impulse, and results in a rapid, dangerous supinatory movement. This movement could be captured by the musculature (peroneus longus and brevis muscles) if these muscles were to receive a pre-impact stimulus. In view of the surprise effect, however, this is unlikely to happen. The vertical ground reaction force has little lever effect in this foot position (Fig 9–7). Consequently, the load is placed on the fibular ligaments, and these are at the limits of tear resistance when the pressure is between 15 and 30 kPa.[10] The last chance to avoid a fibular injury rests with the shoe (perhaps with taping). Unfortunately, the currently used, soft shafts and heel counters are not stable enough to produce a "saving" pronatory movement. This leads to an overload of the fibular ligaments.

For the purposes of shoe construction, this means that stiffening

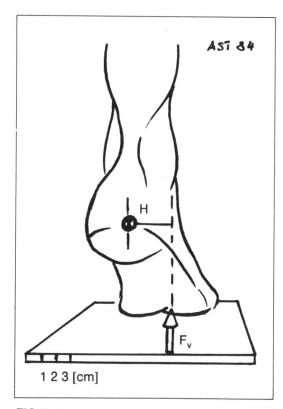

FIG 9–5.
Order of magnitude of the lever relationships during a forefoot landing. F_v = the vertical ground reaction force; H = the lever around the subtalar joint (STJ) axis.

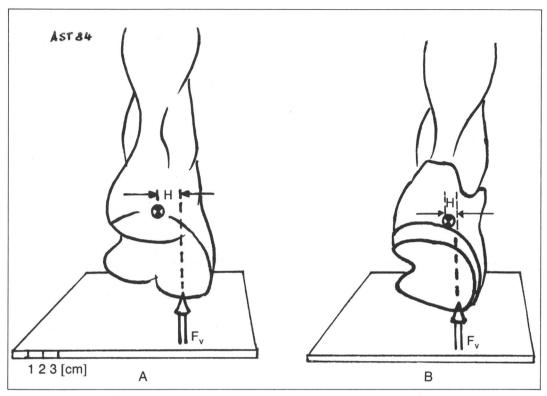

FIG 9–6.
A, forefoot landing with internal rotation of the tibia and adduction of the foot. **B,** effect of the sole on the lever action around the subtalar (STJ) axis. F_v = the vertical ground reaction force; H = the lever around the STJ axis.

Lateral Movements

the shaft to prevent lateral movement is highly desirable, provided it does not interfere with flexion and extension.

In lateral movements, an additional force component appears, namely the friction force, which can be ignored during the landing maneuver. This friction force during lateral movement and rapid braking is of the same order of magnitude as the vertical force, i.e., approximately 100 kPa.[6] During landing, the lever arm of the STJ axis is long on the inner edge of the sole (Fig 9–8,A), but is reduced during the flexion maneuver, since the force impact point is shifted laterally. A thicker sole extends the lever arm (Fig 9–8,B) and thus increases the supinatory movement. It is therefore not surprising that many volleyball and tennis players prefer a flat shoe and thus decrease the load on the muscles and ligaments during a lateral move.

The friction coefficient between the shoe and the ground is the important component of the ensuing friction force. The course of movement of the lower extremity is adapted to and independent from friction.[13, 14] The occasional athlete generally prefers a slight sliding potential and is thus

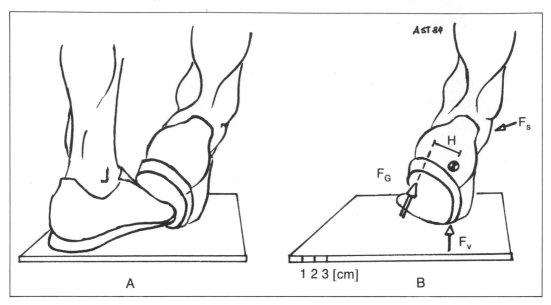

FIG 9–7.
A, landing on the opponent's foot. **B,** the effect of forces acting on the subtalar joint (STJ) axis. F_G = the force exerted by the opponent or team mate; F_v = the vertical ground reaction force; F_s = force-effect of the shaft of the shoe; H = the lever around the STJ axis.

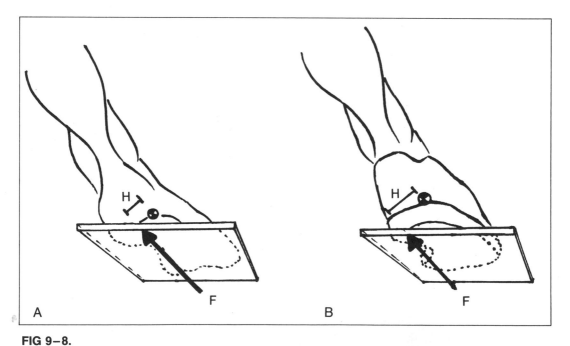

FIG 9–8.
A and **B,** running sideways: Effect of the sole on the lever action around the subtalar joint (STJ) axis; F = the outcome of the vertical ground reaction force and the friction force; H = the lever acting on the STJ axis.

satisfied with a less "gripping" sole. Based on experience, the performance player prefers greater friction (a more "gripping" sole) that permits more rapid braking and takeoff. This naturally also increases the forces generated.

Shoe construction is influenced by other factors as well, e.g., the torsion resistance of the shoe along its longitudinal axis. According to Luethi,[6] this must be optimal (i.e., neither too stiff nor too soft) to prevent injuries.

CONCLUSIONS

The search for the ideal court shoe presents fundamental problems. Good cushioning during landing requires a thick sole, but a thick sole increases the length of the lever arm in lateral movement.

In the hasty attempts to optimize these properties, two things *must* be kept in mind:

1. Cushioning and lever action can be affected by shoe construction technology, such as hardness of the sole, width of the sole, design of the edge of the shoe, torsion resistance, stiffness of the shaft and heel counter.
2. Athletes make very individual demands of their shoes, since they consider not only the function of their feet, but also the design of the shoe, when they select their shoes.

It is therefore important to meet these demands on different levels, i.e.

the marketing of shoes must be a conscious, integrated effort. This is also apparent from the manifold uses to which court shoes are put. This presents the shoe industry with a difficult task. It must recognize these different demands; it must classify them and translate them into shoe technology that is clearly understandable to both the seller and the purchaser. In this way, each athlete would be provided with the appropriate shoe for the optimal performance of his chosen athletic discipline.

REFERENCES

1. *Cavanagh, P.R.:* The running shoe book. Anderson World, Mountain View, CA 1980
2. *Clarke, T.E., E.C. Frederick, C. Hamill:* The study of rearfoot movement in running. In: Sport shoes and playing surfaces. *Frederick, E.C.* (ed.). Human Kinetics Publishers, Champaign, Ill. 1984
3. *Frederick, E.C.:* Measuring the effects of shoes and surfaces on the economy of locomotion. In: Biomechanical aspects of sport shoes and playing surfaces. *Nigg, B.M., S. Kerr* (eds.). The University of Calgary, Calgary 1983
4. *Inman, V.T.:* The joints of the ankle. Williams & Wilkins, Baltimore 1976
5. *Kaelin, X., J. Denoth, A. Stacoff, E. Stüssi:* Cushioning during running—material tests contra subjects tests. In: Biomechanics: Current interdisciplinary research. *Perren, S.M., E. Schneider* (eds.). Martinus Nijhoff, Dordrecht 1985
6. *Luethi, S.M.:* Biomechanical analysis of short term pain and injuries in tennis. Ph.D. Thesis in Biomechanics. The University of Calgary, Calgary 1983

7. Nigg, B.M., J. Denoth: Sportplatz-beläge. Juris, Zürich 1980

8. Nigg, B.M., J. Denoth, B. Kerr, S. Luethi, D. Smith, A. Stacoff: Load, sport shoes and playing surfaces. In: Sport shoes and playing surfaces. Frederick, E.C. (ed.). Human Kinetics Publishers, Champaign, Ill. 1984

9. Platzer, W.: Taschenatlas der Anatomie. Thieme, Stuttgart 1979

10. Sauer H.D.: Experimentelle Untersuchungen zur Reißfestigkeit des Bandapparates am menschlichen Sprunggelenk. Hefte Unfallheilkunde 131 (1978), 37−45

11. Sommer, H.M.: Disposition zur Sprunggelenksverletzung beim Basketballspiel. Dt. Z. Sportmedizin 8 (1983), 254−257

12. Stacoff, A., E. Stuessi, D. Sonderegger: Lateral stability of sport shoes. In: Biomechanics IX. Winter, D.A. (ed.). Human Kinetics Publishers, Champaign, Ill. 1983

13. Stucke, H., W. Baudzus, W. Baumann: On friction characteristics of playing surfaces. In: Sport shoes and playing surfaces. Frederick, E.C. (ed.). Human Kinetics Publishers, Champaign, Ill. 1984

14. Tiegermann, V.: Reaction forces and EMG activity in fast sideward movements. In: Biomechanical aspects of sport shoes and playing surfaces. Nigg, B.M., B. Kerr (eds.). The University of Calgary, Calgary 1983

15. Valiant, G.A., P.R. Cavanagh: A study of landing from a jump: Implications for the design of a basketball shoe. In: Biomechanics IX. Winter, D.A. (ed.). Human Kinetics Publishers, Champaign, Ill. 1983

PART 4 _____ The Soccer Shoe

10 Typical Soccer Injuries—Their Effects on the Design of the Athletic Shoe

M. Masson

H. Hess

Soccer is a team sport, and like most team sports, it is a body contact sport. This makes it particularly prone to produce injuries (Fig 10–1). The increase of injuries in recent years is due to the increasing speed with which soccer is now being played, the increasing use of the body in the game, and the increasing number of active participants.

A statistical study of athletic injuries, done in the Saar region of Germany, put soccer in first place with an incidence of 3.9%. Despite this depressing figure, there was consolation in the fact that the soccer injuries were generally of a minor nature, and that only occasionally were they more serious. The injuries were incapacitating only rarely when compared to other sports, e.g., sailing, flying, diving, or riding, which were responsible for the most serious injuries.

In soccer, the lower extremities were involved in 56% of cases, the

FIG 10–1.
Soccer does produce injuries.

FIG 10–2.
Distortion of the boot and foot.

upper extremities in 23%, and the head in 14%. One quarter of the head injuries involved the central nervous system.

In evaluating this activity, the entire spectrum of ball, soccer shoe, and

FIG 10–3.
The evolution of the soccer boot over time.

playing surface must be taken into consideration. When the ball reaches a velocity of 120 to 140 km/hour, a collision energy of 250 to 300 kPa is generated, and if the ball is wet, this may reach nearly 600 kPa. Needless to say, this leads to a distortion of both the ball and the foot (Fig 10–2). This, in turn, leads to constant microtrauma and, over time, to degenerative changes in the foot and toe articulations. These are specific to soccer players and consist of arthrosis of the ankle joint and of the joints of the great toe.

With the spikes solidly anchored in the soil, substantial forces are generated. These, combined with rotatory and flexing movements, can cause acute injuries to the knee joint. Minor trauma, repeated over time, leads to osteoarthritis of the knee and meniscus damage.

If one examines the development of the soccer shoe, illustrated in Figure 10–3, and sees the evolution from a simple ridge on the sole of the shoe, through leather cleats to the modern plugs and spikes of variable length, all in the name of better fixa-

FIG 10—4.
The configuration of the sole affects the anchoring of the foot to the ground.

tion of the foot to the ground, no further comment is necessary.

The problems produced by indoor soccer are well known. On indoor playing surfaces, the foot is solidly anchored to the playing surface. The normal slipperiness of a natural surface is gone. This results in an increased load on the ligaments and cartilages, particularly in the ankle and knee, as well as in a greater than average load on the Achilles tendon. As a consequence of the increased load on the Achilles tendon, we see an increasing number of achillodynias and even tears of the Achilles tendon. The active locomotor apparatus, the musculature, is subject to injuries through increased loads caused by sudden stopping. Thus the musculature is the victim of its own energy, rather than of external influences.

Only a bristle-soled shoe, which would permit both sliding and sufficient anchoring, could solve this problem. The manufacturers are invited to make improvement by increasing the cushioning potential of the shoe and by designing an appropriate sole.

The problems of designing a shoe for playing on an artificial turf are also well known. These shoes bear little resemblance to the shoes used on a natural turf (Fig 10—4).

KNEE INJURIES

Soccer-specific injuries can be seen in the knee joint. During falls or during a sudden stop accompanied by a rotatory movement, while the foot is firmly anchored to the ground, serious injuries of the joint itself can occur. Injuries can also be caused by collisions during the struggle for the ball, running into the railings, or falling on a hard surface. Meniscus tears, accompanied by a "locking" of the knee, are common. Intra-articular effusions and tears of the menisci, damaged by repeated microinjuries, are equally frequent.

The forces acting on the knee usually produce a tear of the medial ligament and less frequently of the lateral ligament. These almost always require surgical repair. Combined ligament injuries—tear of the medial collateral ligament, medial meniscus, and anterior cruciate ligament, the so-called "unhappy triad"—are fortunately rare, but always require surgical repair. Frequently missed, and therefore more frequent than ordinarily believed, are the isolated anterior cruciate ligament injuries. They are usually caused by a direct fall on the knee and represent one injury for which the composition or design of the shoe cannot be blamed. Other injuries include the flake fracture and the separation of pieces of cartilage with fragments of bone attached. There is also the well-known separation of the cartilage from the underlying cortical layer.

Another, not uncommon result of repeated microinjury is a distinctive cartilage injury. This is usually an early sign of arthrosis and is seen particularly when the ligaments of the knee joint are loose.

ANKLE INJURIES

Soccer also produces some characteristic ankle injuries. Direct impact or excessive buckling of the joint on an uneven playing surface leads to a supination injury and to a related partial or total rupture of the ligaments. These ligamentous injuries may be accompanied by cartilage injuries, particularly of the talus or the distal articulating surface of the tibia. These injuries require immediate treatment.

Swelling in the ankle area can be observed after a simple "jamming" or after ligamentous tears. It can also be seen with arthritic changes in the joint, where the acute injury only acts as a trigger and where the traumatic aspects of the injury are only of secondary importance.

The regular, high soccer shoe cannot prevent supination injuries. If the high shoe were to provide a stabilizing influence, it would necessarily limit motion and thus interfere with mobility and performance. A stabilizing tape bandage can be beneficial. Joints having loose ligaments should be taped up before every game.

The high shoe does make sense, however, since by protecting the ankle and the Achilles tendon against

FIG 10−5.
High-shaft boot as additional protection.

soft tissue injuries from kicks, it does reduce the likelihood of injuries (Fig 10–5). This shoe is not well accepted in Germany, but is seen more frequently in Holland and Belgium.

The high shoe also generates a weight problem. The shoe should be light and not add an unnecessary burden to the runner. The modern soccer shoe weighs only about 250 g, and this weight is not appreciably increased when the shoe gets wet. Considering that during a game a player may run as much as 6,000 to 8,000 m, this reduction in shoe weight considerably reduces the work of the leg muscles.

Players usually object to padding and to strengthening of the toe area, since this may lead to a decreased "feel" for the ball and to less accurate ball control. Many players request that the leather on the outside of the shoe be rough, rather than smooth, to allow more precise ball handling and control.

ACHILLES TENDON INJURIES

Achilles tendon problems and residual injuries in the area of the Achilles tendon can apparently be helped by a well-designed shoe. Such a shoe may have padding in the area of the Achilles tendon or a strap pulled up at the back of the shoe. With the shoe material in use today, great care must be taken to avoid chafing between the hard upper posterior edge of the shoe, or in the area of the heel. This is particularly important in the presence of Haglund exostosis, where additional irritation must be avoided.

SOFT TISSUE INJURIES

The soccer shoe itself can act as a weapon and be responsible for soft tissue injuries. This is frequently related to the shape of the studs. Soft tissue injuries due to worn leather studs with protruding nails, to aluminum studs, or to studs that are intentionally sharpened can be totally prevented. The referee should check the studs before the player is allowed onto the field.

The shoe industry has developed new material for soccer shoe studs, which are now made mostly of plastic. These have no sharp edges, are less likely to split, but tend to wear out more rapidly (Fig 10–6). There are also metal studs that do not split and thus tend to cause fewer injuries. Finally, studs are now designed from a safety point of view, with a metal core and a plastic outer layer, thus minimizing soft tissue injury.

CRITERIA OF THE SOCCER SHOE

The modern soccer shoe must meet the following criteria: It must be "right" for the foot, i.e., it must conform to both orthopedic and hygienic demands. It must be constructed on a last that conforms to the shape of the foot and it must allow for modifications, e.g., the insertion of a variety of inner soles for the correction and support of existing pedal malformations. If there is a difference in length between the two legs, this can be corrected by the shoes without affecting athletic performance and without adding substantial weight.

FIG 10–6.
New, interchangeable, plastic studs.

In the professional ranks, individual shoe design is common and meets the personal requirements and desires of the professional athlete. The individualized shoe must also be designed so that it provides both protection and support.

The shoe must be constructed so that it does not limit the physiologic range of motion and that the rocking motion, particularly in the area of the forefoot, is absolutely guaranteed by inner soles and by the proper flexibility of the sole. The studs and cleats must be placed to avoid isolated pressure points and unnecessary irritation of the foot. In the area of the hindfoot, they must be located slightly towards the edges of the sole to avoid buckling. The shoe must be suited to the athletic activity.

The shoe must be as light as possible to avoid unnecessary loads for the athlete. When inner soles or arch supports are added, it is important that appreciable weight increases be avoided by the use of appropriate materials.

The foot should be hindered as little as possible in its freedom of motion. The sole of the shoe must be designed so that it resists plantar flexion

FIG 10–7.
Soccer boot from 1920.

in the midfoot area while maintaining a good rocking posture. This will allow for better foot position for the instep kick.

The shoe must assure good contact with the playing surface, and the sole must adapt optimally to all types of surface. On hard surfaces, including hard natural turf, "nubby" shoes of differing configuration are used. On softer turf or on wet ground, shoes with detachable studs of varying length provide the best anchoring to the ground. On snowy surfaces yet another configuration is required, and here the recommended shoe has rubber studs since under these conditions, rubber studs appear to provide the best anchor. The shoe industry is very much interested in developing and testing antiskid properties. On icy surfaces a quite different shoe is required. The current recommendation is for a so-called "samba" shoe, which bears only superficial resem-

blance to a regular shoe. It is a further requirement that the shoe not hinder rotation too much, but this property may be very difficult to predict.

To clarify these issues, a series of biomechanical studies and tests should be performed. In view of the manifold requirements of the soccer shoe, this may prove very difficult.

If these concerns were followed to their logical conclusion, an improvement in performance and a decrease in the risk of injury should ensue. The risk of injury can never be totally eliminated since the shoe must be attuned to increasing demands and increased performance. If we compare the soccer shoe used in 1920 (Fig 10−7) with the modern soccer shoe, the changes are obvious. The evolution is far from complete, and many biomechanical investigations must still be performed over a considerable period of time.

PART 5 _____ Other Athletic Shoes

11   The Surfing Shoe

K. Steinbrück

T. Engels-Zewko

Of all the athletic disciplines, none has grown as rapidly during the past few years as windsurfing. It is estimated that there are over 1 million surfers in the German Federal Republic, with approximately 100,000 neophytes added each year. Surfing became an Olympic event in Los Angeles in 1984. The rate of development of materials, equipment, technique, and training have been phenomenal.

When windsurfing injuries were first studied at the Sylt windsurfing school,[4] a considerable number of such injuries were found. In those days, the only garb was the bathing suit, and neoprene wetsuits were a rarity. The Ostermann metal joint caused numerous compression injuries to the feet. Lacerations were caused by shells, stones, glass fragments, and metal objects, which were common in the muck of the mud flats. At that time, the use of old tennis shoes was recommended. The first and only discussion concerning the surfing shoe was presented at the South German Congress of Orthopedics.[5] It was recommended that plastic toe guards be used to prevent injuries to the toes and ankles. No progress was made, however, beyond some improved prototypes. In the meantime, the sportswear industry discovered the tremendous market that this phenomenal increase in windsurfing created, and there was a corresponding increase in the production of equipment.

THE RISKS OF INJURY IN WINDSURFING

Studies of Mass Participants

The results of a 3-year study were presented at a symposium in Heidelberg in 1983.[1] It was interesting that among the 190 casual windsurfers, 90 participants suffered a total of 109 injuries. Analysis of this remarkably high incidence revealed that 62 injuries (56.9%) involved the lower extremity (Fig 11–1). The feet were damaged in only 25%. The injuries consisted primarily of bruises and lacerations but also included dislocations and fractures (Table 11–1). Numerous injuries were due to sharp stones, shells, and coral reefs. The surf board itself was responsible for 80% of the injuries. The feet were most

99

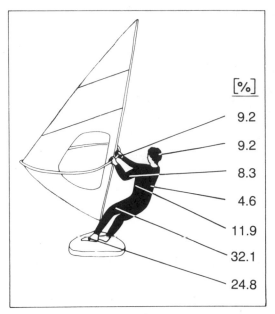

FIG 11−1.
Distribution of 109 injuries according to the area of the body affected. Of the 56.9% of injuries in the lower extremities, the feet were involved in 24.8%.

frequently compressed between the surfboard and the mast, but injuries were also caused by the daggerboard and the foot straps (Table 11−2).

It is interesting that practically all injuries were suffered by surfers who wore no surfing attire and no shoes. Women suffered far fewer injuries, since in contrast to the males, they wore appropriate surfing attire in most instances. The reason for this may be that the attire provides a greater feeling of security and also tends to protect against cystitis and other pelvic problems.[2]

Studies in Competitive Windsurfers

The surfing practices and the risks of injury were the subject of a particular study in 16 top class, competitive athletes, who spent the entire winter in Hawaii, at the Kailua Surf-

ing Center. These were all high-wind and high-surf skiers, who also engaged in ski jumping. These professionals also injured their feet in about 50% of all cases. The primary injuries were lacerations, but there were also contusions, dislocations, and fractures (Fig 11−2). The injuries were due mainly to coral reefs and sea urchins, but there were also injuries caused by the daggerboard, the skegs, and the sharp tail skegs. These athletes regularly wore a wetsuit, but two thirds refused to wear shoes, since these interfered with a good contact with the board.[3]

THE CHARACTERISTICS OF A GOOD SURFING SHOE

The relatively large number of foot injuries and the risk of hypothermia are the principal reasons why appropriate surfing shoes should be designed and worn. A number of im-

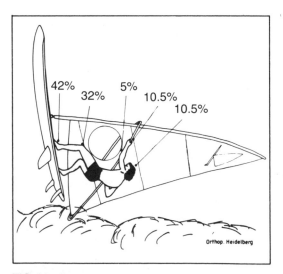

FIG 11−2.
Incidence of injuries in relation to the area of the body in world class surfers; 74% of the injuries were in the legs; of these injuries, 42% were in the feet.

TABLE 11–1.

Typoo of Injury Rolativo to tho Aroa of tho Dody in Windsurfors

	Head	Trunk	Arms	Hands	Legs	Feet	Other	Total
Contusion	3	10	4	3	13	10	2	45
Dislocation		2	2	3	3	3	1	14
Fracture	2	1			1	3		7
Myalgia			1				2	3
Concussion	1							1
Lacerations	4		2	4	18	10		38
Crush injury						1		1
Total	10	13	9	10	35	27	5	109

TABLE 11–2.

Injuries to Specific Body Areas Relative to the Surfboard

	Head	Trunk	Arms	Hands	Legs	Feet	Other	Total
Board	3	6	3	4	18	8	2	44
Daggerboard					6	5		11
Fin						1		1
Shaft of the thill	1	5		2	1			9
Mast	5		2	1	4	1		13
Foot strap						3		3
Mast seat		1			1	5		7
Total	9	12	5	7	30	23	2	88

provements must still be made, and the most important principles and problems will be discussed below. The discussion will cover not only the different types of shoes but also the different soles and closures.

Types of Shoes

We must distinguish between the slipper, the neoprene wetsock, the ankle-high surfing shoe, and the surfing boot (Table 11–3).

The Slipper.—The slipper protects against sharp stones and is light, but provides little support and practically no protection against heat loss.

The Neoprene Wetsock.—Neoprene wetsocks are light and tight fitting so that they permit surfing in foot straps. They provide good protection against heat loss and, depending on the sole, against sharp objects.

They are like socks, however, and provide no support and become very heavy when wet. When wet, they also swell, which may make it very difficult to take them off (Fig 11–3).

Ankle-High Surfing Shoes.—This shoe also protects against sharp objects, but protection against heat loss is significantly less. A disadvantage of this shoe was the frequent occurrence of blisters at the instep and ankles. Support is relatively poor. Water can get into the shoe and make it heavy (Fig 11–4).

Surfing Boots.—Surfing boots provide good support and good protection against sharp objects and heat loss. Pressure points are rare, and the boot is easy to put on and take off.

TABLE 11–3.

Types of Shoes—Advantages and Disadvantages

Shoe	Advantage	Disadvantage
Slipper	Very light	Little support
	Moderate protection against sharp objects	No temperature protection
Neoprene wetsock	Very form fitting	Little support
	Protection against stones	Very heavy when wet
	Heat preservation	Spreads when wet
	Small—can be used with foot straps	Hard to take off
Ankle-high surfing shoe	Protection against stones	Blisters on the instep
	Heat preservation (moderate)	Little support
		Permits entry of water
Surfing boot	Good support	Water may enter (depending on model)
	Very good heat preservation	Frequently too heavy
	Good protection against injury	Usually too wide (cannot be used with foot straps)
	No pressure points	
	Easy to put on and take off	

The disadvantage of the boot is that, depending on the model, water may get into it more or less easily. When fully saturated, the boot is very heavy. Generally, the boots are too wide to allow surfing with foot straps.

Types of Soles

Generally there are three types of soles: the smooth sole, the contoured sole, and the suction cup sole (Fig 11–5, Table 11–4).

The Smooth Sole.—This sole gives a very good "feel" for the board and permits surfing with foot straps. It breaks easily, is slippery, and, because of its thinness, provides little protection.

The Contoured Sole.—This sole provides a good grip and good protection against injuries. The "feel" for the board is decreased, and it is bulky

FIG 11–3.
Neoprene wet sock.

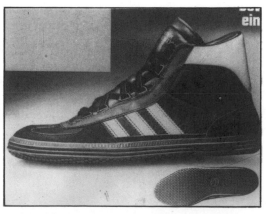

FIG 11–4.
Ankle-high surf shoe.

FIG 11–5.
Different types of soles.

enough to prevent the use of foot straps.

The Suction Cup Sole.—The suction cup sole provides a very secure grip and protects against injuries but has the same disadvantages as the contoured sole, i.e., a decreased "feel" for the board and the inability to surf with foot straps.

The removable inner soles, required in the past to adapt the footbed better to the foot, and the ridge at the level of the first phalangeal joint, are no longer needed. The elongated shaft, particularly with lateral padding, provides very good lateral stability, especially during turning and canting.

The Closures Used in Surfing Shoes

In this discussion, we must distinguish between the shoes that have no closures at all and those which are closed by laces, with a zipper, or with a Velcro strap.

No Closures.—These shoes swell when they get wet and are very hard to put on or take off.

Laces.—Laces of all types provide a solid closure but wear out rapidly and are cumbersome to manipulate.

Zipper.—Because of the possibility of pressure sores, the zipper

TABLE 11–4.

Types of Sole—Advantages and Disadvantages

Type of Sole	Advantages	Disadvantages
Smooth sole	Good "feel" for board Usable with straps	Rips easily Slippery Little protection
Contoured sole	Good grip Good protection	Poor "feel" for board Usually hard and thick Usually cannot be used with foot straps
Suction cup sole	Very good grip Very good protection	Poor "feel" for board Usually hard and thick Usually cannot be used with foot straps

FIG 11–6.
The top performance athlete frequently surfs barefoot.

should be on the side of the shoe. It is convenient and easy to operate, unless it jams.

Velcro Straps.—These are the best since they can be manipulated very rapidly and can even be adjusted during the ride. This is important since the shoes tend to swell when they get wet. A disadvantage is their relatively short life span.

Advice on Buying a Surf Shoe

The following matters should be considered when buying a surfing shoe.

Material.—It must provide good protection against heat loss and should not absorb too much water. It should be neither too flexible nor too rigid.

Workmanship.—There should be good padding over the ankles, the heel portion should be reinforced, and there should be no areas of pressure.

Shape.—The neoprene wetsock is to be preferred since it is most suit-able for surfing with foot straps. On the other hand, the surf boot is the best all-around footwear.

Closure.—It should be easy to manipulate and should not be subject to too much wear.

CONCLUSIONS

The surf shoe is still in a stage of development. It offers great protection against injuries and heat loss to the leisure-time surfer. It should always be worn in unfamiliar waters and among rocks or sea urchins. Almost all shoes share the disadvantage that they can readily fill with water and become heavy and distended. The competitive surfers tend to avoid the surfing boot, particularly in competitions. With bare feet, they have a better "feel" for the board and are more agile when maneuvering (Fig 11–6). In the future, the abovementioned shortcomings should be corrected, and a shoe should be designed that has a sole adapted to all board surfaces and that can be used with or without foot straps.

REFERENCES

1. *Steinbrück, K.,* et al.: Windsurfen. Symposium in Heidelberg, 1983
2. *Steinbrück, K., T. Engels-Zewko:* Sportverletzungen—Sportschäden bei Windsurfern. In: Windsurfen. *Steinbrück, K.* (Hrsg.). perimed Fachbuch-Verlagsgesellschaft mbH, Erlangen 1985
3. *Steinbrück, K., K. Kemmer:* Untersuchung bei Leistungssportlern im Windsurfen. In: Windsurfen. *Steinbrück, K.* (Hrsg.). perimed Fachbuch-

Verlagsgesellschaft mbH, Erlangen
1985

4. *Steinbrück, K., C. Schmidt:* Verletzungsanalyse der Windsurfingschule
Munkmarsch/Sylt 1976.
Unveröffentlichte Untersuchung

5. *Steinhaus, M., H. Laturnus:* Der
Surfschuh—Erfordernisse zur Vermeidung von Verletzungen. Orthop.
Praxis 11/XIV (1979), 819

12

The Throwing Shoe— Providing Discipline- Specific Shoes for the Athlete

A. Thiel

The throwing disciplines, also known as the technical disciplines (javelin, hammer, discus, and shotput), are all part of the track and field sports that require particularly strong and agile athletes. The throwing shoe must therefore be able to withstand intensive loads during starting, turning, and braking maneuvers (Fig 12–1). These throwing shoes are exposed to such extreme demands that they evolved into very special items that can be used exclusively in the discipline for which they were designed.

DISCUS THROWING

Hein Direck Neu, the many-time German champion and "old man" of discus throwing, considers the throwing shoe to be much more than just footwear. He views it as a special shoe for the thrower—one that is intimately involved in the performance and that really becomes as much a piece of athletic equipment as the discus itself. Just like the discus, it

must be continuously improved so that it can contribute to improved performance. There is no such thing as an ideal throwing shoe. All shoes must be programmed for two things: the foot of the athlete and the environment, i.e., the surface of the ring. Thus the outer surface of the sole becomes the most important component of the discus throwing shoe. What is needed is a shoe that is quick but permits a sensitive contact with the ring, that can turn rapidly but does not slip. Neu points out that, during the rotation, the left foot is particularly prone to slip, and this is the reason why Danneberg had different soles on his two shoes.

During this evolution, a number of different materials were tested, e.g., the nubby sole, the all-leather sole, the smooth sole, and the light pyramidal sole. It is important that the sole be drawn up at the edges to allow for the freest and most harmonious rotational potential (Fig 12–2).

The surface of the ring is critical. There are rings that are fast without

FIG 12–1.
Intensive utilization of the throwing shoe during the throwing motion.

being slippery, and there are some that become like a skating rink when wet. Some are rough and prevent the athlete from completing the turn rapidly. According to the athletes, the ideal sole for all surfaces has not yet been invented. Industry will have to try to find the optimal surface both for the ring and also for the throwing shoe.

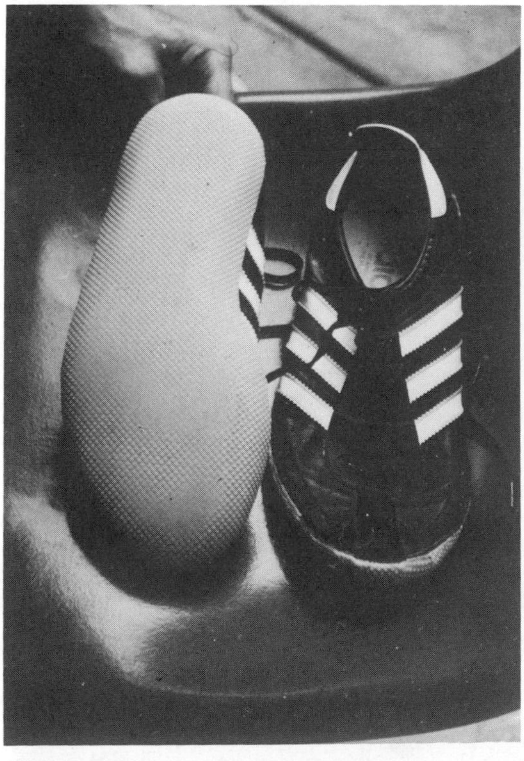

The wear resistance of the sole is of considerable economic importance to the athlete when one considers that in daily use the sole can wear out in 2 weeks and has to be replaced. The throwing shoe must fit as well as possible, and it is well known that to assure an optimal fit, some companies build the throwing shoe on individual lasts for the world class athlete.

The uppers must meet the same kind of requirements. They must hold the foot firmly and should not be affected appreciably by moisture or sweat. The footbed should decrease the "feel" for the ring surface as little as possible and should cause the least possible loss of energy. In the competition shoe, the footbed will be minimal, although in the training shoe it should be more substantial and should also have some padding in the heel area. The entire sole must be both flexible and elastic.

Athletes with sensitive ankles may use shoes with higher shafts. These are particularly beneficial in

FIG 12–2.
Laterally raised sole and strong leather upper.

bad weather but have the disadvantage of limiting and restricting the mobility of the ankle.

The athlete requires several different shoes during the complete training cycle to deliver the best possible performance: running shoes for the running training and for gymnastics, spikes for speed training, weight lifting shoes for strength training, and a variety of throwing shoes for training and competition in good weather and bad and for a variety of surfaces.

HAMMER THROWING

The load conditions on the shoe in hammer throwing are very similar to those described for the discus throw. In this sport, there are also extraordinarily intense rotational and pressure demands on the shoe, which must be met by appropriate material. During the Los Angeles Olympic Games, we had the opportunity to discuss the problems of the throwing shoe and a reasonable approach to the shoe problem with the German athletes and their coaches. It became obvious that the hammer thrower had the same requirements as the discus thrower. The critical elements were the condition of the surface, the weather conditions, and the bottom of the sole.

Hammer throwers also used shoes with different shaft heights (Fig 12–3). The lower throwing shoe interferes less with the motion of the ankle, while the higher shoe provides better protection and support for those athletes who have sensitive ankles. The shoe of the hammer thrower should have the edges of the sole rounded off laterally to provide additional protection and to allow harmonious management of the rotational load. Since the rotational load varies considerably between the two shoes in hammer throwing, the two shoes show a very different wear pattern, one in the forefoot area and the other in the heel area. The uppers are made of leather. The soles used by the German throwers were very smooth or slightly roughened on the bottom. To preserve the "feel" for the ground and to minimize the energy loss, the footbed was kept to a minimum in the

FIG 12–3.
Medium-high or low hammer throwing shoes.

FIG 12–4.
Javelin throwing shoe with strap reinforcement.

FIG 12–5.
Used javelin throwing shoes with markedly stretched uppers.

shoes of the hammer thrower. Thus the requirements are generally the same as for the discus shoe. The heel must be protected, and the forefoot must be stabilized by a good upper and by appropriate lacing.

JAVELIN THROWING

A very special and specific shoe was developed for javelin throwers to meet the highly individual requirements of this discipline. The shoe must provide a secure grip for the foot and ankle joints of the javelin thrower and must also meet all the requirements of the discipline-specific motion sequence.

These shoes will be characterized by a higher shaft and a lighter, but very tough upper material. Both nylon and leather are suitable. The tarsus is typically protected by a wide thong (Fig 12–4). The forefoot cap must also be made of strong, wear-resistant material, since otherwise the dragging motion will rapidly lead to wear. Lacing must be particularly strong and effective (Fig 12–5).

The sole must be very stable and is provided both in the forefoot and

heel area with spikes. It is much less flexible than the sole of the other throwing shoes and is more reminiscent of a jumping shoe. The arrangement of the spikes can vary, and they may even be omitted on the medial aspect of the heel on the bracing foot, since ground contact is made almost exclusively with the lateral edge of the sole (Fig 12–6). For several years now, a leading German athletic shoe manufacturer has offered a javelin

FIG 12–6.
Arrangement of spikes on the javelin throwing shoe.

throwing shoe that has only three spikes on the lateral side of the fore-foot.

The firm heel counter must provide the hindfoot with solid support, and the heel must be protected from "jamming" by an appropriate heelbed.

SUMMARY

The throwing shoes discussed above are highly specialized and de-signed for a very specific purpose. Future developments will be shaped by biomechanical advances, by the special demands made by the surface of the competition sites, and by the development of new materials for the bottom layer of the sole and the foot-beds of future throwing shoes.

13   The Jumping Shoe

K.H. Graff

H. Krahl

The large number of injuries among track-and-field athletes at the Olympic Games raised serious concern among the experts as to etiology and prevention. Of the 58 track-and-field athletes from the German Federal Republic who attended the Olympic Games in Los Angeles, fully 76% suffered locomotor system injuries requiring medical attention. It would be a gross oversimplification to blame the athletic shoe for this alarming increase in injuries. All possible causes must be carefully examined.

The jumps performed by track-and-field athletes are impressive because of their explosive kinetics. In all four competitive forms of jumping, a common, characteristic feature is the one-legged "takeoff" required by competition rules. Of the four events, two can be characterized as "horizontal" (long jump and triple jump) and two as "vertical" (high jump and pole vault).

All of the jumps are high-speed, high-intensity disciplines. They are very demanding on the locomotor apparatus and can affect the body of the athlete biopositively or bionegatively, particularly when the demands are interpreted primarily from a mechanical perspective. The end result of the load on the body of the athlete is stress placed on all organ systems and on all structures.[1]

The talus is particularly heavily involved in all forms of jumping. At the moment of takeoff, it is the recipient of all the reactive forces, and it has the responsibility to provide the dynamic impulse for the locomotor process in the shortest possible time. It is the duty of the athletic shoe, and, in this particular situation, of the jumping shoe, to establish an intensive contact between the ground and the foot. Positive and negative forces of acceleration and distortion act through the shoe onto the foot of the athlete and are modified by it.

The jumping shoe is not a street shoe. Its design represents a compromise between its two primary responsibilities: the improvement of performance and the prevention of injuries and harm. The jumping shoe must also attempt to meet individual requirements, despite the extensive anatomical variations on the one hand and the strongly stereotyped locomotor process on the other. There are

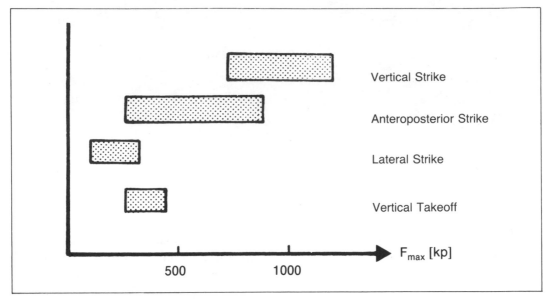

FIG 13−1.
The ranges of maximal force on takeoff in the long jump. (From Nigg, B.M.: Biomechanik. Juris Druck & Verlag, Zürich 1977. Used by permission.)

jumping shoes for long jump, high jump, triple jump, and pole vault, but there is no generic "jumping foot" to meet the individual requirements of these jumps.

To generate rational and useful improvements, the manufacturer needs feedback from the athlete who wears the shoe and whom the shoe serves, from the biomechanicist who measures the reactive forces generated, and from the physician (usually an orthopedic surgeon) who sees the results of these reactive forces in the office or emergency room.

LONG JUMP AND TRIPLE JUMP

The fact that we can now measure the various physical forces and responses generated by jumping is a tri-umph of biomechanical investigations. The maximal force generated during takeoff in the long jump (Fig 13−1) gives an idea as to the loads that can be expected. The maximal vertical force generated at the time of contact with the board can exceed the body weight by a factor of 10.[6] In addition to the bracing force, which is considerable both anteriorly and posteriorly, there is also a significant lateral force. These great lateral forces can be measured, but they are also experienced by the jumper as a feeling of lack of lateral stability. This lack of lateral stability becomes particularly important in the triple jump, since here the jumper cannot concentrate on a single takeoff but must perform three takeoffs in rapid sequence. Thus the lack of lateral stability may significantly affect the optimal utilization of force during the last phase of the triple jump. This must be recognized in the design of the jumping shoe. The top German triple jumpers had a steel plate incorporated into their jumping shoe, which reaches from the spike plate to the heel (Figs 13−2 and 13−3).

HIGH JUMP

During the early development of the "flop" in the technique of high jumping, there appeared a number of characteristic injuries and problems, e.g., medial and dorsal foot problems and stress fractures of the navicular. These observations led to the kinematographic studies of Krahl et al.[5]

Their studies do not measure the active loads precisely but clearly illustrate their effects (Fig 13−4).

In this type of load, the jumping foot assumes a forced pronatory position at the heel in the form of a pes planovalgus. The ankle joint and the subtalar joint are involved in directions other than their normal axis. The soft tissues in the medial areas of the dorsum of the foot and the navicular bone are particularly heavily affected (see Figs 13−4 and 13−5).

The extent to which the foot is distorted depends on the angle between the long axis of the foot and the direction of the approach run, as well as on the jumping shoe. A study of this relationship will allow the es-

FIG 13−2.
Triple jump just before foot placement at the "step."

FIG 13–3.
Triple jump shoe with built-in metal splint (*top* and *middle*). Long jump shoe (*bottom*).

tablishment of the criteria necessary for the avoidance of injuries and overload problems in the locomotor sequence. These are the correct placement of the foot in the direction of the approach run and a significant reduction of the pronatory buckling and foot distortion by properly constructed jumping shoes. This latter is accomplished by providing the heel

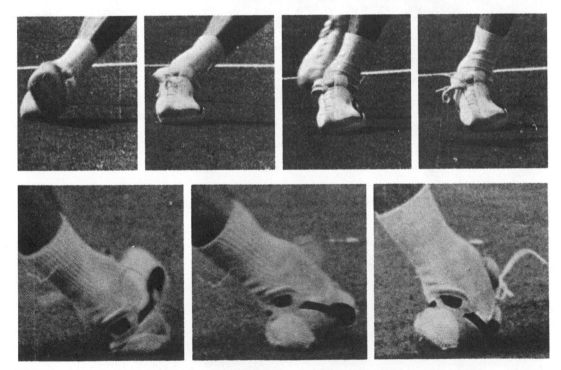

FIG 13–4.
Typical takeoff phase at the "flop" photographed from the front and back.

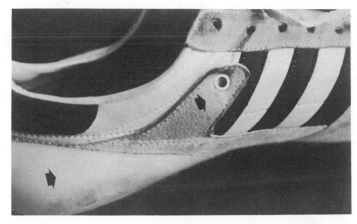

FIG 13–5.
High jump shoe. Stable heel counter and midfoot lacing.

and the medial portion of the hindfoot with a solid support and by individualizing the footbed. Stabilization will be accomplished by extending the heel counter medially (Figs 13–5 and 13–6) and, to some extent, by replacing the standard heel with a slanting takeoff plateau. Whether this latter step is effective in reducing pronation has not been established. Pronation can also be decreased by reinforced nylon in the construction, by installing full-thickness nylon straps into the shaft, and by having additional lacing in the area of the midfoot.

Individual footbeds, like the one installed for the winner of the Olympic competition, cannot be provided in commercial production by the manufacturer. In our view, however, it is precisely the young and coming athlete who needs this kind of support. Presently, it is only the experienced athlete, i.e., the athlete who has had bad experiences, who is provided with an individualized footbed. The argument that this leads to a loss of the "feel" for the ground holds no water, since it does not occur provided suitable materials are used.

THE DEMANDS ON THE LOCOMOTOR SYSTEM

The degree to which the locomotor system is stressed can be mea-

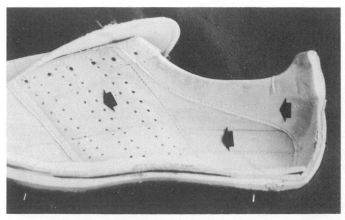

FIG 13–6.
Nylon reinforcement and full-thickness nylon bands (*arrows*).

TABLE 13–1.

Distribution of 99 Foot Injuries in 37 Jumpers (September 1980–September 1984)

	No. of Injuries	(%)
Achilles tendon	18	(18.2)
Ankle joint	51	(51.5)
Subtalar joint	23	(23.2)
Midfoot	2	(2.0)
Tarsal tunnel	1	(1.0)
Plantar fascia		
Talus	3	(3.0)
First metatarsophalangeal joint	1	(1.0)

sured by the injuries and complaints of the athletes. Our experience with jumpers has yielded the following findings:

Thirty-seven jumpers of both sexes had 99 foot injuries requiring treatment in a period of 4 years (Table 13–1). In 51.5%, the injury involved the ankle joint, and in 23.2%, the subtalar joint (subtalar-talo-navicular-calcaneal joint) was involved; 18.2% involved the Achilles tendon. To state it differently, the hindfoot was involved in 97% of all cases, while the midfoot and forefoot accounted only for 3%. A total of 21 surgical interventions were required of which 16 involved the foot.

We have good records of injuries and also of the shoes used by 27 athletes. It is interesting that 3 athletes had no problems of any kind, while 24 jumpers reported intermittent or ongoing problems with one or both feet. Considering that in 8 athletes both feet were involved and in 4 only the "nonjumping" foot was a subject of intermittent or ongoing complaints, one comes to a somewhat surprising conclusion: during training or competition, there was pain intermittently or continuously in 20 "jumping" feet but also in 12 "non-

jumping" feet. The question as to what form of load was responsible for these complaints may well be extended to a consideration of the training shoe.

Even though 20 of the 27 athletes attributed their problems to competitive events, incidents arising during the training period were mentioned just as frequently and repeatedly. This supports the suspicion that the "discipline-specific" injuries have their roots in training and not in competing.

In this context, another surprising observation must also be made. The stress facture of the navicular was considered specific to the "flop" jumper. Between 1974 and 1978, we reviewed six cases treated at the University of Heidelberg Orthopedic Clinic.

During the past 4 years, we saw 29 stress fractures in 25 athletes, all involving the same skeletal area. This serious injury constitutes 50.8% of all stress fractures seen in our athletes (Table 13–2). Of the 25 cases, 23 were track-and-field athletes, of whom 68% were females. On closer inspection one finds a high incidence among short-distance runners and participants in combined athletic events;

TABLE 13-2.

Frequency of Stress Fractures in Individual Athletic Disciplines (January 1901 to September 1984)

Discipline	Tibia	Fibula	Calcaneus	Navicularis	Metatarsals	Sesamoids	Talus	Total
Long-distance run	1	1		2	2			6
Middle-distance run	2			4*	1			7
Sprint	2	6		7†	2			17
Hurdles		2		4‡	2			8
Triple and long jump				1				1
High jump				3	1			4
Pole vault				1				1
Decathlon							1	1
Pentathlon				4‡				4
Discus						1		1
Javelin				1		1		2
Shotput			1					1
Gymnastics				1		1		2
Volleyball					1			1
No athletics				1				1
Total	5	9	1	29	9	3	1	57

*4 stress fractures in 3 athletes.
†7 stress fractures in 6 athletes.
‡4 stress fractures in 3 athletes.

18 stress fractures of the navicular fall into this group. This group also included 4 female athletes who had bilateral stress fractures. The jumpers, with a total of only 5 stress fractures, look good by comparison.[2, 3] While the total number of this injury is alarming, its distribution is not surprising.

In all high-speed, high-intensity events in track-and-field athletics, elements of major reactive forces are an essential condition of achieving a passable level of performance. These athletic disciplines include primarily the various jumps: one-legged jumps, hurdles, ski jumping, and other jumps with or without additional load (Fig 13-7). In these activities, the feet are exposed to the same type of loads as those that have been described for the long jump and high jump. Since it is well known that it is not only the magnitude of the forces, but also the number of incidents that are responsible for material fatigue and overload problems, the source of some of these serious injuries may well lie in this area. Sprinters and participants in combined events perform, on the average, 100 to 300 jumps per week and, during a training period, even more than that. This comes to 20,000 jumps per year, or more.

SUMMARY

The contributions that sports medicine can make to the principles of athletic shoe design must depend on the experiences of the athletes, clinical evaluation of certain injury patterns, and some basic biomechanical considerations. Emphasizing the

FIG 13–7.
Reactive force training. Hurdle jumping *(top).*
Jumping run *(bottom).*

first two areas, the following conclusions can be drawn:

1. There is no such thing as *the* jumping shoe. Even within a single discipline, championship class athletes wear a variety of shoes. There are pole vaulters who wear the so-called long-jump shoe, and there are others who prefer to wear a sprint

shoe for jumping competitively. There obviously is no single shoe designed for a specific jumping discipline that has gained undivided support among the athletes in that field.

2. If the design of the athletic shoe should consider not only performance, but also protection from injury, it is well to remember that 97% of the jumpers suffered injuries to the hindfoot (primarily on the medial side). These findings encountered among jumpers can also be extrapolated to short-distance runners, including hurdlers, and to participants in combined events. We attribute this pattern of injury to the intensive training in takeoff that is common to all light athletic, high-speed, high-intensity disciplines. This view is supported by the experiences of the athletes.

3. Recognition of this fact demands that both a jump competition shoe and a jump training shoe be developed. In jump training, the athletes today wear shoes that have good shock-absorbing qualities but provide only very poor protection for the hindfoot. Of all the criteria that make up a good training shoe for the athlete who has to perform a large number of jumps, a solid, medially projecting heel counter is the most important. The shoe obviously also has to have good cushioning effects both horizontally and vertically.

4. There should be a trend towards the use of individual footbeds. The loads in world class competition are so great that a single type of footbed cannot possibly provide adequate support, particularly along the medial edge of the foot. This is emphasized by the almost incredible increase in navicular bone stress fractures, a severe athletic injury. The challenge can be met only if the manufacturers are willing to incorporate an appropriate insert into their training shoes. To date only a very small number of athletes have succeeded in having the manufacturer install an individual footbed into their shoe. The experiences of this tiny group cannot be extrapolated to the "normal" athlete. Of the 27 athletes questioned, 19 had individually designed jump shoes; 22 had personalized training shoes.

5. It appears that occasionally economic considerations prevent desirable developments. From the perspective of the manufacturer, the cost-benefit ratio is unfavorable in certain disciplines (pole vault, triple jump), since the total number of participants in these disciplines is relatively small. It is hoped that improvements will be made in this area as well. Only then will the high-load performance sports obtain the kind of shoes that will do them justice.

REFERENCES

1. *Ballreich, R., P. Brüggemann:* Sportmotorische Leistungsdiagnostik aus der Sicht der "Präventiven Biomechanik". In: Die Belastungstoleranz des Haltungs- und Bewegungsapparates. *Cotta, H., H. Krahl, K. Steinbrück* (Hrsg.). Thieme, Stuttgart 1980
2. *Graff, K.H., H. Krahl:* Überlastungsschäden im Fußbereich beim Leichtathleten. Leichtathletik 3 (1984), 81–87
3. *Graff, K.H., H. Krahl, R. Kirschberger:* Streßfrakturen des Os naviculare pedis beim Athleten. 1984 noch nicht veröffentlicht

4. *Krahl, H., K.P. Knebel, K. Steinbrück:* Fatigue fracture of the os naviculare pedis in flop athletes—a kinematographic and clinical study. XXI Weltkongreß für Sportmedizin, 7.–12. 9. 1978 in Brasilia

5. *Krahl, H., K.P. Knebel, K. Steinbrück:* Kinematographische Untersuchungen zur Frage der Fußgelenkbelastung und Schuhversorgung des Sportlers, Orthop. Praxis 11 (1978), 821–824

6. *Nigg, B.M.:* Biomechanik. Juris Druck + Verlag, Zürich 1977

14   The Golf Shoe

W. Pförringer

B. Rosemeyer

There are about 120 million people in the world who play golf regularly. It is one of the most widespread sports. The nongolfers have just as little understanding for the popularity of this sport as for the intricate rules by which it is played. Beside the clubs and the ball, the only piece of athletic equipment in golf is the shoe. The golf shoe is recognizable by the metal spikes and by the fringed tongue that covers the lacing.

Aside from some minor stylistic considerations, these criteria appear to be the only ones that guide the majority of the golf shoe manufacturers in the design of their product. Williams and Cavanagh[3] have found that the currently available, mass-produced golf shoe is made just like any other mass-produced street shoe, and that no scientific, athletic considerations are devoted to it. By comparison, the clubs and the ball receive a disproportionate degree of technical consideration.

Even when one considers that the golfer must walk long distances (unless this is eliminated by the electric golf cart, as it appears to be the case in the United States), the shoes are not even particularly suitable or designed for this activity. This is true not only for the last and the basic shape of the shoe, but also for the type, number, and location of the spikes. It is apparent that the most important aspect of the game, i.e., the time period of the golf stroke, has not received and is not receiving any attention, as far as the golf shoe is concerned.

Even from a sports medicine perspective, practically nothing has been done, and the only serious and fundamentally sound work was done by Williams and Cavanagh.[3] The biomechanical aspects of the golf shoe can be fully derived from their work.

BIOMECHANICAL CONSIDERATIONS

The principal movement in golf occurs during the swing. It is a lateral move in a frontal plane and involves a rotational motion that takes place along a longitudinal axis and is more pronounced than in most other sports. Except for the final phase of the swing, this rotation causes a relatively minor motion of the sole in relationship to the ground. Ideally, the shoes should make the work of the lower extremity easier and should provide a solid base of support. They should allow the engagement of appropriate muscular forces while simultaneously providing both increased ease and increased comfort. The interaction between the shoe and the ground is the link that allows the golfer to perform the body movements necessary during the golf swing and that culminates in the contact between the club head and the ball. Since the motion of the various body parts triggers reactive forces from the shoe-ground contact, a study of this interaction creates an excellent opportunity to analyze the biomechanical conditions prevailing during the golf swing. There are very few studies that have looked at the kinetic and kinematic aspects of the events occurring during the golf swing. With the exception of the study by Williams and Cavanagh, there is no other work that has investigated the possible effects of the golf shoe or the implications of shoe design.

Earlier work focused on the dynamics of the swing alone. In 1967, Carlsoo[1] analyzed the ground reaction forces during the golf swing in a Swedish player. By using a pressure-sensitive plate, he studied the three components of the ground reaction forces for each foot of the player during the swing. The shifts in vertical forces at various important points during the swing were described, as were the anteroposterior and mediolateral shifts in amplitude and direction of these forces. The direction of the shear forces were clearly different between the two feet during the different phases of the swing. Repeated measurements of the ground reaction forces showed little variation in the force-time curves. Electromyographic studies were used to correlate the force generated with the position of the involved muscles.

Cooper et al.[2] analyzed forces generated by each foot separately by using two force measurement plates. The primary objective was to see the shift in the axis of the central load, with the axis itself being determined by kinematographic techniques. While some general force patterns could be established, there were subtle differences when different clubs were used. At the moment when the head of the club made contact with the ball, approximately 75% of the maximal vertical force was acting on the leading foot (the foot closest toward the green). This varied from 150% of body weight when a wood was used to 133% of the body weight when a no. 7 iron was used. The peak vertical forces were generated just prior to club-ball contact when a wood was used, but just after the contact when an iron was used. The least vertical force, 80% of the body weight, occurs shortly after the moment of impact and must be attributed to the force of the club, which pulls the body of the player upward. The rotational momentum, determined for both feet by a measuring plate, showed a clockwise motion peak initially (in right-handed players) during the early phase of the swing. This changed to a contrary, counterclockwise movement shortly before the impact, with a peak at the beginning of the second phase of the swing. Unfortunately, the rotational momentum was not determined for each foot independently.

Kinematic data show that there is a functional difference in the biomechanics of the golf swing when different clubs are used. The woods had the highest club-head velocity and the no. 7 iron the lowest. The velocity of the club head was still increasing at the time of contact, when a wood or a no. 3 iron was used, but was already decreasing when a no. 7 iron was used.

Williams and Cavanagh studied the movements and the forces generated by the feet during a golf swing to develop a descriptive kinetic and kinematic illustration of the feet during this activity. The results led to recommendations concerning the shape of golf shoes that should have been of great benefit to the golfers. This study also demonstrated that there was no symmetry in the motion of the two feet and that, therefore, the motion of the two feet had to be studied independently and in relationship to each other (Figs 14–1 and 14–2). While the data vary depending on the club used, it appears that using three different clubs is sufficient for the purposes of this study.

THE MOTION SEQUENCE

An analysis of the motion sequence to which the golf shoe must adapt can be divided into two phases:

1. A long phase of straight walking, i.e., covering the distance between strokes. In this activity, the golf shoe fulfills a role different from that of the ordinary athletic or hiking shoe. The spikes or spikelike projections on the sole serve to improve ground contact with unimproved surfaces and also to perforate the surface of the greens, thus contributing to the aeration and hydration of the greens. For this reason, most golf courses have established regulations governing the use of shoes without spikes. This is necessary to protect the delicate grass surface of the greens. The shoe with small rubber nubs is very comfortable for walking and assures solid contact but does show an increased pressure under the individual nubs and is therefore frowned on by greens keepers. A new design, particularly in light golf shoes, favors a low profile for the shoe in the form of

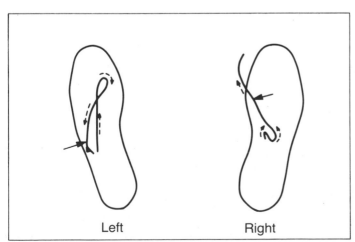

Left   Right

FIG 14–1.
Average path of the center of pressure points under both golf shoes (14 subjects, 4 strokes each with a driver). The position of the shoes corresponds to the beginning of the swing. --> = direction; → = ball contact. (Adapted from *Williams, K.P., P.R. Cavanagh:* The mechanics of foot action during the golf swing and implications for shoe design. Medicine and science in sports and exercise 15/3 [1983], 247–255.)

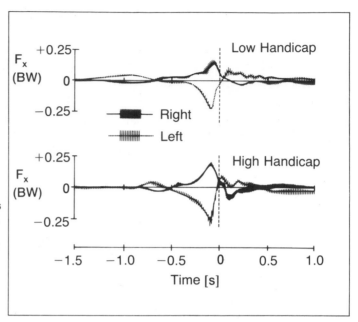

FIG 14–2.
Anteroposterior force (F_x)-time curves for two golfers, one with a high handicap and one with a low handicap. The average curves (± SD) are shown after four swings. The level of competence did not appear to produce any obvious alterations in the force-time curves of the individual strokes. (Adapted from *Williams, K.P., P.R. Cavanagh:* The mechanics of foot action during the golf swing and implications for shoe design. Medicine and science in sports and exercise 15/3 [1983], 247–255.)

small squares no more than 2 mm in elevation.

2. The phase of the swing places entirely different demands on the right and left golf shoe (the following discussion pertains to right-handed players. For left-handed players, the same is true in reverse).

The right foot of the golfer performs a rocking movement during the swing, and at the end of the swing, the player rests first on the anterolateral edge of the big toe and finally on the tip of the shoe, i.e., on the terminal phalanx of the hallux. The left foot behaves quite differently (Fig 14–3,A and B). There is a shift of the weight from the medial to the lateral edge of the foot and a supination of the left foot in both the ankle and subtalar joints. In extreme cases, this movement terminates in a "buckling" of the foot of almost 90 degrees and comes to rest on the lateral edge of the foot, i.e., on the lateral edge of the shoe (Fig 14–3,C). All toes are

pressed against the toe cap, i.e., against the upper, as in a braking maneuver. This can be analyzed nicely during a barefoot golf swing, where there is no upper to oppose the movement of the toes and where the toes then assume a clawing or grasping position, as a reflex, to gain a "toehold" (Fig 14–3,D). It was possible to analyze the motion of the feet inside the golfing shoes by motion picture studies and also by studies using a pressure-sensitive plate. This permitted a graphic display of the distribution of pressure and a simultaneous mathematical assessment, i.e., a measurement of absolute values of pressure (Fig 14–3,E).

The demands placed on the right shoe during the most important phase of golfing, the moment of the swing, are relatively minor. They consist of the ability to rock without generating much force and to provide some support by having an appropriately flexible sole and by not being too stiff. The demands on the left shoe are

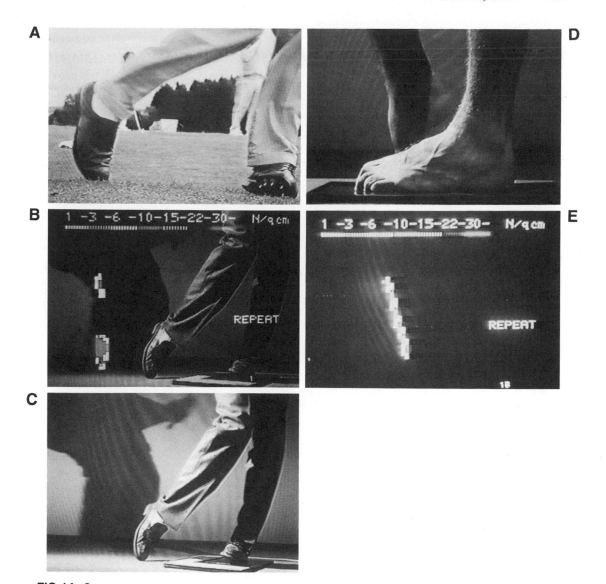

FIG 14–3.
A, end stage of the swing after a drive. The positions of the two feet are quite different. The demands on the two golf shoes must obviously be quite different also. **B,** testing the end phase on a pressure plate. **C,** distribution of pressure under the left foot at the end phase of the stroke. Note the very great load on the lateral edge of the foot. This small area must carry the whole load in the presence of an unstable equilibrium. **D,** end phase of stroke (barefoot). Note the flexed position of the toes. This is the opposite of the position in the golf shoe where the toes are in hyperextension and pressing against the toe cap. **E,** pressure recording in the end phase of the swing (barefoot). Compared to the pressure contact area of the golf shoe, the area of pressure here appears to be somewhat larger.

considerably greater. At the time of the swing and primarily just before the contact of the club head with the ball, the left foot supports a very labile equilibrium, i.e., an insecure stance with a simultaneous, limited, mechanical shifting of the foot and of the force from the medial to the lateral edge. This mechanical limitation can easily be explained by the predictable fact that the existing shoes were never designed for such a medial to lateral tilting motion, and thus the weight-bearing surface is totally inadequate (Fig 14–4,A through E). To date golf shoes have been designed so that the lateral edge does not have sufficient holding power and does not provide the best possible stability. It also does not provide the greatest safety during the rocking maneuver of the foot. If the golf shoe were modified accordingly, it could, within limits, albeit perhaps unconsciously, eliminate the insecurity of the stance during the critically sensitive phase of the swing, and thereby permit more intensive concentration on the movements of the upper extremities, the spinal column, and the hips.

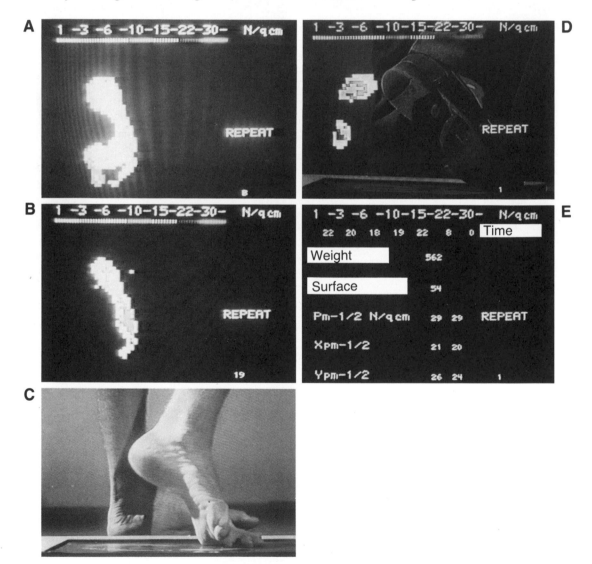

FIG 14–4.
A, pressure distribution on the measuring plate (barefoot). **B,** pressure distribution on lateral rocking of the left foot during the swing. **C,** end phase, right foot (barefoot). **D,** end phase of the swing, right foot (in golfing shoe). The superimposed pressure measurement images are just before the indicated foot position. **E,** numerical display of the data gathered on the pressure plate. These data are immediately available for each phase of the study.

In addition, extensive play involves a substantial number of strokes that require some force from the lower extremities of the golfer. Thus, developing fatigue can also lead to insecurity during the swing and thereby to a lack of precision in the movement. This could almost certainly be reduced if a properly designed shoe were to provide better support.

The fact that certain world class golfers (by no means all) rock only minimally on their left foot during the swing is not an argument against the above statements, since these golfers represent less than 1% of all golfers.

ASYMMETRICAL SHOE CONSTRUCTION

In designing a biomechanically and biodynamically sound shoe the following must be considered:

1. An asymmetrical design must be chosen, i.e., the right and left shoe cannot be mirror images of each other but must be constructed quite differently.

2. Spikes should be eliminated and the contours of the sole designed so that they support the course of the movements rather than impede them. This seems eminently logical.

Consequently, the sole of the right foot should be designed so that it is provided with a better ability to rock in the area of the metatarsal joints. This will support and facilitate the already described rocking during which the right foot finishes up by resting on the tip of the toes.

The profile of the sole of the left shoe should be slanted towards the lateral edge of the sole as viewed from the proximal side. This will support the end position of this foot on its lateral edge. An angle of 45 to 60 degrees is required to accomplish this, and this would provide a very much wider contact surface than the presently used, very thin lateral edge of the shoe. These things must be considered in the design of the golf shoe. The correctness of this theoretical model is clearly demonstrated by the changes and distortion seen in golf shoes that have been used for some time. The strain placed on the uppers is clearly visible to the naked eye. A golf shoe designed according to these criteria is presently under development. It will be the first one to be designed strictly according to the biomechanical and biodynamic requirements of golf.

Similar considerations were presented by Williams and Cavanagh,[3] who suggested that the same objective could be achieved by a rearrangement of the spikes. In theory, this may be correct, but in practice it would not be acceptable, since a nonvertical arrangement of the spikes would limit the usability of the shoe prior to the time of the swing. Walking on such a shoe would be almost impossible, and it would also be quite destructive to the soft ground, particularly on the greens.

SUMMARY

The following constitute some fundamental biodynamic considerations in the design of a golf shoe:

The totally different demands

placed on the two golf shoes during the drive or other strokes must be considered in the design of the shoes. The same considerations, in reverse, must be given to left-handed players. It remains to be seen whether individual problems of each shoe can be worked out simultaneously.

The two different functions of the golf shoes must be recognized. They must serve as walking shoes for substantial distances over varying terrain (turf, rocks, woods, etc.), and they must also serve during the drives and other strokes, which are complex movements and which affect the two shoes quite differently. Other considerations, e.g., water resistance, should not change the internal shoe environment to the point of hyperthermia but should be considered in the selection of materials. The selection of materials is important both from the point of view of strength and weight. It is also desirable that the golf shoe have a flat sole and no heel. The function of the heel can be assumed by an in-ternal wedge, and this will also provide a better and more solid contact with the ground. The introduction of a so-called valgus wedge into both shoes is only one way to counteract the shear forces. It is certain that the development in this area is not yet complete and that it will take years before a truly adequate golf shoe becomes a reality.

REFERENCES

1. *Carlsoo, S.A.:* Kinetic analysis of the golf swing. J. Sports Med. Phys. Fitness 7 (1967), 76−82
2. *Cooper et al.:* Kinematic and kinetic analysis of the golf swing. In: Biomechanics IV, pp. 298−305. *Nelson, R.C., C.A. Morehouse* (eds.). University Park Press, Baltimore 1974
3. *Williams, K.R., P.R. Cavanagh:* The mechanics of foot action during the golf swing and implications for shoe design. Medicine and science in sports and exercise 15/3 (1983), 247−255

15 Mountaineering Shoes—An Overview

W. Treibel

Parallel with the increase in mountain climbing, the last few years have experienced a phenomenal evolution in the mountaineering shoe, an evolution that is far from complete. Contrary to many other athletic activities, mountain climbing is performed in a natural environment and on a natural soil. Alpine activities can be divided into walking, hiking, scrambling among rocks, climbing in rocks and on ice, the recently developed activity of "sports-climbing," exploratory mountain climbing, and mountain skiing. This wide range of activity places demands on the mountaineering footwear that cannot be met by a single shoe. There have to be a number of specialized shoes, although the various individual areas show considerable overlap. Because of the environmental differences (rocks and ice), the differences within the group of mountaineering footwear are greater than all the differences between running shoes or other athletic footwear combined. This has led to the inevitable conclusion that the modern mountain climber has to have more than one type of shoe. The trend towards specialization is enormous. Even a single climb may require two different pairs of shoes.

As in other athletic activities, the shoe in mountaineering is both an item of clothing and also a piece of athletic equipment. It is not the only piece of mountaineering equipment, but it may be the most important one. Mountaineering is a dangerous sport, and the safety of the climber may well depend on the shoe. Gym shoes or loafers have no place in the mountains. They are very slippery and thus can endanger the climber's life. No other piece of equipment gets as much wear in climbing—no other piece of equipment needs to be of such high quality.

Since the middle 1970s, there has been a development that has turned away from the heavy leather boots that had been used almost exclusively until that time. Almost simultaneously, a number of new types of boots were made available. Some of them were distinct improvements and have completely changed the market from the early 1980s on. The dominant type today is a light comfortable boot, which has almost completely replaced the old leather boot and has also led to the rediscovery of the flat, high-friction climbing shoe for high-altitude climbing. In this latter area, the artificial fabrics have taken over, and in the field of ski touring, nothing else is used besides the synthetic (plastic) outer shell and the removable, inner leather boot.

All mountaineering and ski shoes are really "boots," the distinction being the height of the shaft at or above the ankle. It has become customary, however, to use the term shoe, even though this is not really correct.

TYPES OF SHOES

To do justice to the entire range of mountaineering, it is necessary to divide it into several areas of activity, all of which place different requirements on the shoe. We have selected four areas (hiking, climbing, high-altitude climbing, and ski touring) for which the recommended footwear has to be further subdivided. Table 15–1 presents a brief overview.

Only the most important criteria of the materials are mentioned. Additional information is provided below in the individual discussions. In climbing, the range of use to which a

shoe is put depends to a great extent on the experience of the climber. Durability depends partly on use, but primarily on material and craftsmanship. Because of this, only rough estimates based on experience can be given when the various types of shoes are compared with each other. The indicated market penetration is an estimate, since there are no reliable, centrally collected statistics.

It must be kept in mind in any evaluation that, depending on the use to which the shoe is put, the advantages of one type may become the disadvantages of another and vice versa. In view of the wide variations in terrain and use, there can be no "ideal" mountaineering shoe. Of the desired characteristics—lightness, comfort, warmth, waterproofness, suitability for crampons, flexibility, wear resistance, breathability, adaptability, ease of care—only a few can be achieved.

Hiking Shoes

In comparing the different types of shoes, certain specific criteria will

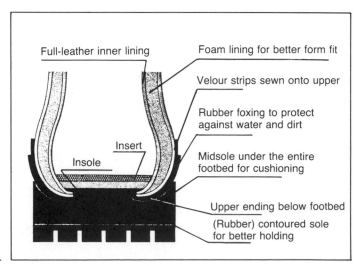

FIG 15–1.
Schematic cross section of the hiking shoe (modified from Lowa).

Full-leather inner lining

Foam lining for better form fit

Velour strips sewn onto upper

Rubber foxing to protect against water and dirt

Insert

Insole

Midsole under the entire footbed for cushioning

Upper ending below footbed

(Rubber) contoured sole for better holding

FIG 15—2.
Hiking shoes may have different sole configurations. The lighter model (*right*) has rubber nubs, primarily for use on dirt and grass. The more stable cleat sole (*left* and *middle*) is more suitable for alpine terrain.

be kept in mind. The so-called hiking shoe (Fig 15—1 and 15—2) evolved from the athletic boot and was placed on the market to fill a void between the athletic shoe and the climbing shoe. Because of the advantages it possessed (light, comfortable, practically no pressure points, no breaking-in period, cushioning, and soil-resistant soles), it has almost entirely replaced the leather mountaineering shoe in hiking. Because of its popularity, it was used increasingly off the beaten paths, but here its poorer wear characteristics (more delicate uppers, lateral seams, decreased stability of the sole, and less firm edges) led to a decrease in durability.

For greater demands, a new, light mountaineering shoe made of suede cowhide was developed. These shoes combine the characteristics and advantages of both the hiking shoe and the mountaineering shoe (Fig 15—3, *right*) and can be used as the universal, original hiking shoe. They are suitable for light and moderately difficult climbing. They are provided with a protective, lateral, rubber foxing, a strong midsole, and cushioning wedge in the heel area of the vulcanized contoured sole. They withstand

FIG 15—3.
An example of the smooth transition from one shoe type to another. The sturdy climbing boot (*left*) has a reinforced, torsion-resistant sole for saving energy while the climber is standing on narrow ledges. The similar light mountaineering shoe, made by the same manufacturer, has more general application for hiking and light climbing.

TABLE 15-1.

Classification of Mountaineering Boots According to the Level of Activity and the Characteristics of the

	Wandering		Climbing	
	Hiking Shoes	Light Climbing (Leather)	Climbing Boots (Alpine)	Special Climbing
Materials	Smooth leather synthetic, soft vulcanized nubby or plugged soles	Smooth or roughened leather; double-stitched or vulcanized contour sole	Chrome-tanned leather; foxing; contour sole with steel inset	Leather or cloth; smooth sole
Primary area of use	Wandering and hiking on improved paths	Wandering (off paths); light climbing	Climbing and wandering	Extreme climbing
Degree of rock difficulty	I	I-IV	I-VI	IV +
Approximate altitude (m)	2,500-3,000	To 3,000	To 3,500	2,000 or 4,000 with second pair
Advantages	Light, comfortable, few if any pressure points; relatively inexpensive	Wear resistant, good support, wide application	Strong; energy sparing with small steps; may be used with crampons	Good adhesion, light; shaft and sole are flexible
Disadvantages	Limited use; not very sturdy; may not be resoleable	Must be broken in; no crampons	Stiff sole is hard when walking; may not be waterproof	Uncomfortable on rough ground; need 2nd pair of shoes
Market share (%)	50-60 40-50	~10	10 ~5	~5
Weight (g)	800-1,800	1,500-2,000	1,800-2,200	800-1,200
Durability	Light to moderate	Moderate	Moderate to good	Light to bad

wear very well and can be used as an all-around boot below the snow level. Since, unfortunately, they were designated as "hiking boots," there is now not only considerable confusion in nomenclature, but also a great variability in quality in hiking footwear.

Climbing Shoes

During the past decade, two different types of climbing boots have been developed. Both types have a relatively thin vulcanized sole for a better "feel" and circumferential rubber foxing for optimal friction in fissure climbing. The alpine climbing boot is a compromise between the heavy leather shoes suitable for crampon wear and the specialized climbing shoe. They usually have a rubber contoured sole and heel and are reinforced with steel in the toe area to provide an energy-sparing toehold on narrow ledges (Fig 15-3, *left).*

Individual Types

High-Altitude Climbing

Leather Boots (Heavy)	Plastic Mountaineering Boots	Ski Touring Boots
Thick, rough, waxed, full leather; double-stitched sole	Plastic shell with leather inner shoe (hut shoe); pointed sole	Like plastic shoes with buckles; integrated or adjustable spoilers; stiff contour sole
Combined climbing on rock and ice	Glacier and ice tours; high-altitude climbing; ice climbing	Ski touring including walking to area of peak climbing
I–IV	I–III	I–III
2,000–5,000	3,000–8,000	To 5,000
Strong; reliable; comfortable; breathe; can be used with crampons	Relatively light; warm; double shoe; waterproof; easy to care for	Good adjustable grip; used with crampons; waterproof; warm; easy to care for
Reliable; heavy; not absolutely waterproof; need breaking in	Relatively stiff; airtight; sweaty	Uncomfortable for longer walks
	10	25–30
5–10	<5	
2,200–2,800	2,200–2,800	3,000–4,000
Good	Moderate to good	Good

Ultralight, special climbing shoes with a flexible sole were already available in the 1930s. They were in the shadow for many years and have returned to general use only recently, in an improved version, from the English-speaking world. In addition to better conditioning, it is the modern, friction-soled climbing shoe with a smooth slippage-resistant, rubber sole that has made possible the tremendous increase in climbs of greater degrees of difficulty (Fig 15–4). Special, soft rubber compounds practically "glue" the sole to the rocks but have the disadvantage of decreased wear. The special climbing shoe—as its name implies—must always remain an optional extra piece of equipment, used only in true rock climbing. In getting up to and walking down from the rock area, a second, different mountaineering shoe should be used that is less likely to slip on grass, loose gravel, or snow.

Newer models tend to blur the di

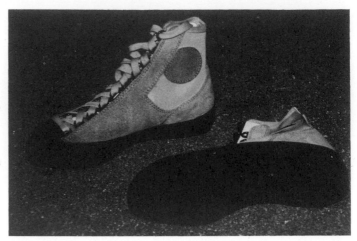

FIG 15–4.
This example of a special climbing shoe, which has a completely flat adhesive sole without a heel, is for the steepest rock-face climbs. The round leather patch in the ankle protects the joint and the underlying nylon-reinforced canvas during contact with the rocks. The special lacing goes all the way to the toes to provide an individualized fit and good pressure distribution in that area.

viding lines between these two types of shoes. This is particularly true for the construction and design of the sole (smooth sole in the forefoot area combined with a contoured heel). The trend is clearly in the direction of the friction-climbing shoe.

High-Altitude Climbing Boots

High-altitude climbing boots are generally used above 3,000 m in the area of snow and ice. The shoe must therefore be waterproof, warm, and have a relatively stiff and nonflexible sole to accommodate crampons. The uppers must also be relatively firm so that the straps of the crampons do not cramp and compress the toes (danger of frostbite). The rigid sides, which are required for crampons, can easily lead to pressure points when the shoe does not fit perfectly. It is difficult to decide between a heavy, leather boot and a shoe of manmade material to meet the extreme demands of high-altitude climbing, since both have distinct advantages (Fig 15–5).

The advantage of leather is that it adapts to the shape of the foot better

FIG 15–5.
In high-altitude climbing, two fundamentally different types of shoes are used. The plastic shoe is completely waterproof and warm. The heavy, leather boot can be used with crampons, breathes better, and is more foot-friendly.

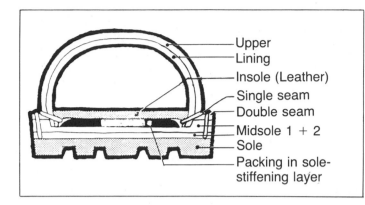

FIG 15−6.
Schematic cross section of a double-stitched leather mountaineering boot. (Adapted from *Meindl, A.*: Wissenswertes über Leder und Schuh, 1. Auf1. Eigenverlag, Kirchauschöring 1982.)

than other materials, although it does require a breaking-in period. In heavy, leather boots, to date, it is customary to find the so-called "double stitch" seam, i.e., the uppers are attached to the midsole with two rows of sutures (Fig 15−6). The heavy, leather mountaineering shoe is usually a very good and durable piece of equipment, which does, however, require regular maintenance to preserve the water-repellant properties of its wax-treated upper.

All experiments to develop a single mountaineering shoe, in which a leather inner part was covered with a waterproof artificial fabric, have failed. It was only at the end of the 1970s that a mountaineering shoe was designed that consisted of an outer shoe of artificial material and a removable, inner leather shoe (see Figs 15−5 and 15−7). This gave the customary leather shoe real competition. The outer shell was made of polyamide or the somewhat less expensive polyurethane, which was also used for the movable-joint sleeve. Compared to leather, the artificial material is lighter, maintains its shape better, is almost maintenance free (needs only to be rinsed with water), and most importantly, is completely waterproof. This makes it particularly suitable for long excursions in snow and on glaciers in exploratory mountain climbing and ice climbing.

Despite this, and contrary to the expectations of the experts, the plas-

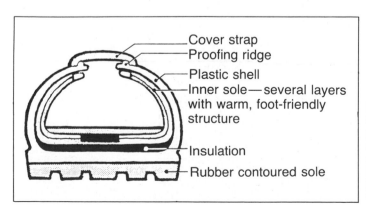

FIG 15−7.
Schematic cross section of a plastic mountaineering shoe with an inner shoe liner. (Adapted from *Meindl, A.*: Wissenswertes über Leder und Schuh, 1. Auf1. Eigenverlag, Kirchauschöring 1982.)

tic shoe did not take over and did not triumphantly replace the leather shoe, as it has done in skiing. The major disadvantage is the inability of the shell to adapt to the shape of the climber's foot. This is particularly unfortunate when the shell and shape of the foot are quite different to begin with. Since with heavy use the human foot tends to widen, the shell has to be wider in the ball and toe area than the adaptable leather shoe. The plastic shoe also leads to increased sweating and, because of its stiffer sole, to less comfort in walking. For this reason, and after an initial "plastics euphoria," the leather shoe regained a part of the market. Its "living" material allows better "breathing," is kinder to the feet, and is still being used widely in today's plastic world.

The Ski Touring Boots

Ski touring is considered to be a part of mountaineering. A touring boot must meet the following criteria: it must permit comfortable walking, since the climb usually takes four to five times as long as the descent; it

must also provide a good grip on the skis. The currently preferred plastic touring boots combine the characteristics of a heavy mountaineering shoe and of a downhill ski boot (Fig 15–8). The laced inner shoe is not sufficiently stable for long hikes, despite its contoured sole and soft-wedged heel. It serves well as a warm ski-lodge shoe. The sole of the plastic shell is made of contoured rubber, slightly rounded for better walking. The frame of the sole is totally rigid to allow prompt release of the binding according to Deutsches Institut für Normung (DIN) standards. To make a good lay-back technique possible during the run, most models have an integrated, adjustable spoiler, which can be loosened for the climb up.

The differences between the currently available models are minor, and there is considerable overlap between them. When the different characteristics are combined, the differences between the models becomes less and less, and an attempt to classify them becomes more and more difficult. Figure 15–9 shows the relationships between the various shoes, their

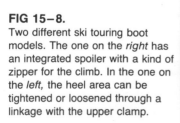

FIG 15–8.
Two different ski touring boot models. The one on the *right* has an integrated spoiler with a kind of zipper for the climb. In the one on the *left,* the heel area can be tightened or loosened through a linkage with the upper clamp.

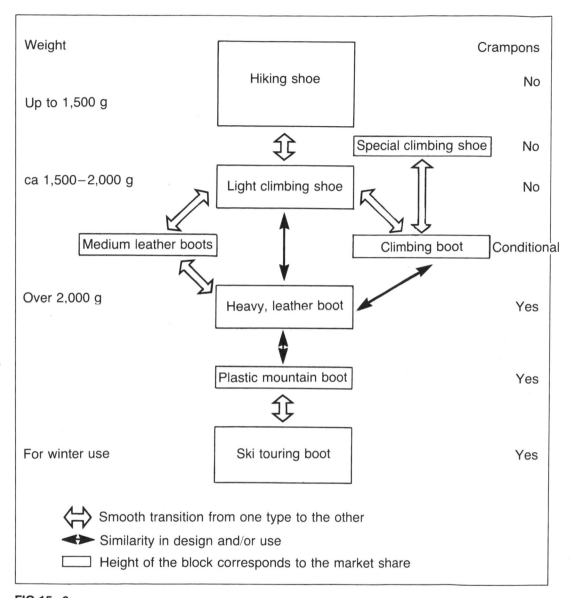

FIG 15−9.
Graphic representation of the individual shoe types with their interrelationships, weight, crampon potential, and approximate market share.

GENERAL CRITERIA

similarities and their differences. They are arranged according to weight and their ability to be used with crampons. The height of the blocks in the figure corresponds to the market share of that particular type.

In leather mountaineering shoes, the upper should consist of a single piece to avoid nonwaterproof seams. In one-piece construction, the only seam is in the back and is covered and strengthened by a superimposed heel counter. Toe caps have not proved successful because of the poor wear characteristics of the lateral seams. Until the 1960s, the medium and heavy mountaineering shoes had smooth leather on the outside. Currently, as a rule, the full-thickness leather is used, but with the rough, less delicate flesh side towards the outside. This arrangement is particularly suitable for rock climbing, since here the water repellant, smooth hide is on the inside and is thus better protected from abrasions by the rocks.

As can be seen in Figures 15–10 and 15–11, most heavier models have an expansion joint in the area of the Achilles tendon and a flexion fold in the area of the instep to allow for better mobility. The tongue must be well padded and must be prevented from lateral displacement by Velcro binding, median hooks, or fixation sutures. The upper edge of the shaft must also be padded to prevent the entry of small stones or snow. The lacing must be easy to handle and therefore is usually provided with hooks in the upper end and with more stable eyelets or rings at the lower end. At the midpoint of the lacing, there is usually a stationary or locking hook that permits a differential tightening of the laces between the anterior part of the shoe and the shaft.

The often relatively stiff soles are usually rounded and anteriorly and posteriorly beveled to allow a better rocking motion. The heel contour tends toward the slanted lateral surfaces and tapered cleats, which are less likely to collect dirt.

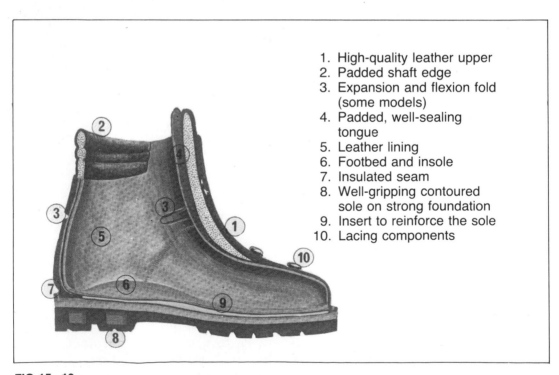

1. High-quality leather upper
2. Padded shaft edge
3. Expansion and flexion fold (some models)
4. Padded, well-sealing tongue
5. Leather lining
6. Footbed and insole
7. Insulated seam
8. Well-gripping contoured sole on strong foundation
9. Insert to reinforce the sole
10. Lacing components

FIG 15–10.
Cross section of a typical leather mountaineering shoe. (Adapted from *Meindl, A.*: Wissenswertes über Leder und Schuh, 1. Aufl. Eigenverlag, Kirchauschöring 1982.)

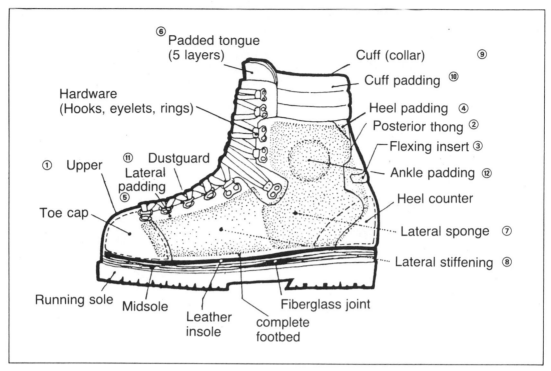

FIG 15–11.
Design and components of a leather mountaineering shoe, suitable for crampon use. (Adapted from *Meindl, A.*: Wissenswertes über Leder und Schuh, 1. Auf1. Eigenverlag, Kirchauschöring 1982.)

Figure 15–11 represents a leather mountaineering shoe having all the above criteria. A truly fine mountaineering shoe consists of a large number of components (Fig 15–12).

FUTURE TRENDS

There are some interesting innovations on the market, but only the future will tell whether they are going to be accepted or not. Industry is beginning to use "breathing" but also totally waterproof materials (e.g., Gore-Tex) in hiking shoes, just as it has in the clothing trades. The quality of the shoe is determined not only by the material, but also by the workmanship, e.g., the absence of seams. The special material cannot be frag-mented, but must be bonded to the inside of the shoe as a single, one-piece "sock." This is technically difficult to accomplish and is therefore frequently ignored. This futuristic methodology must still prove itself in practice as far as durability and strength are concerned. The new materials also tend to make the shoes warmer. Recently, these principles were incorporated in high-altitude boots, both in the single, solid leather shoes and also as the inner shoe in synthetic (plastic) boots. Whether this will solve the sweating problem of the synthetic shoes remains to be seen.

For the same reason, an air duct was developed for the sole of the plastic shoes to channel moisture and water to the outside. Since each step

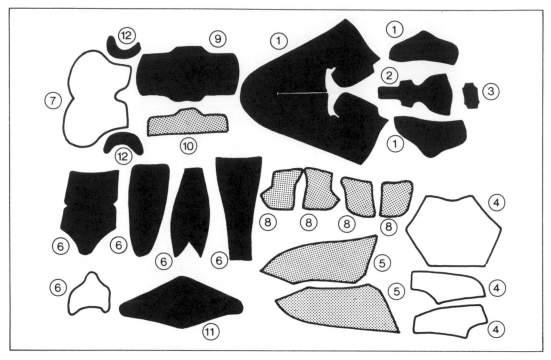

FIG 15–12.
Individual components of the mountaineering shoe from Figure 15–11 with corresponding numbers. The eyelets, rings, hooks, rivets, laces, toe cap, heel counter, and the components of the sole are not shown.

will squeeze air out through this vent, fresh air will be sucked in from above. This is supposed to lead to better ventilation in the synthetic footwear.

In the so called "combination mountain shoes," the inner shoe in the plastic boot was designed to serve as a friction-climbing shoe. Generally, it is too thin and too narrow for this purpose, nor does it provide good temperature insulation or adequate cushioning. In France, for reasons of weight, a light overshoe with integrated gaiters was developed for the approaches to the high Alpine climbing areas. These compromises have to date not been well received.

The newest development in the area of the friction-climbing shoe is the shaft height: for the first time there are some mountaineering shoe models, where the shaft does not extend above the ankle, thus permitting more mobility for the extremely difficult climbs. The disadvantages of the "half shoe" (Oxford)—no ankle protection and no lateral stability—are relatively less important here, since the climbers using these shoes are mostly highly experienced, top climbers, who can provide ankle stability with their well-trained muscles and who use the shoe strictly for climbing.

A new type of ultralight climbing half shoe has no laces and resembles a ballet shoe. It is designed primarily for training or for short practice climbs. Other than providing friction, its only purpose is to protect the sole of the foot and the toes from direct contact with the rocks. Another manufacturer has installed a rapid-release closure in the back of the shoe, in the area of the Achilles tendon, that can regulate the length of the shoe. This assures an optimal position for the toes and the heel during the climb, but the closure can be loosened for walking. Much has been done in the area of the special climbing boots, and there are some further developments under way that are anxiously anticipated.

MEDICAL AND HYGIENIC CONSIDERATIONS

Bothersome pressure points, which appear after several hours of wear, can be softened by pounding with a hard object. Synthetic boots can also be widened for people with particularly wide feet. The shell has to be immersed in hot water and can then be shaped with a special machine. Ski touring boots as well as downhill boots can be adapted individually to problem feet by injecting foam into the inner shoe.

The toe area must not be too small, and there has to be adequate room, particularly for the big toe. The toes must have some "breathing space" and should never be in contact with the front of the shoe (Fig 15–13). In downhill runs, the foot necessarily moves forward, and this can easily lead to blister formation. The lateral sides of the big toe and the fifth toe are obviously the most frequently affected areas, but the dorsum of the other toes is also in danger. Only a good fit and tight lacing at the instep can prevent the forward motion. There must also be adequate lateral space. This is frequently ignored, so that the toes are compressed during a downhill run.

The French and Italian shoes are often built too narrowly by our (German) standards. Apparently the "Germanic" feet are wider than the "Roman" ones. One wonders if these

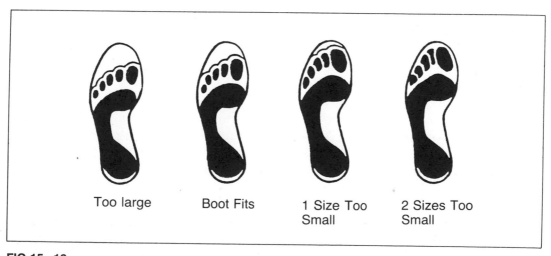

Too large	Boot Fits	1 Size Too Small	2 Sizes Too Small

FIG 15–13.
Survey of the foot outline in various size shoes. Climbing shoes are bought too small for an improved "feel." Explorer shoes are bought too large for fear of freezing. (Adapted from *Meindl, A.*: Wissenswertes über Leder und Schuh, 1. Auf1. Eigenverlag, Kirchauschöring 1982.)

shoes could not be built in different widths and not just in different lengths. This is already done in some "orthopedic" models. Furthermore, some people have asymmetrical feet, i.e., they are not the same size, and it would therefore be very helpful if they could purchase a right and left shoe of different sizes (e.g., one half size apart). This option would solve a large number of medical problems.

Mountaineering shoes, as indeed all other shoes, must be of correct length and width (see Fig 15−13). Yet there are two exceptional situations in mountain climbing where the shoe is intentionally kept too large or too small. In travel over ice above 4,000 m and in winter travel, the shoe should be slightly too large to allow the toes free mobility. Any pressure on the toes (e.g., crampon straps) reduces the circulation and increases the danger of frostbite. A large shoe also makes it possible to wear several pairs of socks in very cold weather. For exploratory travel, the shoes are usually one size (occasionally two sizes) too large.

Under difficult climbing conditions, on the other hand, the shoes are kept intentionally small to provide a tight fit and thus a better "feel" for the ground and better stability on very narrow ledges. In this case, the toes should have no extra space at all.

Since most shoes tend to spread somewhat after extensive use, climbing shoes are often bought one size too small. In exceptional cases, for very demanding climbs and to achieve the best possible "feel," some climbers dispense with socks and wear a climbing shoe two sizes too small. Since this is not only uncom-

fortable, but actually painful, the climbers are usually anxious to take the shoes off as soon as possible, even at every rest stop. This is another reason why many climbers use a different pair of shoes for the approach to and retreat from the actual rock face.

The tight fit can lead to circulatory problems in the feet. The problems are compounded by the fact that the climbing shoes are generally symmetrical and come to a narrow point at the toe (see Fig 15−4). The toes are compressed, and the big toe is strongly deviated toward the other toes. From a pure climbing technique point of view, this makes some sense, since a narrow, pointed shoe can enter a narrow cleft more easily.

The toe area is used extensively in climbing. A certain pressure generated in this area will provide the shoe with greater stability. It was found that more anatomically designed, asymmetric shoes, while providing more medial space, were not satisfactory for the most demanding rock climbs. The reason for this was lack of sufficient stability. When under pressure, the big toe automatically deviated toward the other toes. Nevertheless, the question must be raised whether the experiences gained by the most advanced climbers should be applied generally to all climbers, since these experiences were clearly detrimental to the good health of the feet. It should be investigated whether a pointed and narrow shoe may not lead to a permanent deformity in young climbers, whose feet are not yet matured and thus softer and more easily deformed. There is a real danger of hallux valgus formation. It would be regrettable if this condition were caused not only by the vagaries of fashion, but also by athletics.

In some foreign climbing shoes, the footbed is of poor quality or practically nonexistent. The footbed is not shaped according to anatomical requirements, but is as flat as the sole. There is clearly a need for improvement, and there are no technical climbing reasons why these improvements should not be made. As far as inserts are concerned, the same principles must apply as for any other type of shoe. Orthopedic adjustment in climbing shoes are more expensive because of the heavy, leather construction common in this footwear.

The lateral stability of the shoe in the ankle region is very important indeed, since even the improved and safe paths are usually not free of obstacles. Stones, roots, and scree material are the natural components of unimproved terrain and substantially increase the risk of "twisting" an ankle, mostly in the direction of supination. This is the main reason why mountaineering shoes are generally designed as boots, with the shaft above the level of the ankle. The light hiking shoes usually provide less than ideal stability, but have the advantage of greater comfort. Climbers who have weak ligaments or a poorly healed earlier injury and are thus more prone to dislocation should be provided with a variety of stabilizing plastic inserts. This would be highly desirable from a sports medicine point of view, and the principle is now made part of the aftercare options following a surgical procedure. There are some indications that this

desirable process is now being incorporated into some hiking boots.

Until recently there was only one model of climbing shoe, without consideration of sex. Now there are special women's models, which are smaller and have a built-in higher heel. The increased slant provided for the female foot has no specific advantages in the mountains and has to be viewed strictly as a tribute to fashion. Women who habitually wear high heels will develop a shortening of the Achilles tendon. This makes it difficult for them to walk on flat shoes, particularly uphill, where increased dorsiflection of the foot is essential. Raising the heel of the mountaineering boot makes uphill (though not downhill) walking easier. It constitutes a symptomatic "therapy" and an acceptance of the realities of daily life.

It was discovered most recently that including a cushioning layer in all mountaineering and ski touring boots can effectively decrease the load on the joints of the foot (see Figs 15-3 and 15-5). In contrast to the hiking boot, usually only the heel is provided with a cushioning wedge, since cushioning here will be particularly helpful in downhill walking and will not interfere with the forefoot during the actual climb. The cushioning wedges were first used in mountaineering shoes about 1980 and have since become a standard feature of these shoes. To date, cushioning wedges of various thickness and material have been used, but their precise effect has not been investigated. Their use is based purely on experience, and it would be reasonable to investigate this shock-absorbing effect from a scientific point of view. It would be useful to know whether the cushioning has any medical significance.

SUMMARY

Mountaineering shoes are highly differentiated and specialized athletic shoes designed for occasionally extreme demands in the mountains. The climber is offered an enormous variety, and there are models for every conceivable use. This makes a choice very difficult and later makes it problematic whether the best shoe is being used in each situation. Since every single mountain excursion may present a variety of demands for the footwear, excessive specialization in mountaineering shoes is irrational, and the need for compromises is obvious. In the face of rapidly changing surfaces, the mountaineering shoe must have certain all-around properties. Carrying a second pair must be limited to very special situations, for reasons of weight alone.

In some models, improvements in certain components are still necessary. This is particularly true for the width of the shoe at the level of the ball of the foot and for the room provided for the big toe. The footbed must also be improved along anatomical and functional lines. The mountaineering shoes have improved considerably in recent years. They have reached a high standard and have given a significant impetus to mountain climbing.

BIBLIOGRAPHY

1. *Hanschke, T.*: Alpine Austrüstung. 1. Aufl. Bergverlag R. Rother, München 1984
2. *Huber, H.*: Bergsteigen heute—Der Leitfaden für die Praxis, 4. Aufl. Bruckmann, München 1978
3. *Kubin, A.*: Bergschuhe—Doppelt genäht hält besser. Alpin-Magazin 8 (1984), 28–30
4. *Meindl, A.*: Wissenswertes über Leder und Schuh, 1. Aufl. Eigenverlag, Kirchauschöring 1982
5. *Ölmüller, K.*: Trekkingschuhe mit Goretex—wirklich wasserdicht? Alpin-Magazin 7 (1986), 30–34
6. *Schrag, K.*: Tourenskistiefel. Bergwelt 1 (1982), 32–34
7. *Schubert, P.*: Alpine Eistechnik, 12. Aufl. Bergverlag R. Rother, München 1981
8. *Spiecker, H.*: Wander- und Bergsteigerschuhe. In: Sportschuhe, 1. Aufl., S. 113–116. *Spiecker, H.* (Hrsg.). perimed Fachbuch-Verlagsgesellschaft mbH, Erlangen 1983
9. *Wagner, H.*: Der Bergschuh im Wandel der Zeit. Schuh-Technik + abc 2 (1984), 86–87

PART 6 _____ The Ski Boot

16 — Biomechanical Considerations of the Ski Boot (Alpine)

E. Stüssi

In contrast to the past, the modern ski boot has assumed a major role in providing optimal interfacing with and control of the ski. The development was due to the evolution of current skiing techniques, the changes in the materials used in the construction of the skis, and changes in the design of the skis. The boot must also serve as the connecting link between the foot and the binding with a precisely defined interface to the complex safety release mechanism of the binding. In addition, we also have such requirements as comfort, foot hygiene, and protection against cold.

To examine the causes of these developments in relation to the biomechanics of injury prevention, we must first determine which external factors were instrumental in bringing about the developments. It seems certain that these etiologic factors must include

- The frequency of lower extremity injury.
- The introduction of safety standards.
- The introduction of safety bindings.
- New techniques in skiing.

It is interesting to observe how these factors influenced the evolution of the modern ski boot, derived from the simple leather boot, which in turn evolved from the hiking boot. The modern boot is different with respect to

- Plastic shell construction.
- Shaft height.
- Design of the sole.
- Entry and closure.
- Design of the inner boot.

All these changes affect the biomechanics of the foot inside the ski boot. The following aspects will be discussed below:

1. Biomechanical considerations of the changes in the ski boot during the past 15 years.
2. Criteria of the modern ski boot.

BIOMECHANICAL CONSIDERATIONS OF THE CHANGES IN THE SKI BOOT DURING THE PAST 15 YEARS

Johnson and Ettinger[1] have shown that the incidence of lower extremity skiing injuries has decreased from

63% to 48% (Table 16–1). This reduction was due primarily to a reduction in the torsion fractures of the tibia and ankle joint (from 17% to 5%). By comparison, the flexion fractures of the tibia decreased only slightly. In absolute numbers, however, the incidence of injuries to the human locomotor system did decrease.

The high incidence of ankle injuries in the late 1960s and early 1970s was due to unsatisfactory ski boot design and to inadequate or nonexistent safety bindings. Modern skiing techniques led to higher downhill speeds. At these high speeds, a fall or an edge failure, combined with the lever action of the ski, placed enormous loads on the lower extremity. The ankle is the weakest link. It is very injury prone and was never designed for such a great rotational momentum.

The alarmingly high incidence of accidents led to the development of safety standards. On the basis of these standards, safety bindings were developed, but unfortunately they were not used with any regularity. Additional changes in ski boot construction led to a reduction of the loads on the lower extremity, particularly on the ankle. Extreme rotational momentum on the ankle is today largely prevented, since the safety bindings automatically release the foot during a fall.

The higher shaft and the shell construction reduced the rotational freedom of the ankle (pronation-supination). The frequent occurrence of congenital or acquired lower extremity abnormalities (genu varum and valgum) forced the boot manufacturers to equip the boot with a correction factor, the so-called canting correction that decreases the incidence of edge failure and thus decreases the risks of injury.

The second degree of freedom of the ankle joint, plantar-flexion and dorsiflexion, was also significantly reduced in the early boots. Since this motion is of great biomechanical significance (springiness of the knee and ankle joints), it will be given particular attention.

The injury statistics of Johnson and Ettinger[1] show that the incidence of flexion fractures of the tibia has not decreased, but the site of the fracture has shifted. The reason for this was found in an incorrect, too stiff, or improperly oriented shaft design.

Three important points have to be considered from a biomechanical point of view:

1. The effective rotational axis of the shaft must correspond to the rotational axis of the ankle joint. This

TABLE 16–1.

Ski Injury Statistics*

	1972–1973 (%)	1980–1981 (%)
All skiing injuries	100	100
Upper/lower body	37/63	53/48
Lower extremity		
Calf	30	15
Other	33	33
Torsion injury	17	5
Flexion injury	12	10
Knee injuries	22	20
Ankle injuries	10	3
Shoe-shaft fractures	5	5
Tibia fractures	7	3

*(Adapted from Johnson RJ, Ettinger CF: Alpine ski injuries: Change through the years. *Clin Sports Med* 1 (1982), 181–197.

means that during flexion the motion of the shaft must correspond to the motion of the tibia.

2. The relative lever length of the shaft and the tibia must be adjusted appropriately.

3. These lever lengths must properly correspond to the stiffness of the shaft.

If the shaft is stiff and the lever-length ratios are unfavorable, the skier runs the risk that the tibia will be sheared off at the upper edge of the shaft during a fall (Fig 16–1). Short shaft lever length leads to extremes in force and momentum (Fig 16–2).

Correct flexibility is not the whole answer. The functional anatomy of the ankle joint must also be an important consideration. If the axis of flexion of the ankle joint is not precisely in line with the axis of flexion of the shaft, an unfavorable lever ratio will ensue, and the advantages of flexibility will be lost (Figs 16–3,A and B).

Figure 16–3,A illustrates the situation where the rotational axis of the shaft is not in line with the axis of the ankle joint. The parallelism existing between the shaft and the tibia in the upright position is lost during flexion. Pressure points and a possible breaking point are created at the anterosuperior edge of the shaft, which can cause severe pain. Figure 16–3,B illustrates an optimally fitting boot with the axes in alignment. The tibia will be parallel to the shaft over the entire range of flexion, and the forces will be distributed along the entire length of the shaft. Under these conditions, an appropriate inner shoe

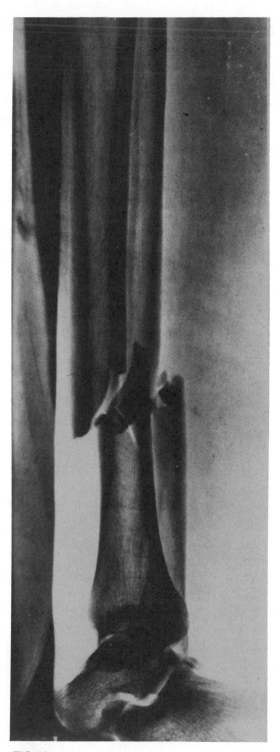

FIG 16–1.
X-ray picture of a shaft-edge fracture.

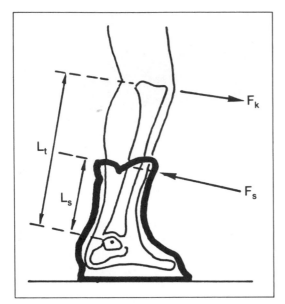

FIG 16–2.
Calculation of the maximal forces—the law of levers.

will be able to prevent pressure points without any difficulty.

To improve the lever ratios in favor of the tibia, the shafts were made longer and longer during the late 1970s. The rationale for this development was the inverse relationship between the force at the edge of the shaft and the length of the shaft, provided that the flexibility of the shaft remained the same. If the shaft covered the entire length of the leg, no flexion fracture could occur during a fall.

This development contributed to the safety of the tibia and the ankle. If the flexion resistance stays the same over the entire range of the flexion of the ski boot, the resulting flexion momentum on the tibia will be decreased. With respect to the safety of the knee, however, this is a very poor solution. The increasing stiffness of the flexion joint of the boot decreases the ability of the ankle to compensate

for the load and places the entire load on the knee. The absence of any decrease in the incidence of flexion fractures of the tibia until 1981 indicates that the trend toward high shafts was a false move. In modern ski boot design, an attempt is made to find a satisfactory compromise between shaft length and flexibility (flexion-extension) by more imaginative design. A very wide variety of adaptive and adjustive mechanisms make it possible for skiers to change the flexibility of the shaft according to their ability and expectations.

The importance of good agreement between flexion in the ankle joint and accurate positioning of the shaft, including attenuation of the flexion and the position of the dorsal extension, was demonstrated by the work of C.Y. Kuo et al.[3] (Fig 16–4). Even in normal skiing, the dynamic forces of flexion may reach 600 newton-meters, which is far above the static fracture limits of the tibia. These forces do not all manifest as a traction force in the heel area (as assumed by the manufacturers of the modern automatic heel release) but as a flexion momentum with a substantial vertical force component in the area of the forefoot. This means that the shaft of the ski boot is compressed primarily in an anteroinferior direction. The findings mandate a fundamental rethinking of the functional principles of safety bindings, particularly in view of the fact that these findings were substantiated by Johnson and Ettinger.[1] The percent incidence of flexion fractures has not decreased appreciably since the introduction of safety bindings and of the automatic heel release.

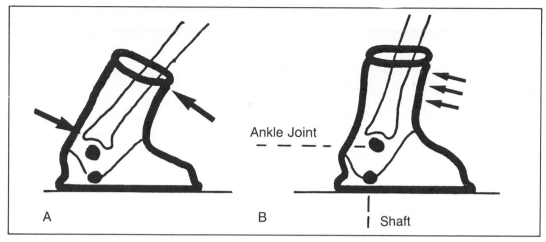

FIG 16–3.
Loss of flexibility due to unfavorable lever relationships. **A,** no agreement between the rotational axis of the shaft and of the upper ankle joint. **B,** optimally fitting boot.

Improvements in the load acting on the ankle make it biomechanically very likely that the problems arising in the rather delicate knee joint will increase (see Table 16–1). Injuries of the upper extremity have increased in recent years, presumably as the result of changes in skiing technique. To what extent these upper extremity injuries are related to ski boot design is unclear at this time.

CRITERIA OF A MODERN SKI BOOT

As mentioned in the introduction, modern ski boot design is the result of several factors. The requirements today are not significantly different from the requirements of 5 years ago. There are, however, some additional aspects that, together with nonbiomechanical considerations, make up the list of the criteria that the modern ski boot must meet. The discussion of these criteria will be presented below in the form of a check list. The criteria of the modern ski boot can be divided roughly into two groups:

1. Technical and biomechanical criteria.
2. Orthopedic criteria.

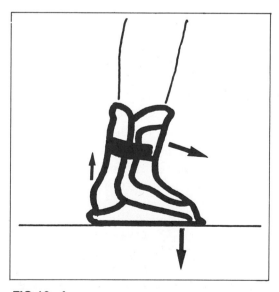

FIG 16–4.
Coordination of the flexion motion, direction of the shaft, flexion, and dorsal extension.

Technical (Skiing) and Biomechanical Criteria

From a technical (skiing) point of view, the ski boot must represent an interface between the human body and the ski. This implies first of all an exchange and steering function, i.e., the skier must be able to steer as well as possible, but must also have a direct feedback from the ski and from the ground. In this way, the skier can adapt to the requirements of the skiing surface and the snow conditions.

These conditions can be met if the height, stiffness, angle, and functions (rotational axes, ankle joint (AJ)/shaft) of the shaft are adapted, as well as possible, to the individual skier. It must be possible to correct for anatomical abnormalities, e.g., genu varum and genu valgum (canting). Excessive movements beyond the physiologic range of the ankle must be prevented by appropriate measures (positioning).

Another important point is the so-called "binding friendliness." As required by the standards, the ski boot must provide an optimal attachment to the modern safety binding. In addition to this, a design solution must be found such that the sole can be used with reasonable safety when the skier walks on snow, ice, wet composite and wood floors, and other surfaces.

Biomechanical considerations must further include all aspects of foot mobility (sliding) in all directions, as well as all loads to which the foot is exposed within the ski boot. Measurements of jolts while the athlete is skiing have shown that the tibia is exposed to considerable acceleration, which leads to a correspond-

ing load on the joints. The ski boot should therefore contain cushioning components in the sole (heel) area that can serve as shock absorbers. It would be a mistake to give the foot too much play in the area of the instep. In case of a forward fall, this would act like a loose seat belt in a car and allow a whiplash effect on the foot, leading to excessive load on the foot and ankle joints as well as on the ligaments and articulations of the knee.

Orthopedic Criteria

From an orthopedic point of view, the most important criterion is that the foot and the leg be in an optimal environment. This, of course, means a good fit so that no pressure areas are created (perfusion and pain). When a boot is designed, it is also important to consider the individual variations in the total foot volume and also in the volume of the forefoot and in the width of the forefoot. There are several methods whereby this can be accomplished (polyurethane foam, special inner shoes, air cushions, etc.). It must also be possible to use orthopedic inserts.

Another consideration is the "climate" in the shoe. The selection of a material for the inner shoe that can absorb perspiration will benefit the foot. In this connection, it is equally important that the functions of the foot not be affected by external temperature and moisture, i.e., the boot must be properly insulated.

The boot must also be user friendly. Entry into the boot from the rear was a major step in the right direction. User friendliness also implies that the boot can be used, at least to some extent, in normal walking. The first step in this context must be the folding of the spoilers and thus the free mobility of the ankle joint. This should not, however, allow too much freedom to the foot and lead to the danger of stepping out of the boot with every step.

SUMMARY

The criteria of modern ski boot can be summarized as follows:

1. The modern ski boot must be designed from a functional point of view, i.e., the design must take into consideration the realities of functional anatomy (axes, etc.).
2. It should not make compromises at the expense of other joints (length of shaft, flexibility, and positioning).
3. It must represent the ideal connecting link between man and ski (steering and feedback).
4. The modern ski boot must be comfortable.

REFERENCES

1. *Johnson, R.J., C.F. Ettinger:* Alpine ski injuries: change through the years. Clinics Sports Med. 1 (1982), 181–197
2. *Kuehne, L.:* Grundlagen Skischuhbau. Kriterien für den Bau. Beschreibung möglicher Meßmethoden. Diplomarbeit in Biomechanik, T & S, ETH-Zürich 1980
3. *Kuo, C.Y., J.K. Louie, C.D. Mote jr.:* Field measurements in snow skiing injury research. J. Biomech. 16/8 (1983), 609–624

17 ———————— Kinematics of the Foot in the Ski Boot

M. Pfeiffer

Changes in the shape of the foot, caused by motion of the shaft of the boot, were observed in the laboratory by x-ray imaging and video tape recording. The movements of skiing were simulated, and the varying behavior patterns in different boot models were observed.

When the foot was in place and the leg was moving forward against the resistance of the shaft at the ankle, the following was observed:

1. "Levering of the foot" in its entirety and in its components. Its original fixed position is lost.

2. In a seemingly passive fashion, the bones of the foot are displaced both toward each other and away from each other. Particularly obvious is the raising of the talus from the calcaneus. This can proceed to the limits of the connecting ligaments. The talus is displaced superoposteriorly.

3. The axis of the ankle joint deviates from the rotational axis of the shaft (Figs 17−1 and 17−2).

4. Depending on the angle of the shaft, there is a continuous change in the spatial and pressure relationships of the foot to the shell. There is also an ongoing change in the areas of contact and an unpredictable appearance of pressure points.

5. Displacement of the calcaneus from the precise "heel position," probably due to traction by the Achilles tendon in the absence of active antagonistic muscle activity.

6. The normal interplay of shifting the load on the arch from hindfoot to forefoot is lost through the compressive effects of the shell.

7. The relationship of the foot to the shell varies considerably from model to model, depending on whether the pressure on the shaft is caused by normal skiing or by a fall. A greater or smaller "crash space" is created over the dorsum of the foot and/or by the elevation of the heel.

(Problems of the binding release will not be discussed).

THE VARIOUS TYPES OF SKI BOOTS DISCUSSED FROM THE PERSPECTIVE OF SPORTS MEDICINE

Type A.—Levering and displacement of the foot along the longitudinal axis of the boot:

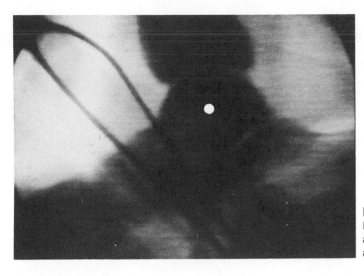

FIG 17–1.
Relationship of the axis of the
ankle (*white spot*) to the rotational
axis in the standing position.

- Unsatisfactory positioning of the
  heel, even at rest.
- Forward displacement of the foot
  during backward motion of the leg
  due to exaggerated forward leaning
  of the rear shaft.
- The shoe is too long.
- Absent or faulty footbed.
- Insufficient adhesion between the
  skin, the sock, and the inner shoe.

Type B.—The shaft comes into
contact with the shell during forward
movement and compresses the foot
from above downward. This may
also be done initially by improper
closure. Therefore the following occur:

- The longitudinal arch can no longer
  function.
- The bones of the hindfoot and midfoot are already fixed in their
  extreme position and hence
- No "crash space" in the boot and no
  activation of the binding-release
  mechanism by an anatomical forward displacement.

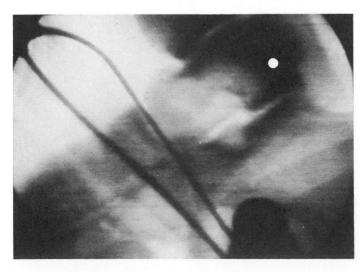

FIG 17–2.
When the lower leg moves
forward, the axis of the ankle
(*white spot*) moves away from the
rotational axis.

Type C.—Early and strong shaft resistance in the presence of good instep contact and good heel position. Therefore, the following occur:

1. The physiologic gliding function of the ankle joint is stopped prematurely and thus
2. The talus is levered posterosuperiorly.
3. The contact of the sole with the boot and the "feeling" of the sole are reduced, and the toes curl under.
4. The synchronous play of the longitudinal arch is passively overcome.
5. In a simulated forward crash, there is a reduced "crash space" over the area of the midfoot and very little elevation of the heel.

Type D.—The shaft exerts its braking action on the forward motion of the leg relatively late, and the forward motion stops barely before the limits of the joint are reached. Therefore, the following occur:

1. The talocrural motion takes place over a relatively long arc and without opposition.
2. Synchronously with the forward movement of the leg, the dorsum of the foot rises and the longitudinal arch is increased, so that
3. The ensuing backward movement starts with a preliminary flattening of the arch and a preservation of the stability of the hindfoot.
4. The heel and consequently the axis of the ankle joint move

posteriorly and superiorly only very little and before the limits of the joint are reached.

Type E.—Ski boot with open shaft and the old leather ski boot:

Free mobility of the ankle, no noticeable displacement of the foot or its bony structures.

All the above points affect the safety of the run and the mobility necessary for optimal balance. They can have a strong negative effect both orthopedically and from the point of view of functional economy. This creates certain medical demands with respect to sports that must be considered in future ski boot design and construction.

MEDICAL CRITERIA IN SPORTS

The shaft of the boot should provide the leg with good support, but not with great resistance for about two thirds of the possible arc, i.e., 20 to 22 degrees. Up to that point, the normal, physiologic function of the ankle should not be impeded. Because of its effects on the foot, the arc described by the shaft is divided into a "lead segment" and into a later "lever segment."

Forward sliding of the foot should not be possible. There should also be no loss of contact of the sole and no decrease in the "feel."

Previous misconceptions concerning the shaft and its role in absorbing energy must be replaced by the realization that shaft pressure generates impulses affecting the motion patterns of the upper body, which, in turn, profoundly affect acceleration and balance.

Pressure of the shell on the dorsum of the foot and interference with the longitudinal arch of the foot must be avoided.

Correct positioning of the foot is more important than forced constraint and "squeezing" the foot. This will prevent misuse of the ligaments and weakening, particularly of the fibular musculature and ligaments. (This will also explain why even competitive skiers can suffer ankle dislocations while engaged in light athletics or even just in everyday activities.)

When the lateral stability of the shaft is properly maintained, the forces acting in a sagittal direction should not be merely passive but should be the result of active muscle participation and tonic muscular tension. If muscular function is inhibited in the ankle area, greater loads will be placed on the knee.

The ski boot and its shaft must be adapted to the technical skill of the skier, and the technical skills of the skier must be adapted to the preexisting biomechanical functions of the leg and the foot.

These medical requirements with respect to sports should not be construed as criticism of the boot industry. It is hoped that they are a contribution to the development of a ski boot designed along anatomical principles. This goal has not yet been achieved.

18 Ski-Specific Injuries and Overload Problems— Orthopedic Design of the Ski Boot

H.-W. Bär

Few forms of athletics place as high demands on the footwear used in their performance as alpine skiing. The reason for this is that, just like the ski or the ski pole, the ski boot is part of the athletic equipment. It functions as a connecting link between the binding and the human body and performs a series of difficult, complex tasks (Fig 18–1). First of all, a functional unit must be established between the ski boot and the binding. On the other hand, this "piece of equipment" must provide comfort on standing and walking, not just for hours, but for days or weeks and, for instructors, for the entire year. It has been known for a long time that of these manifold activities relatively little time is spent in actual downhill skiing, even by experienced skiers, and that the time spent in standing and walking may be many times as long (Table 18–1).

Several years ago the Stiftung Sicherheit im Skilauf (SIS) or Skiing Safety Foundation distributed questionnaires to more than 10,000 people with questions relating exclusively to the health aspects of the ski boot. It was found that 25% of the respondents were dissatisfied with their ski boots. This has motivated the industry in recent years to improve the design of the inner shoe. A glance at the catalog of the manufacturer reveals that today almost every boot has an "orthopedic assistance" feature of some kind that can be used to modify the inner shoe.

The rules of both technique and physics set rigid criteria for the design of the sole so that the sole may have the required rigidity, the resistance to torsion, and the low friction potential that will assure the proper functioning of the so-called safety bindings. (These criteria, incidentally, are not fully provided by the Deutsches Institut für Normung [DIN].) The Internationaler Arbeitskreis Sicherheit im Skilauf (IAS) International Skiing Safety Working Group sets firm attenuation limits for the rigidity

FIG 18–1.
Alpine skiing places great demands on the ski boot.

of the shaft in forward and backward motion. The human foot that should function in a standard shell, unfortunately cannot be standardized. Just like every face and every hand, every foot has its own individuality.

Twenty years ago, if skiers wanted a properly fitted boot, they went to a shoemaker who made them an individually designed leather boot that, naturally, fit well (Fig 18–2). These boots remained "firm" for 2 to 3 years, at which time they were exchanged for new ones. Today the situation is much more complex, and the foot must be fitted into a ready-made shell designed according to rigid specifications. This means that the boot, purchased in the specialty shop, on "dry" ground, may prove the next day and on snow to be too soft, too hard, or too much inclined forwards. This is unfortunate, since one of the most important functions of the boot, i.e., the establishment of an intimate contact between athletic equipment and the body, is lost.

The boot must provide the following:

1. The best possible, direct transfer of force from the body to the ski through a form-fitting inner shoe and a corresponding total fit.
2. Reasonable thermoregulation and comfortable and relaxed standing and walking, even for feet with deformities and injuries.
3. Purposeful performance of prevailing skiing techniques through appropriate forwards and backwards mobility.

The multiplicity of options in providing a well-fitting inner shoe, ranging from plastic inner soles to ad-

TABLE 18–1.

Time Spent in Downhill Skiing, Walking, and Standing*

	Downhill Skiing	Walking	Standing
Beginners	1	8	40
Average skiers	1	4	20

*Adapted from Hoppichler.

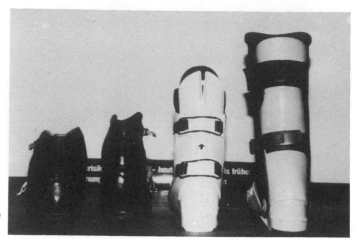

FIG 18–2.
Evolution of the ski boot over the years.

justable air chambers and insufflated polyurethane foam indicates that the ideal method has not been discovered yet. A significant factor in all this is that in the presence of an existing defect in the pedal arch or the pedal skeleton, the above described inserts only perpetuate, but do not correct the defect. This is particularly true in the adult. A footbed should be first of all an active participant in establishing physiologic functioning of the muscles and ligaments of the foot by correcting any existing deformities.

In designing ski boots for children, it must be kept in mind that approximately 40% of the youngsters up to age 10 years will have some pes valgus, pes planus, or genu valgum deformity. This helps in the snowplow position, but is a handicap in a straight run. Axis deviations are very difficult to correct in a stiff, plastic boot, and even the insertion of plastic wedges under the boot, known as "canting," frequently ignores the fact that correcting the pes valgus leads to an axis deviation in the knee. Since children make up one third of the ski injury statistics, this is a fruitful area for further work by both medicine and industry.

Substantial progress has been made in a number of ski boot models in that they now permit standing in the neutral-0-position, rather than the previously unavoidable 20 to 30 degree forward slant. This slant caused cramping of the muscles and muscle tightness of the entire lower body up to the spinal column. A singularly unpleasant side effect of this position, so common to skiing, was a load-induced chondropathy of the patella. The studies of Plitz demonstrated that this position can cause retropatellar pressures of 1,000 kg/cm^2. Hauser showed that, in addition to the sole, the shape of the shaft was also a contributing factor in the prevention of injuries and fractures. Further studies, in which pressure-sensitive plates are used, are being planned.

Investigations by Pfeiffer have shown that the foot maintains some spontaneous mobility in the ski boot. Thus the total immobilization by foam injection or compression by

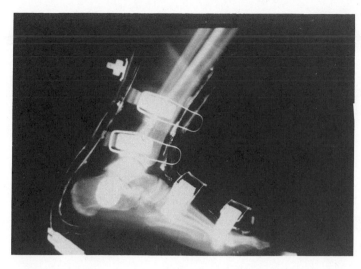

FIG 18–3.
Forward leaning in the ski boot.
The foot maintains some mobility.

tight buckles are unphysiologic (Fig 18–3). For this reason, and for more than 10 years, individually shaped insoles have been recommended. These are covered with a soft material that allows spontaneous motion of the foot along physiologic lines, but at the same time takes into account the existing pedal abnormalities, which must be assumed for at least 50% of all people. Correcting the sole permits the complicated tendon and ligament system of the pedal arches to function without undue fatigue while also protecting the vascular and nervous system of the foot (Fig 18–4 and 18–5).

The boot must assure freedom of mobility to the toes. This is accomplished by having a large enough inner shoe. Only in the case of major congenital or post traumatic deformities should foam injection with an elastic plastic material be used to provide a satisfactory fixation of the foot in the boot. The evaluation of such pathologic conditions is beyond the ability of the manufacturer or merchant and requires the active participation of the orthopedic surgeon.

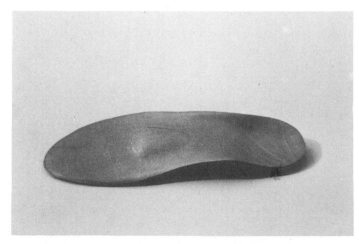

FIG 18–4.
Adjustable insert with a soft cover.

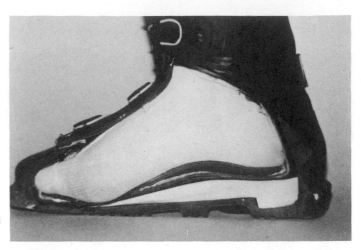

FIG 18–5.
Longitudinal section through a ski boot with corrected foot support.

The importance of the shape of the tongue was also recognized in the meantime. It was noted that after extensive or long-term use, the tongue tended to slide to one side. This leads to pressure damage and irritation, particularly on the medial surface of the tibial edge. This is seen quite regularly in racing. The inner shoe must provide continuous cushioning for the medial edge area of the tibia. This is accomplished by tailoring the tongue to conform to the anatomical requirements of the tibia. Furthermore, the tongue must be designed so that it will adapt to the forward and backward movements of the shaft without developing folds and not wrinkle even during maximal forward ventral displacement of the shaft.

Finally, it should be noted that the inner shoe must be made of a material, felt or one of the new artificial fibers, that can "breathe" and that allows the transfer of moisture and creates an acceptable climate for the foot. This implies both humidity control and thermal regulation. Problems in this area are more likely to lead to circulatory disturbances than even the greatest compression by tight buckles.

REFERENCES

References are available on request from the author.

19 Sports Medical Criteria of the Alpine Ski Boot

W. Hauser

P. Schaff

Many alpine skiers have insufficient mobility in their knees and ankles. The range of motion, particularly in the ankles, is much too small. This results in a static, stiff run. It does not correspond at all to the ideal of a wide range of mobility in the area of the knee and ankle, which was proposed and taught during the early alpine skiing lessons. Even the best didactic methodology is not always successful in imparting to the student the full range of motion. The lack of proper technique seen so often is not due to lack of ability, but to an unsatisfactory functional configuration of the shaft in so many ski boots. This is particularly true in the models designed for children, adolescents, and women.

FUNCTIONAL CONFIGURATION

The configuration of the shaft in the modern ski boot is such that the vertical force directed upward from the area of the heel is critical to the release of the conventional binding. This force is markedly affected by the function and configuration of the shaft. In different shafts, totally different forces may be generated in the region of the heel, even when the angle of flexion at the ankle is the same. The load on the tibia relative to its longitudinal axis also differs markedly in different boots, even though the angle of flexion may be the same.

To set physiologically correct criteria for ski boots, it is critical to measure the distribution of pressure along the anterior edge of the tibia in the different models. In a study sponsored by the Stiftung Sicherheit im Skisport (SIS), or Skiing Safety Foundation, of the Deutscher Skiverband (DSV), or German Ski Association, and carried out by the Internationaler Arbeitskreis Sicherheit beim Skilauf (IAS) or International Skiing Safety Working Group jointly with the Technischer Überwachungs-Verein Bayern (TUV-Bayern), or Bavarian Technical Monitoring Association), the configuration of the shaft of the ski boots was investigated, together with the load conditions of the human leg and their effects on performance. A special pressure-distribution measurement system was designed for laboratory use.

The Pressure-Distribution Measurement System

The pressure-distribution measurement system consists of

- A pressure-measuring mat.
- An integrator with a video signal generator.
- Several peripheral units to record and/or display the data.

The Pressure-Measuring Mat.— The pressure-measuring mat is based on a capacitance pressure measurement system that functions according to the following principles: when a force acts on a plate capacitor (condensor) (Fig 19–1), which has a compressible substrate as the dielectric medium, the distance (d) between the capacitor surfaces is reduced and the dielectrical constant changes. This raises the capacity of the condensor, and this increase in capacity reduces the high-frequency impedance. If a network of such condensors is set up and a specific, high-frequency signal is put through it, the amplitude of the output will be a measure of the forces acting on the network.

If parallel metal strips cross at right angles both over and under a compressible dielectric medium, each intersection becomes a pressure-sensitive condensor (Fig 19–2). The shape of such a pressure-measuring sheet can be varied widely. It is also possible to select a dielectric medium that is flexible along either the longitudinal or transverse axis. Acute angulation must be avoided since this may also compress the dielectric medium and thus generate a false signal. For these experiments, a measuring

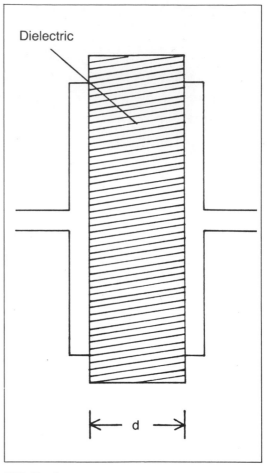

FIG 19–1.
The individual elements of the pressure-measuring mat consist of a plate condensor and a compressible dielectric.

mat was used that roughly simulated the shape of the tongue in a ski boot. It consisted of three 1.2-cm wide longitudinal metal strips and twenty-four 0.8-cm wide transverse strips. This produced 72 pressure points. The integrator can handle 192 pressure points simultaneously.

The measuring mat is so thin (3 mm) and so flexible that it fits between the sole of the foot and/or the leg and the boot without affecting the range of motion.

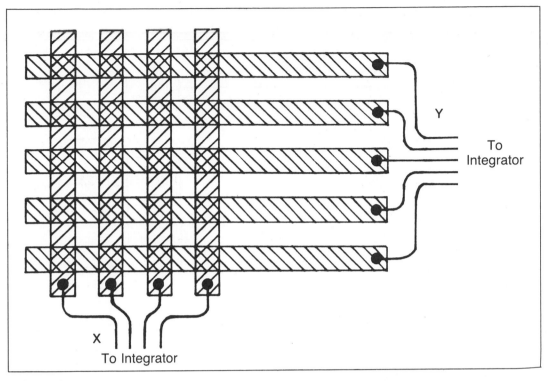

FIG 19–2.
A pressure-measuring mat consists of parallel measuring strips that are woven at right angles above and below a compressible dielectric.

The Integrating Unit.—In Fig 19–3 a block diagram is shown. The integrating unit consists of a high-frequency sine-wave generator, two integrators for input and output signals, a differential amplifier, a 6-bit analog-to-digital (A/D) converter, a color video signal generator and an RS 232 C-interface. These components were controlled by an 1802 CMOS computer.

The Peripheral Units.—The unit was controlled from a keyboard. The display units consisted of a color television screen, a video tape recorder, a microcomputer with floppy disk storage, and a matrix printer. Storing the data on a video tape recorder makes it possible to review the entire motion sequence in slow motion or on individual stills.

When measurements were made inside the ski boot, the medial ankle was used as the reference point. Measurement point no. 6 was located at this level (Fig 19–4). The measuring sheet extended another 20 cm above this point.

Methodology

Three different ski boot models were selected for the study: a low-shaft model, a model with a medium-high shaft of adjustable stiffness, and a model with a high shaft. The diagrams show superimposed curves for

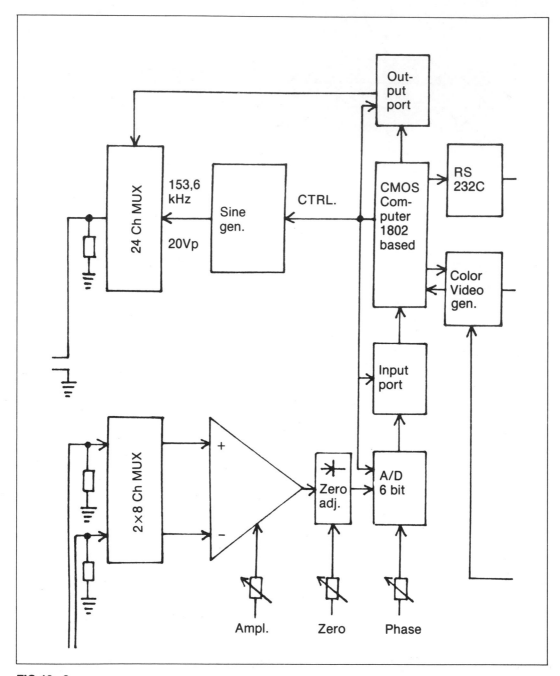

FIG 19-3.
The block diagram illustrates the experimental setup. It consists of a high-frequency sine-wave generator (*Sine gen*), two multiplexers for input and output signals (*MUX*), one differential amplifier (+ −), one 6-bit A/D converter (*A/D 6 bit*), one color video generator (*color video gen*), one RS 232 C-interface, and an 1802 CMOS computer as the control unit.

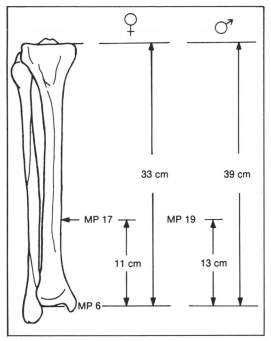

FIG 19–4.
Position of the measuring mat in relation to the average length of the tibia. *MP =* measurement point.

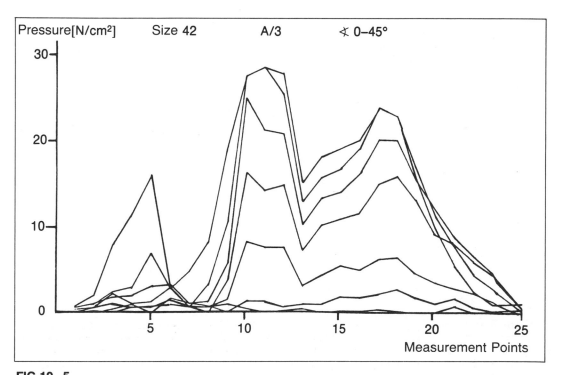

FIG 19–5.
The distribution of pressures in the low-shaft boot model **A,** determined by measuring sequence *3.* The individual curves represent the distribution of pressures at various forward angles. The *top curve* was obtained at an angle of 45 degrees. The *lower curves* each represent a decrease of 5 degrees in the forward angle of the shaft (size 42 boot).

the different forward angles. These are defined as the angle between the longitudinal axis of the shaft and the vertical. Starting with an angle of 0 to 10 degrees, measurements were made at 5-degree intervals until a 45-degree angle was reached for a size 42 boot and 40 degrees for a size 38 boot.

When we look at the values obtained from the low-shaft boot (Fig 19–5), it is apparent that the maximal pressure lay fairly far forward and that it was biphasic in the area of the leg.

The midshaft boot, at a soft setting (Fig 19–6), showed little pressure over the entire range until 45 degrees was reached. At this time, a relatively high value was obtained. There was a very marked increase in pressure between 40 and 45 degrees, and there was only a single peak.

The high-shaft model demonstrated a triple peak curve (Fig 19–7). The peaks were small until 40 degrees were reached. The pressure increased significantly only at 45 degrees.

If one compares the maximal pressure of all three shoes at 45 degrees, there is practically no difference. There are appreciable differences in the area between 0 and 30 degrees. It is critical to examine the pressure in the heel component of the binding at the same time (Table 19–1). At 45 degrees, this measured 26 daN for the low-shaft boot, 45 daN for the medium-shaft boot at a soft setting, and 51 daN at a hard setting.

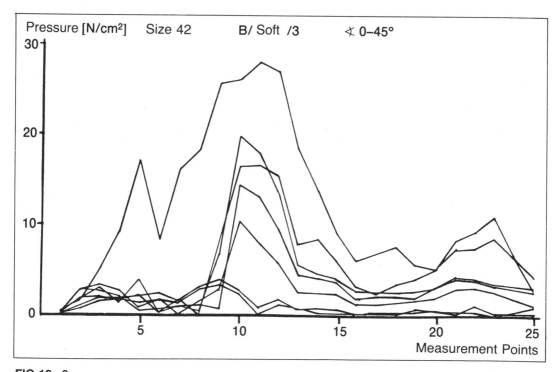

FIG 19–6.
The pressure distribution curves for the medium-high boot **B.** The forward angle attenuator was set at "soft" (size 42 boot).

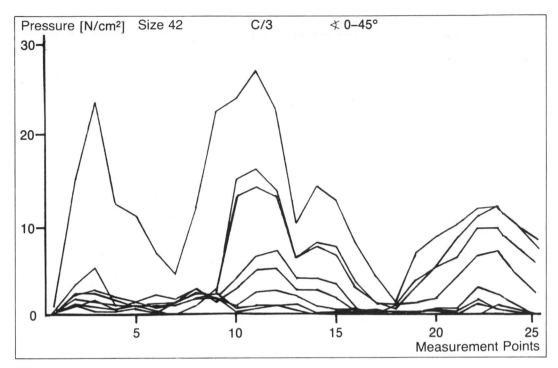

FIG 19–7.
The pressure distribution curves in the highest-shaft boot *C* (size 42 boot).

The value for the long-shaft boot at the same angle was 58 daN. Only high-shaft boot C generated enough power to release the binding. The low-shaft boot generated only half as much power at the heel-binding component, even though the peak pressure was just as great as in boot C.

If one compares the distribution of pressure in model A with model C at identical pressures at the heel, one notes a definite difference in the mean values (Fig 19–8). The flexion momentum on the tibia was also clearly different. The forward angle reached by model A at this point was 35 degrees and by model C only 20 degrees.

It must be remembered that these data were obtained in the laboratory at room temperature. The situation at the low temperatures of the ski slopes

TABLE 19–1.

The Vertical Force at the Heel (F_{AV}) at Three Different Angles for the Various Models Tested

Forward Angle (Degrees)	Force (daN) at Heel Component (Size 42 Shoe)			
	A	B (Soft)	B (Hard)	C
35	0	13	26	38
40	13	29	38	45
45	26	45	51	58

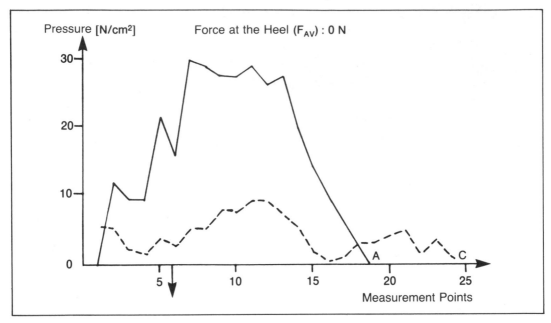

FIG 19–8.
Pressure distribution curve for model A (*solid line*), compared with that for model C (*broken line*). Both are at the same force at the heel component (F_{AV}). Model A is at a forward angle of 35 degrees, model C at 20 degrees.

may be quite different. The currently used ski boot materials have a twofold to sixfold rigidity factor. A number of ski boot models that rely on their material for rigidity may undergo significant changes under these conditions. It can be expected that, at the forward angle necessary for alpine skiing, the pain threshhold will be exceeded in women and children. Telemetric measurements, planned for the future at these temperatures on the ski slopes and under marginal conditions, should give us the answer.

SUMMARY

On the basis of the available data, the following criteria can be determined for the shaft configuration of a functional and safe ski boot:

- The boot must be safely locked at a forward angle of no more than 40 to 45 degrees.
- Dorsal flexion of the ankle must be assured for the entire range necessary in skiing.
- The development of pressure should be as even as possible over the entire range of forward flexion.

On the basis of the completed studies, the following concrete criteria can be established:

- When a forward angle of 40 to 45 degrees is reached, the force exerted on the heel-binding component must exceed the 95th percentile of the lowest setting for that particular group of skiers.
- To enable the ankle to dorsiflex as far as is necessary for good skiing, the maximal pressure generated in

the shaft must not exceed the 95th percentile of the pain threshold between 0 and 35 degrees.

- Pressure must increase linearly between 0 and 35 degrees. This should be true for the development of pressure at individual points as well as of the pressure across the length of the shaft. "Linear" must be defined individually for every ski performance target group, and this has to be done empirically.

Furthermore, the forward momentum generated by the distribution of pressure must not exceed the mean potential forward momentum that can be generated by the weight of the skier at 35 degrees.

In the future, ski boots will be designed rationally and according to the increasing requirements of the ski performance target groups. We also hope that these studies will answer the questions concerning the effects of shaft height on knee injuries and of a combined flexion-torsion momentum on the tibia.

PART 7 _____ Other Winter Sport Shoes

20 The Figure Skating Boot

W.-D. Montag

It is distressing for an experienced orthopedic surgeon to see all the things that emerge from a skating boot when skaters change their clothes. Ten to 20 pieces of foam rubber, pieces of felt, and styrofoam from a single skater's boot are no exaggeration. All this is put into the boot to provide cushioning against pressure points. It is impossible to convince a figure skater that these items actually increase the pressure.

Seeing this was the start of an odyssey from boot manufacturer to boot manufacturer years ago, when I became responsible for the medical care of championship figure skaters. The makers of skating boots for world-class athletes are regular shoemakers, without qualifications as master orthopedic shoemakers. Any criticism was met with the repeated and convenient response: "This is the way we have always done it. These are the shoes with which Manfred Schnelldorfer, Marika Kilius, Hans Jürgen Baümler, and others became world and Olympic champions. If the boots were no good, they would not have won." The sports physician can say only one thing: "Just imagine how much better they would have done, if they had a better pair of boots!"

The skating boot makers in Germany and neighboring countries are all famous. "Their boots" are in great demand, since everybody in the world—European champions and Olympic medalists—get their boots from them. These shoemakers used the same arguments and were not about to listen to well-intentioned advice or respond to urgent requests.

The problems confronting the skating boot are determined by the following factors:

1. Strong lever action is exerted on the boot by the blade, which is approximately 5-cm high. It is well known from biomechanical theory that the lever force depends on the distance between the boot and the surface (ice) (Fig 20–1).

2. The boot should protect the ankle against supination and pronation, but should not affect dorsiflexion and plantar flexion to any great extent.

3. There are three different levels of load: (1) solo and pair skating, (2) ice dancing, and (3) compulsory exercises. The design of the boot must be quite different for each of these categories.

4. For so-called recreational skating, one can rent a pair of boots for 1

FIG 20–1.
The height of the skate acts as a powerful lever.

to 2 hours. In competitive skating, one can find 5-year-olds who can no longer use "ready made" boots.

For the championship class, a "made-to-order" boot is mandatory, and it will be a different boot for the compulsory exercises and for free skating.

The skating boot is not a mass-produced item that a manufacturer can make in sufficient numbers and at a large enough profit to allow for the financial burden of doing research. Small athletic-shoe companies repeatedly engaged in the production of skating boots, and the results were consistently unsatisfactory. To find an orthopedically oriented boot maker who could meet all the criteria for a good skating boot

was not difficult. Unfortunately, the athletes did not accept these men, since they were not part of the "in" group. They were not known, and their boots had not yet been worn by a master.

PRESSURE POINTS

Figure 20–2 illustrates a skating boot that was worn for 3 weeks. Even after only 3 weeks, the upper developed a crease that was bad enough to cause a pressure ulcer and prevent the skater from skating for several weeks. Almost one half of all German master-class skaters had to have surgery performed on their medial or lateral malleolus because of pressure sores, inflammatory bursitis, and significant tissue damage of the malleoli.

One case was particularly troublesome. The skating boot was pressing on the external malleolus, and this resulted in bursitis. No treatment was given. Bursitis led to such severe tissue reaction and tissue damage that the peroneal tendon was dislocated at the external malleolus.

At the time of surgery, the following were found: The external malleolus was skeletonized and denuded of periosteum. It could be said that the malleolus sat in a "soup" of tissue fragments. The retinaculum was totally separated from the bone, and the peroneal tendon was anteriorly dislocated over the skeletonized bone. The effort it took for this passionately devoted figure skater to continue to skate, despite excruciating pain can be appreciated only by someone who treats such injuries regularly. Follow-

FIG 20–2.
This skating boot was worn only for 3 weeks. It already shows evidence of wear on the shaft.

ing the operation and the construction of suitable boots, the injury was healed, and this lady is today one of the most elegant and appealing members of the German master class.

Figure 20–3 illustrates the boot of a runner-up in the world championship. She had to stop all athletic activities at the beginning of the 1983–1984 season, just before the German championship, because of pressure sores on her feet. Improper coaching also led to spinal column complaints, and she could not re-sume training until July of the following year.

This shoe was sliced open to show its construction. It can be seen that, through a kneading process inside the boot, the stiffening middle layer was so distorted that it caused pressure sores on the foot and on the leg, right through the soft leather lining. It is not only poor workmanship that can cause injuries, but using unsuitable materials can cause them as well.

In general, the skaters do not consult the attending physician about

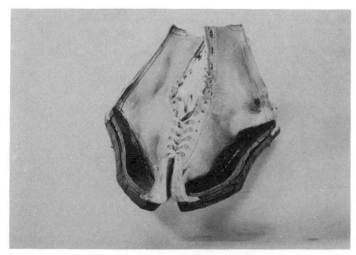

FIG 20–3.
Boot sliced open showing typical pressure points.

poorly fitting boots. It took great effort and repeated discussions concerning the importance of appropriate footwear before the attending sports physician was even consulted. The coaches, particularly the older ones, were reluctant to cooperate. These coaches had the same attitude as the manufacturers since they were coaching the European and world champions and the Olympic medalists of the day. Only when a younger generation of coaches took over, who had personal experiences with the miseries of badly fitting skating boots, was there a marked improvement in cooperation.

JUMPING TECHNIQUES

A further problem is created by the extremely variable loads placed on the boot by differences in jumping technique. Today a triple jump is a standard expected even from a junior skater. This produces a much greater load not only on the skater, but also on the boot. Today even youngsters are exposed to loads that were previously expected only from a master-class skater. To get a proper boot for a young skater, the parents must spend over $600. How quickly youngsters outgrow boots is well known to all who have children. If then this boot does not even last through the period of annual competition and has to be replaced at least once and sometimes twice each year during the years of growth, it is obvious that an impossible situation exists. Truly high-quality boots cannot be provided under these circumstances.

ARTISTIC ACCESSORIES

A third difficulty is created by the fact that the boot must contribute to the "artistic appearance" of the skater. Figure skating is an athletic activity in which the artistic impression created by the skater is important and where the performance of the athletic program is affected by the clothing of the skater. The wide lacings, narrow tongue, and construction of the skating boot did not do justice to the shape of the foot or the leg. Male skaters have worn a boot cover for many years now, so that the boot cannot be seen at all. This is not possible for female skaters and has given rise to serious problems.

THE LAST

A problem of workmanship was identified when it was recognized that the skating boots were made on a regular shoe last. Major improvements were made when a plaster cast was prepared of the foot and lower leg under load conditions. The last was then made from this mold.

Figure 20−4 compares the foot last with the so-called foot-leg last, now used by orthopedic boot makers. Furthermore, the layer between the lining and the outer leather, used to stiffen the boot, is no longer bonded to its neighbors but is mobile so that all three layers can move in relationship to each other. The formation of creases is now much less likely, if not impossible. The contact area between the tongue and the boot was also ex-

FIG 20–4.
Special last made for the individual skater.

amined critically. It was found that the edges of the tongue were directly over the malleoli. Further improvements were made by dividing the lacing into two or three segments that could be tightened individually and thus more vigorously. This is significant, since during skating the lacing becomes uneven and loose over the instep and overly tight at the top of the boot. This problem was attacked and solved satisfactorily.

EDGE SKATING

A fifth problem is purely technical. Skating takes place on the edges, i.e., on the inner or outer edge of the blade. The inner edge is used more and more vigorously. If there is a slight crus varum or valgum and/or a genu varum or valgum, this affects the position of the boot and determines whether the weight is placed on the inner or outer edge when the skater is standing still and straight. This must be taken into consideration. The coaches are fully aware of the problem and know all the tricks to help the skater. The position of the blade can be shifted slightly anteriorly or posteriorly, medially or laterally, and this is not a major problem for sports medicine.

The practicing sports physician must be advised to focus his attention on the internal and external malleolus and to the region of the shaft edge, particularly at the end of a training session. It is best to sit next to the skater and observe all the things that may emerge from the boot. It would be most desirable if the sports physician would support the legitimate complaints and reproaches that the athletes make against the refractory boot makers. It would also be beneficial if the sports physician would not only advise the coaches but also actively cooperate with them.

SUMMARY

Criteria for the skating boot are as follows:

1. Basic research investigating the figure skating boot from a biomechanical perspective.
2. Transmission of these findings and of the orthopedic–sports medicine experiences to the

boot makers and material providers so that a model boot can be designed.

3. Preparation and wide distribution of this test boot.

4. Assembly of all theoretical, practical, and empirical findings into a basic model.

Obviously, fabrication of the skating boot represents a hitherto unresolved problem.

21 ———————— Ice Hockey Boot Requirements

D. Winklmair

The hockey boot market shows a number of divergent trends at the present time. In the area of leisure and spare-time hockey, the ratio between shell boots and ballistic nylon mesh boots was 1:2 last winter, with a very marked trend toward increased market penetration for the shell boot. The reason for this was the unlimited capacity of the shell manufacturers, who flooded the market with inexpensive shells. In championship and professional circles, the number of shell boots is very much smaller. In this area, there is a clear trend towards the sewn, reinforced nylon mesh boot. Practically all ice hockey boots today (even on championship teams) are equipped with plastic-coated blades (Fig 21–1). Very few players still use the conventional steel blades.

Ice hockey demands that the boots be highly maneuverable and permit rapid starts and stops. To accomplish this, several characteristics of the boot must be brought into harmony:

- The arc of the runner and the grinding of the running surface.
- Lateral stability.
- Mobility of the shaft forward and backward.
- Vertical transfer of the rotational momentum.

THE ARC OF THE RUNNER AND GRINDING OF THE RUNNING SURFACE

The runner of the blade is approximately 3-mm wide, and thus these blades are considerably thinner than the blades of figure skates. The profile of the runner is a segment of an ellipsoid. The length of the runner in contact with the ice is usually about 8 cm. Players who demand maximal maneuverability hone their blades down to a contact area of only 2 cm. This will reduce the maximum achievable speed, since speed depends on the ice contact area of the blade.

The running surface of the blade must be ground hollow. If the edge is too sharp, some maneuverability is lost. Top players, whose blades are sharpened after every game, will have only a minimally hollow-ground blade.

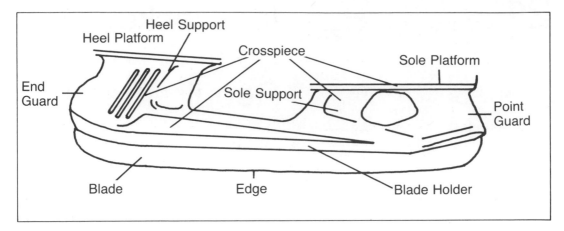

FIG 21–1.
Plastic-coated ice hockey skate.

LATERAL STABILITY

Strong lateral stability is particularly important in ice hockey since it can prevent serious ankle injuries to the players. Adequate lateral stability can only be achieved by having a sufficiently rigid upper material attached to a solid heel counter that extends anteriorly on both sides. Support for the joints should be incorporated in the area of the longitudinal arch to prevent internal flexion. These are the characteristics that determine the usefulness of the ice hockey boot. They determine maneuverability, starting, and stopping.

A plastic-shell boot appears at first sight to have certain advantages as far as lateral stability is concerned. The advantages of this rigid material should not be underestimated, particularly for the untrained or technically inept, occasional player.

Highly trained and accomplished professionals are less dependent on the support of rigid materials, since their musculature is able to assume a major role in the maintenance of the foot position. For these players a shell boot becomes a limiting factor in training. The shell construction also makes it more difficult to fit the boot properly. When the foot "floats" in the boot, both lateral stability and force transfer suffer. The reinforced nylon mesh used for the top quality boot is expensive, but it is sufficiently rigid and yet form fitting.

SHAFT MOBILITY

The typical rigidity values for the shaft of the shell boot are between 70 and 80 joules/radian and for the nylon mesh shaft 40 to 50 joules/radian. Top quality shell boots may have a rigidity value as low as 50 joules/radian.

The limited mobility of the shaft in shell boots is obvious from these figures. The position of the shaft also influences the proper fit of the shaft much more in the shell boot than in the nylon mesh boot. The reason for this lies in the fact that most shell boots have a fixed pivot point at the ankle. This is the reason why top players do not use shell boots, although psychologic reasons, e.g., the "bulky" appearance of the boot, may also possibly contribute to this rejection.

Shaft mobility is also affected by the shape of the tongue. The tongue should be high, wide, and not too soft.

TRANSFER OF THE ROTATIONAL MOMENTUM

The problem of rotational momentum transfer exists in all athletic shoes and boots. Only one aspect of the problem will be mentioned here: shell boots must be provided with a soft liner. The poor resistance to distortion of these liners causes a reduced transfer of force, and this is yet another disadvantage of the shell boot.

PROTECTION AGAINST INJURY

The limited use of shell boots by top players is further restricted almost entirely to defensive players. This observation leads to another, very important criterion of the ice hockey boot, i.e., protection against injury from the puck or from the stick or from the blade of another player.

Hard hit pucks can achieve a velocity of 150 km/hour. Lateral impact of the puck against the blade, the blade attachment, or the boot is a real, practical, dynamic concern. To prevent injuries, the ice hockey boot must be able to withstand this impact.

The prevailing Canadian standards for the ice hockey boot require that the effects of such an impact be tested with a mechanical simulator. The test mechanism consists of a vertical pipe in which a weight of 3.5 kg can fall from a height of 3 m onto a blade held by a clamp at right angles to the longitudinal axis of the pipe. The weight has a puck attached to its end that strikes the blade. Since damage and distortion are dependent on the energy generated at the moment of impact, the test is performed under conditions of energy equivalence. For a puck weight of 110 g and an impact velocity of 150 km/hour, the equivalent energy can be calculated to be a weight of 3.5 kg and drop height of 3 m. To protect against injury, the blade and blade attachment must be able to withstand such impacts without being broken or separated from its attachment to the boot. The extent to which such a test is applicable to the body of the boot has not been determined to date.

Falling players frequently smash horizontally into the goal post. This dynamic stress can also be tested by simulation. Instead of a falling weight of 3.5 kg, a heavy cylindrical weight of 22.7 kg is used with a piece of steel pipe soldered to its lower end. The drop height is 60 cm. The steel pipe hits the running edge of the blade at right angles. The impact corresponds to the player sliding into the goal post at 7 km/hour. The boot must also survive this test without distortion of the blade or separation of the attachments from the boot.

SUMMARY

The development of safety features for the body of the boot lags far behind the same concern for the blade and the blade attachment. The developments in the area of hockey boot design show no consistent direction.

BIBLIOGRAPHY

1. Norm ASTM F 737–81: Standard performance specification for ice hockey skate blades, Philadelphia 1981

22 The Cross-Country Ski Boot

A. Vogel

The cross-country ski boot has considerable influence on the performance of the skier. Since the boot must provide a running function, a secure walking function, and a certain amount of comfort for a wide variety of feet, it must meet a number of different requirements. These requirements vary considerably, not just from individual to individual, but also from performance level to performance level (Tables 22−1 and 22−2).

The motions of the skiers depend on their performance level. Their kinematics (lengths of stride, rate, and acceleration) and dynamics vary considerably as a function of the amount and duration of the energy expenditure.

In addition, different performance level groups have different requirements in the area of safety features and insulation. The available boots vary accordingly, from the high boot of the "wanderer," to the low, racing boot for the championship caliber skier.

Since many of the functions can be achieved only jointly by the boot and the binding, there are different bindings for different boots. These are standardized as Nordic 75 (achievement groups W and L), Nordic 50 (as

TABLE 22−1.

Cross-Country Ski Boot Criteria—Strongly Dependent on the Level of Performance of the Target Group

	Functional Configuration
1. Running	Kinematic, dynamic, and energy requirements
2. Binding compatibility	Requirements in contact areas of the shoe-bindings system Nordic 75 Touring 50 Racing 50
3. Walking	No protruding components Gripping sole
	Fit and General Configuration
1. Foot-friendly configuration	Room for toes, footbed, and tongue Room for the joints
2. Comfort and protection	Waterproof on the bottom Absorb sweat Conserve heat Protect ankle

Racing 50 and Touring 50, for several achievement groups) and specialized boot-binding systems (for optimal performance).

Since many of the problems of the cross-country ski boot are shared by many other athletic shoes, only those features will be discussed that are specific to cross-country skiing. A

TABLE 22–2.

Requirements of Performance Target Groups on Which Manufacturers Base Their Product Design*

Performance Group Symbol	Capacity of Skier	Terrain	Performance and Motivation of Skier
S	All techniques, speed, endurance	Well-prepared track, no limits on difficulty	Performance oriented
A	The important techniques, endurance	Well-prepared track, moderate difficulty	Athletically oriented
L	Modest technique, not for downhill	Prepared track easy (pref. flat) terrain	Leisure activity oriented, health oriented
W	Dependent on terrain until important technical aspects are mastered	Primarily easy to moderate terrain other than prepared track	Wandering, nature watching
I	This group contains all those skiers who have individual requirements and who cannot be assigned to groups S,A,L,W. Skiers in this group may demonstrate widely varying characteristics.		

*The definition of each performance target group makes it possible for every skier to select the appropriate group. The manufacturers design their products specifically for a certain target group and label them with the appropriate target group symbol. Ski, binding, and boot are all adapted to the requirements of a particular target group, and so the choice of equipment is made very easy for all cross-country skiers. S= superior; A= average; L= low; W= wanderer; and I= individual.

few general remarks will address the general requirements.

GENERAL REQUIREMENTS

The inner space must provide sufficient room for the toes, must provide lateral support, and must assure a solid seat for the foot. This is accomplished by high and laterally extended heel counters and toeboxes. The boot must be provided with a removable insert, which, if necessary can be replaced with an individually shaped insert. The tongue should cover well but should not interfere with the rocking motion and must be secure from displacement. For achievement groups W and L and for those using the skating technique, a higher shaft must be provided that limits lateral mobility and thus protects the ankle.

The boot must be watertight for at least the lower 6 cm, both during walking and skiing. Good insulation is a requirement. In the high boots for groups W and L, the entire foot must be kept warm. Both the cover and the lining materials must not only be able to participate in all movements of the foot for long periods of time, but must also serve as a heat exchanger, absorbing and releasing heat rapidly in the internal space. The lining must be able to absorb water and channel moisture away from the foot. This function, so important for the internal environment of the boot, can be par-

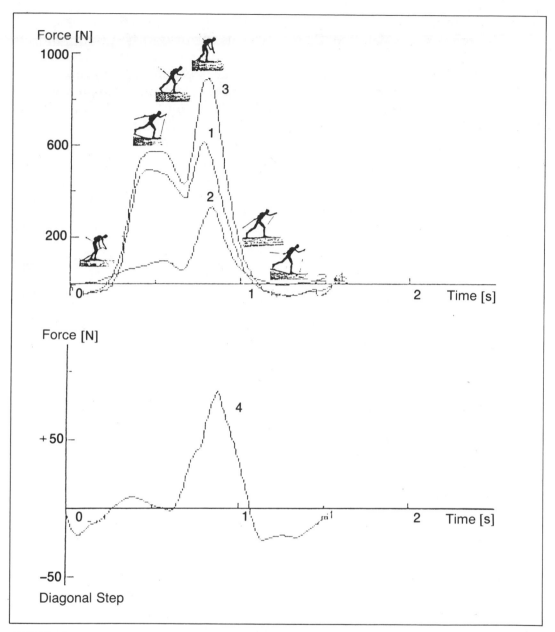

FIG 22-1.
Course of the vertical takeoff pressures, measured at the tip (*1*) and at the heel (*2*). Total pressure (*3*) and the course of the horizontal pressure (*4*), all in one diagonal step.

tially assumed by the sock. The boot must be able to dry rapidly.

The cross-country ski boot must enable the skier to walk securely, even on slippery surfaces. For this purpose, the front end of the boot, de-

signed to fit into the binding, should not be too long. The sole must be able to grip well, perhaps by having some areas made of rubber.

When designed to be used with a standard Nordic binding 75 and

50, the measurements of the boot are regulated by the standard Deutsches Institut für Normung (/) ISO 6959. Coordination of the combined boot-binding system is assured, since the same manufacturer is usually responsible for both components.

THE SEQUENCE OF MOTIONS

The diagonal step is the most common technique in cross-country skiing, both for skiers in group A, who use it in its basic form, and also for the average skier, who uses a dynamic pushoff and swing phase. Elements of the diagonal step are incorporated into other forms of motion, e.g., the two-pole pushoff, the circling step, the herringbone step, and the gliding step of the L group skier, who achieves forward motion by shifting his or her weight from ski to ski. The point of the exercise is to give the body the greatest possible

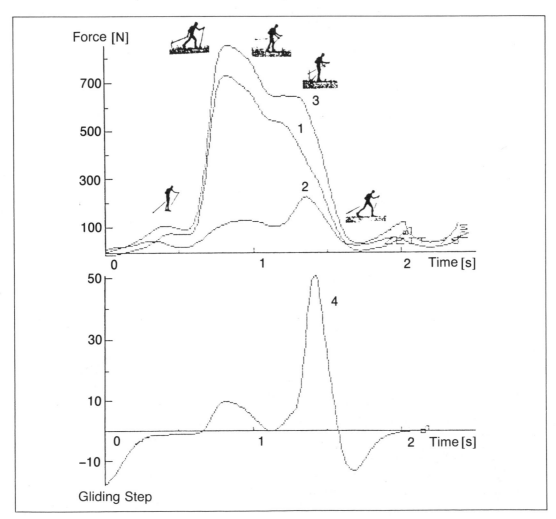

FIG 22–2.
Same as Figure 22–1, except that it represents the gliding step.

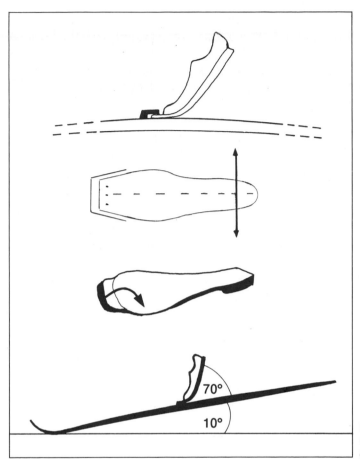

FIG 22–3.
Characteristic movements of the cross-country ski boot.

impetus with the legs and the arms, whether the skier is gliding on one ski or two. The glide should cover the greatest possible distance, several meters, before another pushoff is required. The greatest impetus will be provided by the greatest force exerted over the longest period of time.

Figure 22–1 illustrates a tracing of the vertical force during a single diagonal step. F_{zs} is the force at the toe, F_{za} is the force at the heel, F_z is the sum of the forces, and F_x is the propulsion force exerted by the skier. The area below the F_x curve is the measure of the impetus generated by the pushoff. Figure 22–2 illustrates

the same for a gliding step in a technically inexperienced skier.

THE ROLE OF THE SKI BOOT IN CROSS-COUNTRY SKIING

To perform the sequence of motion described above, the cross-country ski boot must be able to transmit the required forces in every phase of the exercise. The front part of the boot must be very flexible (Fig 22–3), but must have enough rigidity to prevent torsion and lateral displacement and prevent the heel from "missing" the ski during a herringbone step. The greatest mobility of the sole must be under the ball of the foot to spare the toes excessive strain during the step. This will also guarantee that the sole is placed firmly on the surface of the ski during the pressure phase.

When the locus of greatest mobility is moved forwards, anterior to the ball of the foot, the length of the stride is increased. A reasonable compromise must be found, unless a "variable" solution is sought, that would permit changes in flexibility to be made according to the requirements of the terrain and the sequence of motion.

During the rocking motion, a certain flexion resistance of the boot is helpful, since it will keep the ski in a better position, particularly during a skating step, and not allow it to dangle loosely from the boot. A solidly anchored boot will also keep the ski oriented in the proper direction and firmly pressed onto the snow surface. On the other hand, flexion of up to 90 degrees during every rocking sequence will require work. Since at the end of the step, the rear end of the ski is usually somewhat elevated (see Fig 22–3), the maximal boot an-

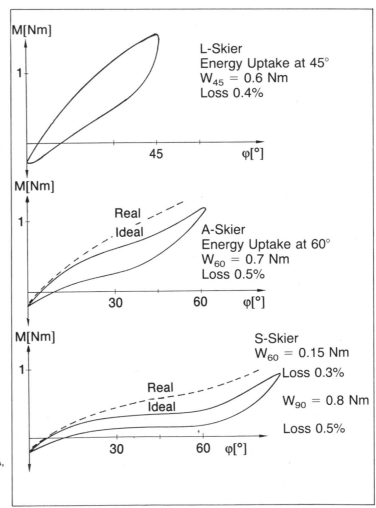

FIG 22–4.
Flexion-momentum angle diagrams for different cross-country ski boots for L, A, and S class skiers. The losses are calculated at 150 joules of energy per pushoff.

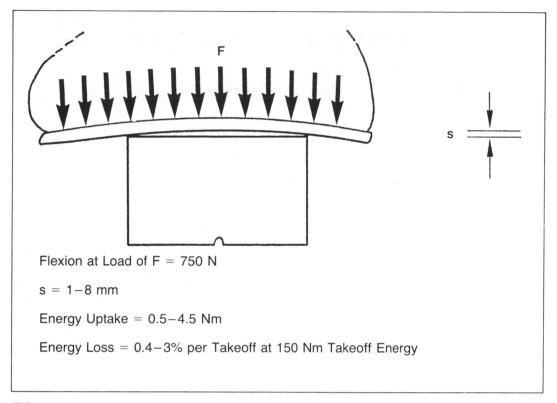

Flexion at Load of F = 750 N

s = 1−8 mm

Energy Uptake = 0.5−4.5 Nm

Energy Loss = 0.4−3% per Takeoff at 150 Nm Takeoff Energy

FIG 22−5.
Cross-sectional flexion of the cross-country ski boot on pushoff.

gle rarely exceeds 70 degrees. The work expended on tilting the ski cannot be usefully recovered, even though the distortion is partially reversible.

When the boots are not satisfactory, this loss of energy can amount to 5% of the total, usable locomotor energy. For this reason, the boot and the binding must be so designed that the energy required for flexion be held to a minimum.

This can be achieved if the flexion momentum rises to the higher ranges necessary for proper ski control only toward the latter part of the flexion process when proper ski control is particularly important. For the skating technique, and to make the her-

ringbone step easier, even smaller angles require an increased momentum. The momentum should not rise much with less than a 30-degree angle in group A and 45 degrees in group S. Both the angle and the required momentum is characteristic for each achievement group. Flexion momentum-angle diagrams are shown in Fig 22−4 for group L, A, and S skiers. The area under the curve is a measure of the energy lost in the boot-binding complex.

The great forces generated during pushoff cause those parts of the sole extending beyond the surface of the ski to bend downward (Fig 22−5). This distortion of material also means a loss of energy. Assuming an energy output of 150 joules for the pushoff on a diagonal step, the loss for optimal boots will be in the range of 1%, and for less satisfactory boots about 5%. This is a "contribution" that can make a difference between first place and tenth place in a race.

The energy transfer in the boot-binding complex can be measured with relative ease (see Figs 22−1 and 22−2). Its effect on performance can also be determined. To do this, a skier is asked to cover a preset distance (uphill, downhill, or level) on repeated occasions, using the same equipment and varying only the boot or the boot-binding complex. Assuming that the heart rate remains constant and does not vary from test run to test run, the time of the run becomes a measure of the effect of the boot on performance. It was shown by repeated studies that these measurements were reproducible and truly reflected the effects of the various boots and bindings on performance.

SUMMARY

The cross-country ski boot evolved from two sources. It was derived from the old, pre−World War II ski boot with which it still shares the squared-off front end. It is also derived from the running shoe and thus has particular requirements. Improvements in these characteristics, so important for the long distance runner, were made possible only by the development of the boot-binding complexes. It can now be shown that the diagonal step and the skating technique put quite specific and different requirements on the ski, on the binding, and on the boot. It can be assumed that the further development of the cross-country ski boot will be a function of skiing technique and will occur as one component in a corresponding improvement in the ski.

PART 8

Athletic Shoes for Children

23

Biomechanical and Dynamic Studies of the Athletic Shoe for Adults and Children

W. Diebschlag

F. Heidinger

Several orthopedic studies have shown that a majority of the population has foot deformities requiring treatment and that even children may have acquired damage. These largely acquired defects were due primarily to the inactivity of the feet and to the constraints of undersized footwear, which was too small in every direction and in every component. The ensuing muscle and tendon atrophy manifests itself as a complication of inadequate footwear.

It can be expected that a good athletic shoe conforms to the anatomy of the foot, as far as its shape and elasticity are concerned (selection of proper materials). This is particularly true for the inner sole that must provide a true footbed and that must be able to respond to the specific requirements and loads of individual athletic activities. Elastic footbeds are particularly desirable in those activities (running, jumping) where high forces and pressures are generated and where protection against these must be provided. The feet of children are still growing and must be especially well protected.

Fig 23–1 presents a simplified outline of the biomechanical regulatory cascade of the posture apparatus. It is evident that the shape of the footbed and the deformities of the foot have a direct effect on the ground reaction forces and thus on the entire biomechanical cause-and-effect sequence. This sequence is, of course, also directly affected by pathologic processes, e.g., arthritis or ligamentous injury, which act on their respective link in the sequence.

THE EXPERIMENTAL PART

To quantitate these effects, several studies were performed in which an electronic pressure distribution measurement system developed at the Institut fur Arbeitsphysiologie der Technischen Universität München (The Physiology of Work Institute of the Munich Technical University)[1-12] was used. Figure 23–2 illustrates one

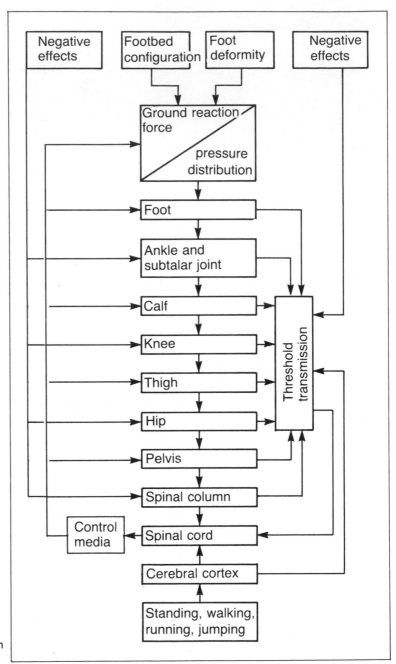

FIG 23–1.
Greatly simplified biomechanical effect cascade of the human posture apparatus.

part of the computer, the monitor, and two miniaturized, pressure-sensitive mats, which can be inserted into the athletic shoe (sensor distribution = 1/cm²). Figure 23–3 illustrates a pressure sensor in various stages of assembly. The graphic display of the data, covering the entire area of the foot, can be done by a block display and by shadings of color. Figures 23–4 and 23–5 illustrate in simplified form (and in black-and-white)

FIG 23–2.
Pressure-measuring soles and a personal computer and screen for the management and display of data.

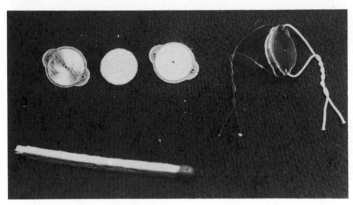

FIG 23–3.
Force sensors for pressure measurement designed on the transformer principle.

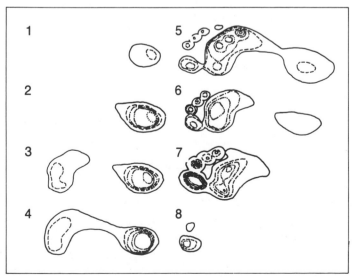

FIG 23–4.
Isobar representation of the rocking sequence in walking at 5 km/hour.

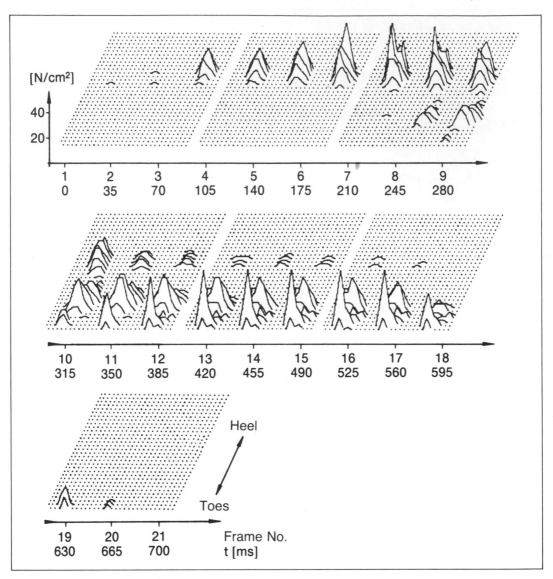

FIG 23–5.
Three-dimensional representation of the rocking sequence of one foot at 5 km/hour.

an isobaric and a three-dimensional representation of the rocking sequence of the foot, respectively. Although not shown here, the use of color allows a good quantitative assessment of the differences between a normal foot and a deformed foot (splayfoot, pes planus and pes valgus). The changes in color represent distinct changes in pressure (newtons/cm^2). It is well known that in the normal step during rocking, the force transfer takes place primarily over the lateral ball of the foot, with less load on metatarsal heads two through four, and the medial ball of the foot. In the splayfoot, the highest loads are observed over metatarsal heads two through four. Figure 23–6 illustrates, in spatial representation, the pressure while the subject is standing still on both feet (*left*=normal, *right*=splayfoot).

To study the effects of different shoe floor designs on the load transfer in the individual forefoot areas, the rocking process was evaluated with a flexible pressure=measuring mat in the shoe with or without an orthopedic footbed (Fig 23–7). The following forefoot areas were studied:

- Area 1: Medial ball.
- Area 2: Metatarsal heads 2 through 4.
- Area 3: Lateral ball.

Figure 23–7 illustrates the changes in the transmitted weight components (N) in areas 1, 2, and 3, during the rocking sequence, with or without an orthopedic footbed. The foot studied was a splayfoot, like the one illustrated in Figure 23–6. The orthopedic footbed consists of an individually fitted torsion pad, according to Hachtmann.

In area 3 (lateral ball), the weight transfer was lower with the orthopedic footbed than without it. Similarly in area 2 (metatarsal heads 2–4), the orthopedic footbed lowered the transfer of the load components. This is a very desirable feature. The load trans-

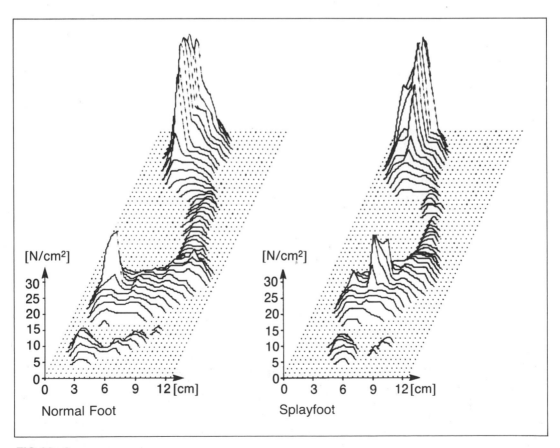

FIG 23–6.
Three-dimensional representation (standing) of a normal foot (*left*) and a splayfoot (*right*).

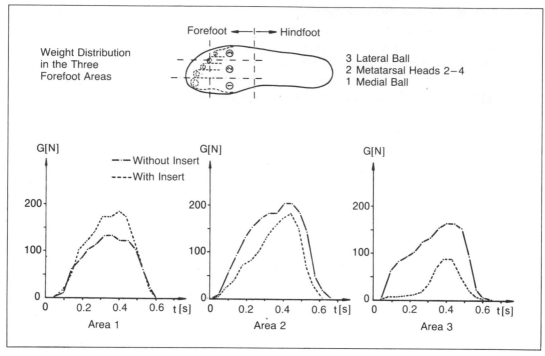

FIG 23—7.
Transference of the weight components on individual areas of the forefoot while the athlete is walking at approximately 5 km/hour in shoes with or without an orthopedic footbed. The subject has a splayfoot (see Fig 23—6).

fer is increased with the footbed in area 1 (medial ball). This showed that, when a torsion-insert was used, there was an immediate change in the load transfer in the different area. In areas 2 and 3, the forces were reduced and shifted in the direction of area 1. This effect is physiologically desirable, since the area of the medial ball was originally destined to accept heavy loads. If elastic materials are used for the insert, the load and pressure values could certainly be even more positively affected. In selecting materials, a fundamental consideration must be that, if possible, the footbed retain some elasticity even under maximal load. This will prevent an unphysiologic rise in pres-

sure, particularly in the area of metatarsal heads 2 through 4.

When the possible elastic materials (different types of foam) are evaluated, the characteristic elasticity curve is very useful, since it indicates the material's compressability in relationship to the force exerted. Figure 23—8 illustrates this relationship in a not very satisfactory standard foam and a good latex foam. A foam having a linear curve is more suitable for a footbed, since it can transform the generated forces into a uniform, elastic compression over the entire surface area.

Having determined by the above-mentioned sports-specific measurements, the values for the forces and pressures acting on the sole of the foot, one can construct appropriate footbeds on the basis of the elasticity curve of the various foams. Thus, it should be possible to combine horizontal and vertical layers of different foams that correspond to the differential loads in the various areas of the foot and to optimize the response of the footbed to the various pressures acting on it. Consideration can also be given to differing body weights, shoe sizes, and the particular requirements of each athletic activity.

Particular attention must be given to the athletic shoes for children to prevent the appearance of foot deformities. Colored distribution diagrams of pressure on the sole of the feet during standing and walking in adults and children have led to valuable conclusions:

1. A child stands with the center of gravity toward the heel and with practically no weight on the toes.
2. The greatest load transfer while the child is standing is in the

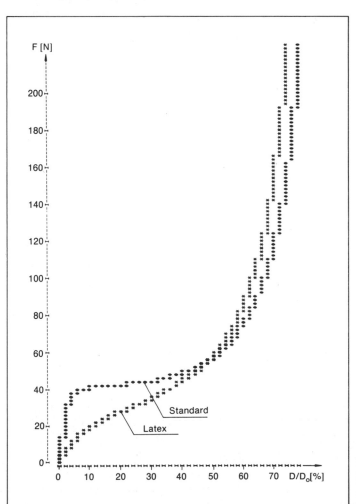

FIG 23—8.
Elasticity curve of two elastic substances: standard and latex foam.

area of the forefoot, on the lateral and medial ball of the foot. This indicates that the anterior transverse arch is intact.

3. During the rocking sequence, both the longitudinal and transverse arches are depressed more sharply and rapidly, but they revert to their original shape immediately after the load is lifted. This physiologic reaction is not seen well in the deformed feet of the adult. Even if the deformity is not painful and produces no handicap to walking (e.g., severe splayfoot) that would initiate medical attention, it can still produce changes in standing and walking. Thus, unbeknownst to the patient, these shifts in pressure and force impacts continue to produce pathologic changes in the muscles, tendons, joints, cartilages, and bones, leading ultimately to severe secondary complications, which require major corrective procedures.

SUMMARY

The determination of forces and pressures acting on the sole of the foot during standing and walking and exposure to the various loads of the different athletic activities allow the development of a footbed that conforms to the requirements of the individual athletic activity. The design of this footbed should take into consideration the behavior of elastic materials as determined by their characteristic elasticity curve and also by the weight of the athlete.

In October 1984, the "child foot-measurement days" sponsored by the German DAK—Gesundheitsdienst (Health Services) came to an end. The results are not yet available. If one looks, however, at the frightening data obtained in a preliminary study —that 60% of all children wear shoes that do *not* fit—it seems obvious that there is still a great need for improvement in children's athletic shoes and in the education of children, parents, and physical education teachers.

REFERENCES

1. *Beierlein, H.-R., W. Diebschlag:* Meßmethoden und Ergebnisse der Druckverteilungsmessung unter der Fußsohle des Menschen. Z. Orthop. 115 (1977), 606–607
2. *Brunner, W., B. Kurz, W. Diebschlag:* Kapazitives Druckverteilungsmeßsystem für hohe Meßstellendichte. Biomed. Tech. 28 (1983), 221–224
3. *Diebschlag, W.:* Quantitative Ergebnisse der Druckmessung an der Fußsohle des Menschen, S. 1–18. In: Kongreßband zum V. Congrès de l'union internationale des techniciens de l'industrie de la chaussure (UITIC), Belgrad/Jugoslawien, 20.5. 1981
4. *Diebschlag, W.:* Some quantitative results of pressure measurements on the sole of the human foot. SATRA Translation, Trans Series 115, No. 9. SATRA, Kettering/Northants, U.K. 1981
5. *Diebschlag, W.:* Die Druckverteilung an der Fußsohle des Menschen im Stehen und Gehen, barfuß und im Schuh. Z. Orthop. 120 (1982), 814–820
6. *Diebschlag, W.:* Die Druckverteilung an der Fußsohle Erwachsener beim Stehen und Gehen, barfuß und im Schuh als Kriterium für die Sohlengestaltung, S. 752–768. In:

Proceedings of the VII. Congress on the Leather Industry. Budapest/ Ungarn 4.–10. 10. 1982

7. *Diebschlag, W.*: Ergebnisse der Druckmessung an der Fußsohle des Menschen. Schuh-Technik + abc 76 (1982), 643–650

8. *Diebschlag, W.*: Résultats quantitatifs de mesure de la pression au niveau de la plante du pied humain. Technicuir 16 (1982), 96–103

9. *Diebschlag, W., H.-R. Beierlein, W. Müller-Limmroth*: Die Komponenten der resultierenden Kraft unter der Fußsohle des Menschen beim Gehen. Das Leder 28 (1977), 202–209

10. *Diebschlag, W., B. Kurz*: Gesunde Füße und angepaßtes Schuhwerk als eine Voraussetzung für dauerhafte Leistungsfähigkeit, S. 22. In: Kongreßband der Gesellschaft f. Arbeitswiss. (GfA), 29. Arbeitswiss. Kongreß, Dortmund 10.–11. 3. 1983

11. *Kurz, B., W. Diebschlag, F. Stumbaum*: Portables Druckverteilungsmeßsystem für biomechanische Gangspuranalysen. Biomed. Tech. 31 (1986), 19–24

12. *Müller-Limmroth, W., H.-R. Beierlein, W. Diebschlag*: Die Druckverteilung unter der menschlichen Fußsohle: Qualitative und quantitative Meßergebnisse. Z. Orthop. 115 (1977), 929–936

24 _____ Children's Shoes— Medical Considerations

B. Rosemeyer

W. Pförringer

It is well known that there is great variability in the shape of the feet. The truly normal foot is rare today, even in the adolescent, and even though most children are born with normal feet. In the normal footprint, the isthmus, i.e., the narrowest point, is approximately one third of the width of the forefoot. It is also known that, as far as the toes are concerned, there are three main types that must be recognized in designing shoes. The three types are

1. The Egyptian foot—the big toe is longer than the second toe.
2. The square foot—the first and second toes are equal in length.
3. The Greek foot—the big toe is shorter than the second toe.

More than half the population has an Egyptian foot, which occurs naturally in childhood as well.

It must be remembered that the foot assumes its proper function only in assuming the erect posture and in walking. This is shown by the fact that the foot of the infant resembles a clubfoot. It clearly is not a clubfoot, however, since it can be converted easily into the normal position. The shape of the foot becomes stable only with the plantigrade habitus.

CHANGES IN THE PEDAL ARCHES

Walking is a very complex movement in which the bones, ligaments, and muscles of the foot are all subject to different loads. This is manifested by the fact that the longitudinal arch of the foot is not rigid and changes during the process of walking.

A number of studies have investigated this problem. Experimental subjects of different age groups were photographed with a high-frequency camera as they were walking in front of an image intensifier. The x-ray pictures were evaluated individually, and the shape and height of the longitudinal arch were measured (Fig 24–1). The individual steps were evaluated on the basis of four characteristic phases. These were

1. Maximal compression of the soft tissues under the calcaneus.

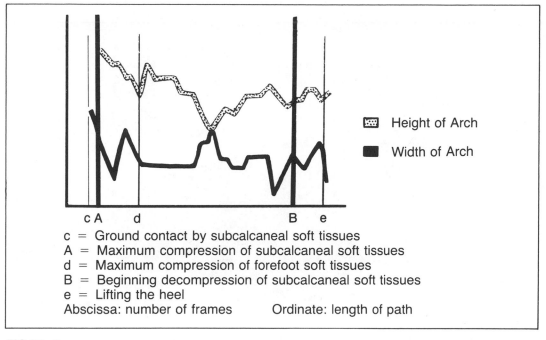

c = Ground contact by subcalcaneal soft tissues
A = Maximum compression of subcalcaneal soft tissues
d = Maximum compression of forefoot soft tissues
B = Beginning decompression of subcalcaneal soft tissues
e = Lifting the heel
Abscissa: number of frames   Ordinate: length of path

FIG 24–1.
Graphic representation of the changes in the arch of the foot during one step. (From *Puff, A., B. Rosemeyer:
Das Verhalten des FussLängsgewölbes beim normalen Gehakt [röntgenkinematlgraphische Untersuchung zur
Gelenkmechanik]. Morphologisches Jahrbuch 105/2 (1963), 274. Used by permission.)*

2. Maximal compression of the soft tissues of the forefoot.
3. Beginning recovery of the soft tissues under the calcaneus.
4. Lifting the heel.

The number of frames was graphically displayed on the abscissa, while the length of the distance measured was shown on the ordinate. This showed the load-dependent changes of the arch of the foot during the course of one step. It could be demonstrated that there were numerous, practically compensated, short-range changes in the height of the arch, with a general tendency to protect the arch. There was a threefold rhythm during the evident changes in the shape of the arch that corresponded to the effect of the maximal force, to the load, and to the contraction of the muscles, which later served to preserve the arch. It was assumed that the load caused a prestretch of the muscles, followed by a reflex contraction, which then strengthened the arch of the foot.

In studying the arch of the foot in children, a second consideration must be kept in mind. This concerns the looseness of the connective tissues. To answer this question, we have studied the range of maximal hyperextension of the metacarpophalangeal joint in 1,000 patients of different ages. This study showed that the hyperextensibility of the metacarpophalangeal joint decreased with age and that the female patients could hyperextend their metacarpophalangeal joint considerably further than the males. After age 6 years, hyperextensibility of the metacarpophalangeal joint decreases rapidly and reaches its maximum rate of change

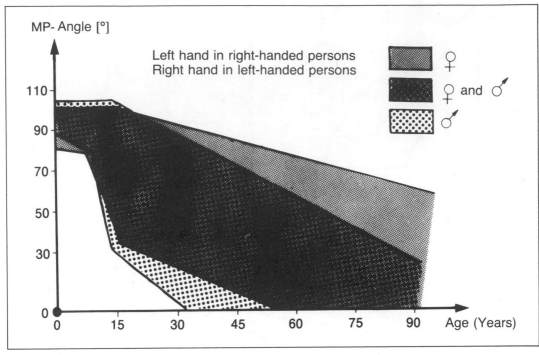

FIG 24–2.

Graphic representation of the relationship between the hyperextensability of the metacarpophalangeal (*MP*) joint and age. There is a particularly marked reduction in hyperextension at about 15 years of age. MP = metacarpophalangeal. (From *Rosemeyer, B., R. Paulig:* Der Metacarpophalangeal-Index. Orthop. Praxix 2/80 (1980), 89. Used by permission.)

at about 15 years of age. This observation could be explained by the fact that, at this age, significant manual labor leads to a stabilization of the joints and to a strengthening of the muscles (Fig 24–2).

In providing inserts for the children, it must be recognized that as part of normal development there is a physiologic valgus position, which can be actively corrected by standing more on the heels. Children who

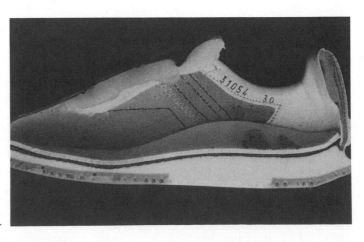

FIG 24–3.

Favorable footbed: The footbed is incorporated into the sole structure.

FIG 24–4.
A dual Velcro strap closure favored for pediatric footwear. This closure assures a uniform, nonslipping contact between the foot and the shoe.

show this physiologic valgus position should not be provided hastily with special inserts, since this is a physiologic developmental stage that does not require any therapy. The majority of the soft leather "C"-foot or pes planus inserts with medial arch support are quite unnecessary.

PROBLEMS IN SHOE DESIGN

In designing an athletic shoe, it is nevertheless very important to make certain that the child's foot is well bedded in the shoe (Fig 24–3). The footbed should ideally be in one piece with the sole of the shoe and should be adapted to the last for a normally shaped foot, particularly in the area of the longitudinal and transverse arch.

It must be recognized that during the rocking phase a sharp angulation occurs between the metatarsals and the proximal phalanges. The rocking sequence is therefore not even a true "rocking" in the shoe, but an isolated sharp flexion of the metatarsophalangeal joint. This flexion must be considered in the design of the shoe and of the sole, so that the uppers do

FIG 24–5.
Pediatric shoe in the shape of an athletic shoe. Closure is by a single Velcro strap. Good control of the heel occurs through a slightly raised heel pitch.

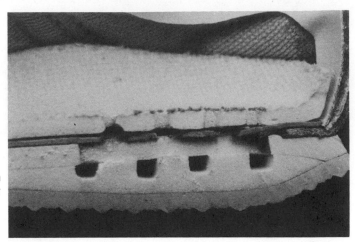

FIG 24–6.
An attempt to improve the ventilation of the interior of a pediatric shoe. Air spaces in the sole and openings through the insole should improve the ventilation of the shoe.

not develop isolated pressure points in this area.

Lacing presents yet another problem in the athletic shoe for children. The regular lacing is definitely unsuitable for children. The shoelace glides poorly, and thus consistent lacing is impossible when the laces are being pulled up. Furthermore, long laces are dangerous, since the child may stumble over them. Velcro closures are well developed and guarantee a closure that does not slip. For smaller children, one Velcro strap is sufficient. In older children, several such straps can be used (Fig 24–4).

If the shoe meets all the requirements, there should be no problem when the child puts on its first athletic shoe (Fig 24–5). If these conditions are met, it does not matter whether the shoe looks like an athletic shoe or not. What is important is that the shoe be well ventilated. Some manufacturers try to solve this problem by incorporating air chambers into the footbed and connecting these with ducts to the inside of the shoe (Fig 24–6). The profile of the sole can be a subject for lengthy argu-

ments. In real athletic shoes, it should conform to the type of load it is expected to bear.

SUMMARY

In children's shoes, it is particularly important not to be swayed by appearances or solicitations. The following points are important:

1. The foot must be seated optimally in the shoe.
2. The hindfoot must be particularly stable. Whether this is accomplished by high straps in the Achilles tendon area or by placing an indentation in this area is immaterial.
3. There must be adequate space for the forefoot.
4. The shoe must not be too short. Even with loose lacing and a slight forward displacement, the child's foot should never be in contact with the toe cap.
5. The edges of the shoe should not be too hard.

6. The closure must be easy to handle and uniform.
7. The foot should be well ventilated.
8. The shoe design must take into account the sharp flexion of the metatarsophalangeal joint during the rocking phase.

This list is valid for the normal foot. It is essential that the foot with special problems be provided with a shoe with special features.

Because of the marked, general weakness of the connective tissues of the foot in children, the ratio between load and load-bearing capacity rapidly shifts in favor of the load-bearing capacity. For this reason, the child's shoe must have the same properties as the adult shoe. It must also be remembered that, in childhood, athletic activities should maintain a playful character. Well-designed shoes can contribute effectively to this requirement. Orthopedic requirements can be met only if the above criteria are carefully considered. Only in this way can the growing foot be helped and damage from improper footwear be prevented.

BIBLIOGRAPHY

1. *Pförringer, W., B. Segesser:* Der Sportschuh. Orthopäde 15 (1986), 260–263
2. *Puff, A., B. Rosemeyer:* Das Verhalten des Fußlängsgewölbes beim normalen Gehakt (Röntgenkinematographische Untersuchung zur Gelenkmechanik). Morphologisches Jahrbuch 105/2 (1963), 274
3. *Rosemeyer, B., R. Paulig:* Der Metacarpophalangeal-Index. Orthop. Praxis 2/80 (1980), 89

PART 9 ———————— Special Problems

25

The Corrective Athletic Shoe— Indications and Biomechanics

B. Segesser

B. M. Nigg

Until a few years ago the provision of inserts for the athletic shoe was a distinct component of orthopedic-technical practice. Today this has changed. It is the athletic shoe itself that has moved onto the center stage of orthopedic-technical and economic considerations. It seems appropriate to devote some thought to the indications for a corrective athletic shoe.

INDICATIONS

There is no agreement on the point whether corrective modifications of the athletic shoe should be prophylactic or therapeutic.

A study of 640 athletes has shown that 34% had static disturbances of their feet. Only a quarter of them had lower extremity complaints that could be traced back to problems developing during the training period. On the other hand, a biomechanical study of 84 athletes with longstanding complaints in the foot-leg area found that 92% had static disturbances in their feet. A static disturbance can be evaluated by clinical measurement techniques. It is an anatomical or functional distortion of the foot and may be the result of a posttraumatic functional disturbance. It can lead, although not necessarily, to overload. It must be remembered that decreased load-bearing capacity is not the only cause for locomotor system complaints. Excessive load can produce problems, even in the face of normal load-bearing capacity, if the choice of footwear or playing surface was poor.

Since not every foot with static disturbances is bothered by excessive loads, and since normal feet can develop problems under such loads, it seems logical that the *indications for corrective athletic shoes should be limited to preexisting problems.* In other words, these shoes should be therapeutic and should rationally complement the therapeutic armamentarium of medications and physical therapy.

Biomechanical studies have shown that athletes with complaints related to the leg-foot area move differently than the healthy athlete.[2] This is true for all phases of motion from the landing to the takeoff. In the landing phase, accentuated pronation (the so-called excessive pronation) can lead to tibial complaints. The tibialis posterior muscle that is responsible for capturing this movement is exposed to excessive loads. Similar problems can arise in the area of the distal tibial edge when the flexor digitorum communis muscle is overtaxed during the rocking maneuver on the lateral edge of the foot. Thus both the pronated and supinated foot can be exposed to excessive load.

Load-induced pain in the leg-foot area can have multiple etiologies. It must be remembered that a faulty rocking posture is not uncommonly the result of a shortening of the gastrocnemius muscle, or of a rotational disturbance of the hip joint. Equally, an insufficiency of the calcaneal ligaments, caused by incomplete recovery from a fibular ligamentous injury, may interfere negatively with the activity of the Achilles tendon or the position of the foot during pushoff (Fig 25—1).

In addition to accentuated pronation and supination of the foot, or disturbances in the ligamentous system, there are some trivial complaints, e.g., ingrown toenail, stress fracture, overloading the sesamoid bones, and last, but not least, a hallux rigidus, that may all be biomechanical factors affecting the rocking posture of the foot negatively.

A pathologic, biomechanical mo-

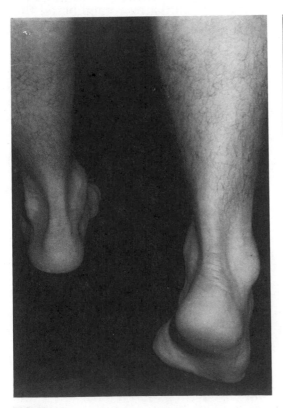

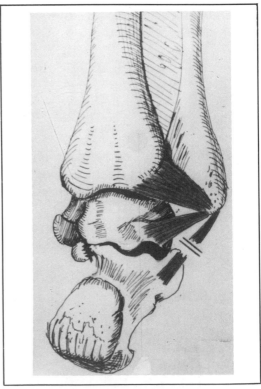

FIG 25—1.
Disturbed traction relationships of the Achilles tendon after injury to the fibular ligaments.

FIG 25–2.
Pronation of the foot affecting the functioning of the knee joint.

FUNDAMENTAL CONSIDERATIONS OF THE CORRECTIVE OPTIONS

There is little agreement in the area of prophylaxis vs. therapy in the field of corrective athletic shoes. As far as the technical corrective options are concerned, there is practically a religious war. Biomechanical studies show clearly that a static footprint in plaster or ink cannot give any indication as to the dynamic behavior of the foot. It is also known that selection of the footwear affects the motion characteristics at least as much as the use of corrective shoes. With the increase in scientific data, nobody can claim any longer that corrective athletic shoes will lead to a "normalization" of the locomotor process, since "normality" and freedom of complaints are by no means synonymous. Changing the pattern of motion is sufficient to affect the excessively loaded foot therapeutically. In view of the recent improvements in running shoes, this can be frequently accomplished by switching to a different commercial shoe. When this does not suffice, there are a number of ways to achieve improvements in 75% of the cases. The cost of making a correction in the athletic shoe may vary from $5 to $200, the benefits frequently have a similar range.

tion disorder of the foot frequently leads to excessive loads on the knee, the hip, and the spinal column. This is particularly true as far as the lateral stabilizers of the knee are concerned, and bursitis is common under the tendons of the pes anserinus and the iliotibial tract. The prosupination of the foot always leads to a torsion of the tibia, which in turn leads to an asymmetrical tension on the patellar ligament, and may even lead to a contraction of the quadriceps and a lateralization of the patella itself (Fig 25–2).

A less common indication for corrective athletic shoes is a falling off in performance due to accentuated pronation. This can be seen in high jump and speed skating.

A study done jointly with Nigg, concerning different approaches to corrective athletic footwear, has shown that similar results could be achieved by expensive, permanent insoles and by pasting in much less expensive components.[3] Measured changes in the angle of pronation are affected the same way by both ap-

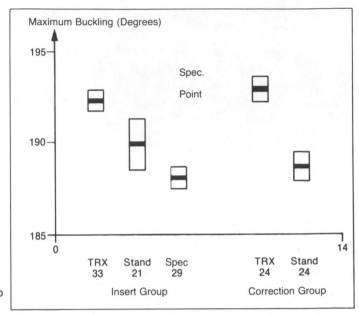

FIG 25–3.

Decrease of pronation through inserts or medial support. TRX = movement in the shoe without correction; Stand insert group = rigid, removable insert; Stand correction group = medial support glued to the sole; spec insert group = insert glued to the sole.

proaches. The maximal pronation and, particularly, the speed of pronation can be reduced by a medial support (Fig 25–3). Placing an insert into the athletic shoe resulted in a wide scatter of the data. It was found clinically that inserts placed into the shoe frequently worked their way through the medial wall of the shoe, thereby losing all their stabilizing effects (Fig 25–4). The stiffer the insert, the less

likely the success of this corrective action.

Medial support will change the pushoff position of the foot. The higher the medial support, the greater the trend towards a lateral displacement of the forefoot, which then must be corrected in turn. This lateral displacement of the forefoot is undesirable in most cases, since it usually leads to the rocking sequence taking

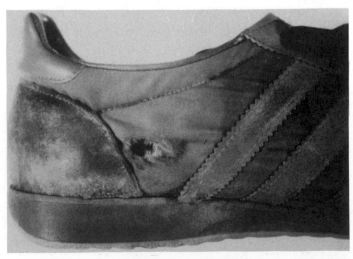

FIG 25–4.
Insert emerging through the lateral wall.

place over the fifth toe and must be corrected in some way by changes made in or with the shoe (Fig 25–5).

Two additional factors can alter the rocking sequence. A leather-cork insert pasted into the shoe will markedly increase the rigidity of the shoe in the area of the hindfoot. This is not necessarily desirable for the maintenance of the position of the foot, particularly for the pronatory movement in the landing phase. The insert, particularly if it is also used to correct a problem of leg length, will significantly affect the behavior of the heel and its heel counter. This will further cast a shadow over the attempts to correct the proper performance of the rocking sequence that, after all, is the purpose of placing a corrective insert into the shoe.

SOME BIOMECHANICAL CONSIDERATIONS

The problem of the corrective athletic shoe can be approached from several directions. One can simply attempt to alleviate the complaints of the athlete, and this is certainly a commendable attitude. If a more systematic approach to the larger question is attempted, the function of the proposed correction should be investigated from three perspectives. The functions that are of importance for the athletic shoe are:

- Cushioning.
- Support.
- Guidance.

Cushioning means shock absorption. Every landing on the ground exposes the locomotor system to impact forces. Corrective shoes may be able to reduce the peak forces of impact. During ground contact, the foot should be in a relatively stable position. It is possible that a corrective shoe may provide additional support during this phase and reduce excessive pronation and supination.

During the pushoff phase, the foot must be guided in a certain direction. It is possible that corrective shoes will give additional guidance in this phase also.

It is assumed that in most cases

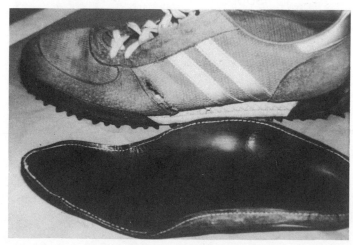

FIG 25–5.
Lateral forefoot advancement through excessive medial support.

the effects of a certain corrective alteration of the shoe can be predicted by "common sense." Until recently, for example, cushioning potential was predicted on the basis of a simple laboratory test. This method obviously has real disadvantages, since it does not take into consideration the response of the athlete. The following thoughts are all based on studies performed with experimental subjects, and thus the behavior of these subjects is a part of these considerations.

Cushioning

The cushioning of peak forces of impact occurring on landing is usually accomplished in biomechanical studies by measuring these peak forces. Biomechanical studies, both at the ETH in Zurich and also, independently, in Calgary have produced some very interesting results. Even though the midsole in the experimental running shoes varied enormously in hardness (from very soft to very hard, in both directions, far beyond the commercially available hardness range), no difference could be demonstrated as far as the peak forces of impact were concerned.

Studies in Calgary, in which a variety of inserts made of a wide range of materials were used, substantiated these findings. Again, there were practically no differences. In the few cases where differences were encountered, these were related much more to the shape of the insert than to its material properties.

When the studies were made with different types of shoes (different ex-

ternal geometry), differences in peak force of impact did appear. These results are surprising and give rise to the following comments:

1. It seems apparent that changing the external geometry of the shoe has a greater effect on peak forces of impact than changes in the materials inside the shoe.
2. It is assumed that inserts can modify the peak forces of impact only to a very limited degree.
3. Whether and how an athlete's behavior can be modified should be the subject of a separate study. If it could be shown, for instance, that an insert could enable an athlete to reduce his landing velocity by 40%, the problem of cushioning would be solved.

In conclusion, as far as cushioning is concerned, the problem of corrective footwear is far from being clearly understood. It appears that over time the athletes can adapt to anything, but it is not at all clear how this adaptive process is managed.

Support

The support function of the shoe is usually defined in biomechanics as producing a change in the relative position of the foot (calcaneus) and the leg (tibia). This change in angle, commonly and simply referred to as pronation and supination, is usually the target of the corrective measures of the shoe. Ordinarily, reduced pronation (in running) or supination (in tennis) is attempted. To understand this process, the effects of pronation on running must be discussed. When running barefoot, pronation at the ankle extends over 7 degrees, with the major portion of pronation taking place in the initial phases. When these same athletes wear running shoes, pronation can be measured at 15 degrees, i.e., it is more than doubled. This means that some pronation is normal, but that the shoe produces additional pronation.

There are two basic ways in which this pronation (which can reach 30 degrees in some cases) can be reduced. An additional component can be introduced into the shoe (medial support or heel stabilizers) that again reduces the shoe-induced pronation, or one can eliminate the cause of the pronation. The additional components do have some effect, but their effectiveness leaves much to be desired. The velocity of the pronation can be reduced, but the total effect on the pronation remains largely unchanged.

This means that the cause of the additional pronation must be identified. Studies have shown that the additional pronation is caused by the lever effect of a slanting heel. The obvious conclusion is that this heel must be cut off. Studies have shown that this method substantially reduced pronation.

In summary, the excessive motion of the ankle (30 degrees) is largely due to the shoe. The best way to reduce this motion is to control its site of origin. This can be achieved by fitting the critical side of the rear of the shoe (lateral in running) as much as possible to the shape of the foot. This will eliminate the strong lever action.

Guidance

The guidance function of the athletic shoe is defined in biomechanics as producing a relative change in angles of the ankle. Experimental studies have shown that the position of the heel and of the leg can be affected by the shoe. It was also shown that this relationship could be changed by the insertion of wedges in the forefoot area. In running, for instance a lateral forefoot wedge can reduce the supination during pushoff and bring it into the range of barefoot running. It was shown further that medial supports under the arch of the foot increased supination during push-off and thus had a negative effect on possible injuries.

SUMMARY

With proper indications, the corrective athletic shoe can complement other therapeutic measures. In 578 cases, corrective shoes produced a marked improvement in 75% of the athletes with longstanding injuries. In fact, they were free of symptoms and could engage in athletics again. When one considers general criteria and realizes that the main thrust is toward changing the rocking posture of the foot, it seems unnecessary to push for custom-made athletic shoes. As long as biomechanical measuring devices are not universally available to make corrections in the athletic shoe, corrections must be judged, rightly or wrongly, solely on the basis of therapeutic success. This should be compensation enough for the practicing sports physician in most cases. On this basis, the incorporation of these simple measures makes good sense.

REFERENCES

1. *Biedert, R., A. Elsig:* Kniebeschwerden bei Sportlern: Behandlungsmöglichkeiten durch Korrektur der Statik. Schweiz. Z. Sportmed. 1984
2. *Nigg, B.M.:* Biomechanics of running shoes. Human Kinetics Publishers, Champaign, Ill. 1986
3. *Nigg, B.M., S. Lüthi, B. Segesser, A. Stacoff, H.W. Guidon, A. Schneider:* Sportschuhkorrekturen. Ein biomechanischer Vergleich von drei verschiedenen Sportschuhkorrekturen. Z. Orthop. 120 (1982), 34–39
4. *Segesser, B., B.M. Nigg:* Insertionstendinosen am Schienbein, Achillodynie und Überlastungsfolgen Fuß—Ätiologie, Biomechanik, therapeutische Möglichkeiten. Orthopädie 9 (1980), 207–214
5. *Segesser, B., R. Ruepp, B.M. Nigg:* Indikation. Technik und Fehlermöglichkeiten einer Sportschuhkorrektur. Orthop. Praxis 11 (1978)
6. *Spring, H., A. Elsig:* Kleines Wunderding im Schuh. Sportinformation 2 (1980), 22
7. *Subotnik, S.I.:* The overuse syndrome of the foot and leg, part 2. San Francisco California College of Pediatric Medicine 1974
8. *Thiel, A., M. Karpf:* Bild und Behandlung der Achillodynie. Sportarzt Sportmed. 24 (1973), 106

26 Providing Inserts for the Athletic Shoe

J. Runzheimer

J. Holder

The steady increase in the number of both recreational and competitive athletes has led to a rapid evolution of athletic clothes and particularly of athletic footwear. The majority of the currently commercially available athletic shoes are more likely to meet requirements of the particular athletic activity for which they were designed than the individual requirements of the athlete. The footbed provided for most athletic shoes conforms to general anatomical principles of the foot. There is no such footbed in most mass-produced street shoes. Thus the tendency of youngsters to use athletic shoes in lieu of street shoes is, from an orthopedic point of view, desirable, even though the parents generally disapprove.

Nevertheless, certain fundamental considerations must be accepted. The repeated loads to which the locomotor and homeostatic mechanisms are exposed during athletic activities can result in injuries and in orthopedic problems in the lower extremity and the spinal column, unless these injuries are prevented or problems corrected by special inserts in the athletic shoe.

Athletes are frequently advised to use individualized inserts. In view of the dynamic loads and the other stresses common to athletic activities in general and the particular demands of the individual athletic disciplines, the commonly recommended orthopedic inserts are not satisfactory. They are made of much too rigid materials, and they are shaped primarily for passive support. Using the so-called half or three-quarter inserts in athletic shoes is not satisfactory. These inserts can slide forward easily and thus no longer provide appropriate support.

An insert for an athletic shoe must be made of elastic and flexible materials and must be shaped so that it reduces the load on the foot during walking and running. The locomotor function of the individual components of the system must be maintained. Friction motion between foot and insert and insert and shoe must be avoided. These lead to a loss of energy and a decrease in performance. These considerations led to the design of a specific athletic shoe insert.

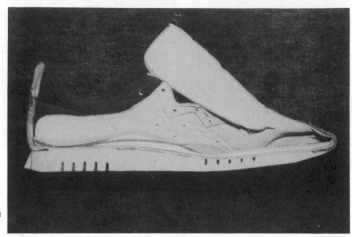

FIG 26–1.
Longitudinal section of the insert in
the shoe.

THE ORTHOSPORT INSERT

The orthosport insert is a full-length insert that must be fitted into the athletic shoe so that it corresponds in shape to the insole. For the insert to fit properly, the athletic shoe may have to be widened. In the hindfoot area, the insert must be weight-bearing and support the heel at a constant height (Fig 26–1). Distally it must consist of flexible and elastic material. The projected support of the foot in the line of impact of the weight of the body must be based on a suitable infrastructure, so that the arch of the foot is properly padded and supported.

In walking and running, some springiness and change in shape, similar to barefoot walking or running, should be maintained. The weight-bearing surface of the insert should be designed so that it can maintain some elastic springiness and some resilience under a superimposed weight load.

The basis for the orthosport-insert is a plaster cast that was made from a foam model obtained under load conditions. The plaster cast is modified

in minute detail by a grinding process. These adjustments are made with constant reference to a blueprint based on the precise corrective requirements of both the athlete and the athletic activity (Fig 26–2). A special substance (Termit plastic) produced as a carrier by a kneading

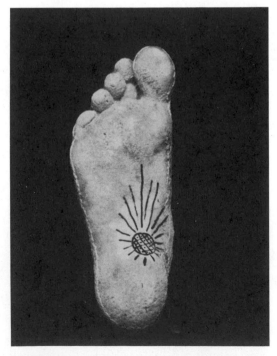

FIG 26–2.
Plaster cast with corrective markings.

process will be used to stabilize the heel.

A soft rubber pad, designed and placed accurately according to the footprint, will be used for midfoot padding. The core of the insert is plastic (polyurethane), shaped by a thermoplastic cold extrusion technique. This material is very light and highly elastic with good cushioning ability and considerable resiliency. It does not lose its positive, corrective capacity after use. Material fatigue is minimal. The dynamic peak forces are cushioned elastically without great loss of energy during the push-off phase. The covering of the insert should be made of a "breathing" material, such as processed leather, pressure-shaped artificial leather, lamb's wool, or felt. In addition to its supportive-corrective role, such matters as body weight and the requirements of the individual athletic activity should be considered in the various phases of the manufacturing process.

Support of the foot is possible without significant interference with function. The flexion and torsion elasticity is maintained and can prevent muscle cramping. The holding ability of the toes, and particularly of the big toe, must be preserved in the shoe.

The measures designed to correct the arches of the foot are kept intentionally small but highly specific to interfere as little as possible with the normal motion of the foot. In addition to their locomotor and holding function, the muscles of the foot that maintain the arch must be given sufficient room to change their shape actively in the shoe.

The insert should weigh no more than 15 to 20 g despite its several components (Fig 26–3). The reinforcing components can be modified thermoplastically, so that minor changes in the shape of the foot or the appearance of complaints can be managed by suitable modifications of the insert. Careful checking of the insert after a period of 3 to 4 weeks has proved useful.

INSERTS

Normal Inserts.—Standard design of inserts for mild splayfoot is such that the foot is supported under the

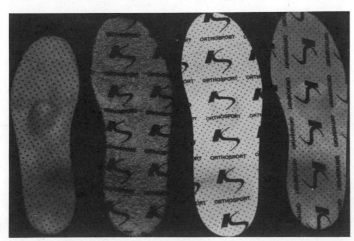

FIG 26–3.
Low-weight inserts covered with "breathing" materials.

calcaneus at the level of the sustentaculum tali and behind the head of the third metatarsal to support the arch under load. The normal functional line of the foot is supported by the shape of such an insert, and additional torsion is prevented.

The Torsion Insert.—A torsion insert can be designed to correct the calcaneus shelf by shifting the weight laterally by a medial extension of supporting and protecting structures for the fifth metatarsal head (Fig 26–4). The lateral edge of the insert should be raised in the hindfoot area and the heel cover should be strengthened. This athletic-shoe insert is particularly appropriate for children who "toe in" when they walk.

The Antitorsion Insert.—If the lateral edge of the foot is under excessive loads in the area of the fifth metatarsal, a small elevation should be placed under the fifth metatarsal head. This will supinate the hindfoot and pronate the forefoot. This produces two results: it corrects the position of the foot, and by activating the muscles of the foot, it causes a re-

verse rotation, i.e., an antitorsion. The stride and the entire walk will be improved.

The Step Insert.—In splayfoot, special attention must be paid to the individual adjustments of the axis of the foot when a transverse arch pad is introduced. The insert has both prophylactic and therapeutic effects, since the placement of a step decreases the load on the forefoot.

Step Insert With Lateral Edge Elevation.—When the lateral edge of the splayfoot is exposed to excessive loads, as manifested by hyperkeratosis in the area of the fifth metatarsal head, the underside of the insert should have a step placed proximal to the fifth metatarsal head. This decreases the tendency to form calluses and to develop other injuries.

Pes Cavus Insert.—The pes cavus should be provided with a so-called stretch pad (Fig 26–5). In addition to an anterior and posterior step to decrease the load on the metatarsal heads, this insert also has a slight elevation in the heel area. It will pre-

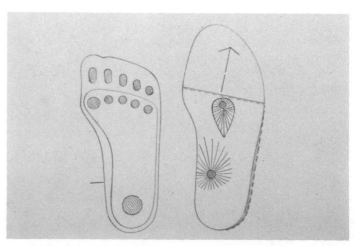

FIG 26–4.
Torsion insert: An example of a corrective insert.

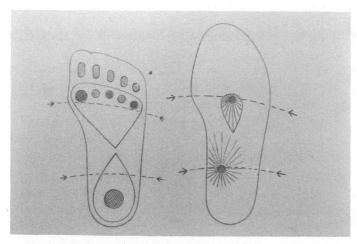

FIG 26–5.
Pes cavus insert.

vent the Achilles tendon problems so commonly seen in patients with pes cavus.

Inserts With Cutouts.—If the base of the fifth metatarsal head is under excessive load, and there is a symptomatic periostosis or periostitis, the shoe should be fitted with an insert having a cutout in that area. The same should be done following a tear fracture at the base of the fifth metatarsal. The cutout area should be filled with a soft material.

Inserts for Calcaneal Spurs.—The insert used for a person with calca-

neal spurs is similar to the one described above. At the level of the calcaneus, there should be good padding with plastic or rubber foam. There should be a cutout in the area sensitive to pressure, usually at the medial calcaneal tuberosity. The cutout should be filled with a soft material and covered with leather, imitation leather, or lamb's wool (Fig 26–6). This should rapidly improve the problem.

Inserts With Padding.—In severe cases of pes cavus accompanied by inflammatory changes in the forefoot, an insert is used that provides pad-

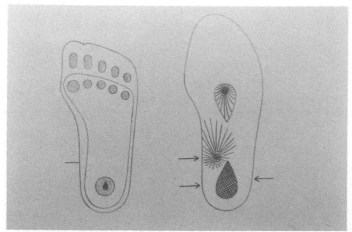

FIG 26–6.
Calcaneus spurs insert.

ding for the forefoot. This not only provides a corrective support, but also decreases the load on the tender forefoot.

Insert With a Butterfly Rocker.— In the strongly flattened forefoot, we use an insert that acts like a butterfly rocker. The special shape of the insert will decrease the load in the area of metatarsal heads 2 through 4 in the forefoot. The material along the edges is firmer in this insert.

SPECIAL INSERT OPTIONS

Orthosport inserts can be modified to serve particular requirements. Some examples follow.

Differences in the length of the legs, not exceeding 15 mm, can be corrected with an insert and with corresponding modifications of the shoe. The shoe modification may consist of a posteroanterior slant, not to exceed 5 mm.

In cases of disturbance of the axis of the leg, e.g., genu varum, genu valgum, or genu recurvatum, with corresponding symptoms in the knee, elevation of the inner or outer edge or a reciprocal lowering of the other side will lead to an improvement in the static distribution of weight in the joint. Corrective inserts of up to 5 mm are tolerated well.

A prophylactic and therapeutic elevation of the lateral edge of the foot, with a laterally elevated insert is indicated in cases of crus varum and a chronic periostitis of the medial edge of the tibia.

In the presence of preexisting ligamentous weakness, or postopera-tively, following repair of capsular or ligamentous rupture in the ankle joint, an insert that is raised along the lateral edge can be very helpful. It will pronate the heel and thus reduce the tension on the ligaments.

In persons with plantar fasciitis or knot formation at the medial edge of the plantar aponeurosis, medial grooves should be built into the insert.

In painful arthoses of the metatarsophalangeal joint of the big toe and of the metatarsosesamoid joints, inserts with soft and deep padding are used. These inserts should also have a special support in the area of the first metatarsal bone.

DISCUSSION

In cooperation with the orthopedic appliance maker, we have prepared approximately 3,000 inserts since 1979. These include the specially designed ones for patients with lame feet, rigid feet, or polio residuals.

Many varieties of orthosport inserts were prepared for athletic shoes of practically all athletic activities. In exceptional cases, inserts were also designed for ballet shoes, dance gymnastics, and golf. The bulk of the inserts (more than 50%) were prepared for the long distance runner.

The durability of the insert depends on a number of external variables. On the average the insert should last for about 10,000 km.

To maintain the therapeutic success of an operation, injection, or physiotherapeutic manipulation, during resumption of athletic activity, an individually designed insert and corresponding athletic shoe may be necessary. If this is not done, the athlete may develop into a chronic invalid.

The practice of trying to maintain the performance of the athlete with injections, series of injections, and drugs is hardly etiologic therapy. The orthopedic surgeon and the sports physician must recognize the importance of functional and anatomical principles and must rediscover the observations made by the fathers of orthopedics.[2, 3]

New materials and new developments in orthopedic technology have made major improvements in insert technology possible. This in turn made it possible to provide the athlete with the best possible orthopedic foot care.

REFERENCES

1. *Baumgartner, R.:* Die orthopädietechnische Versorgung des Fußes. Thieme, Stuttgart 1972
2. *Hohmann, D., R. Uhlig:* Orthopädische Technik, 7. Aufl. Enke, Stuttgart 1982
3. *Hohmann, G.:* Fuß und Bein, 3. Aufl. Bergmann, München 1939
4. *Lequesne, M., M. Samson, S. Braun:* Eular Bulletin, Zeitschrift für Rheumatologische Fortbildung und Information XIII, 2 und 3 (1984)
5. *Rabl, C.R.H., W. Nyga:* Orthopädie des Fußes, 6. Aufl. Enke, Stuttgart 1982
6. *Thomson, W.:* Pflege deine Füße— gesunde Füße, gesunder Mensch. Thieme, Stuttgart 1972

27   Corrective Athletic Shoes—A Program

K. Liebig

To implement corrective changes in the athletic shoe is not a new idea. A number of attempts were made some time ago to improve performance by making changes in the athletic shoe and by using changes in the biomechanics of locomotion to accomplish this purpose. Foot deformities in athletes mandated corrective changes in the shoe. Even major deformities, proved by footprints, do not necessarily keep athletes from becoming championship class performers (Fig 27–1). Even though from a static perspective these feet are grossly abnormal, they are functional and do not decrease performance.

For top athletes, athletic shoes are made on an individual basis with full recognition of foot abnormalities. Differences in leg length and axis deviations can be corrected by appropriately designed athletic shoes, without interfering with performance or individual style.

In leisure activity and athletic activity in which the masses participate, the situation is quite different. The spread of athletics for the masses has generated increasing numbers of participants with congenital or acquired foot deformities. Needless to

say, the incidence of athletic shoe complaints has increased proportionately.

ORTHOPEDIC FOOTWEAR PROBLEMS

To provide individually designed athletic shoes is not possible for reasons of cost and production capacity. Orthopedic corrections and improvements must therefore be made on the mass-produced athletic shoe. In doing this, two diametrically opposed concepts must be brought into harmony. The athletic shoe must be light, fit well, provide a good seat, and be flexible, but must also provide good protection for the heel and good cushioning in the hindfoot area. On the other hand, there must be room for orthopedic inserts to support the foot and to provide corrective positioning. The inserts must be made from rigid or semielastic materials that do not conform to the biomechanical requirements of the athletic shoe and thus act in a counterproductive fashion.

The use of different materials with very different properties and the

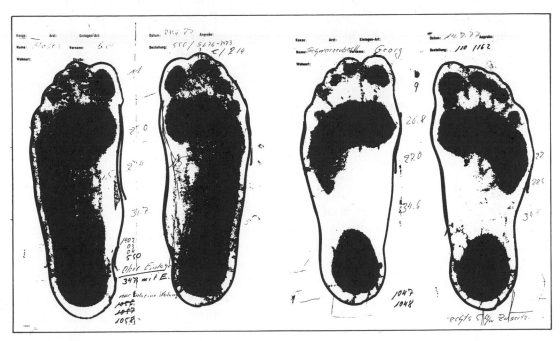

FIG 27–1.
Footprints of two leading athletes with marked foot deformities.

use of different adhesives led, at times, to these substances working against each other. This led to a rapid loss of the corrective function and was also esthetically unappealing. Making such shoes created very serious problems for the orthopedic shoemaker. If the correction had to be made in the area of the sole, the rubber sole had to be ground away. This generated heat that could affect the midsole, and the rubber that was ground off of the sole could not be used again. To date, good rubber soles that can conform to the contours of an athletic shoe have not been available.

In recent years an additional dimension has been added to the athletic shoe. The athletic shoe has become a social status symbol that is worn not only by people who engage in very limited or no athletics, but also by people who have more or less severe locomotor system pathology and who would normally wear a corrective orthopedic shoe. This group also wants to wear athletic shoes in order to imitate the "gym shoe generation." Using the athletic shoe as a symbol of mobility and dynamism, they wish to be integrated into the ranks of the "normal" society. It was quite particularly important to provide this group with good shoes.

CORRECTIVE MEASURES

Segesser summarized the problems encountered in designing corrective measures for the athletic shoe in 1978:

- The last must be wide enough.
- The upper must provide stable sides.

- There should be buffer heels or a buffer sole, and the profile of the sole should not interfere with the motion sequence.

To make proper corrections, the technical problems must be mastered, and the corrective features must be solidly incorporated into the shoe. The materials used must be light and conform to the design principles of an athletic shoe. The sequence of motion of the foot should not be disturbed. The flexibility of the sole must be maintained, and correcting the length of the leg must be accomplished in the area of the sole, since the heel area is intentionally kept low. If the heel is raised to make up for the shortness of the leg, the foot may very easily start sliding forward.

There are a number of areas in which corrective measures can go astray. One sees the same mistake being made over and over again, and this is the reason why, to date, orthopedic corrections in mass-produced athletic shoes have not been very successful. The corrective measure can be unstable, the insert can slide around in the shoe, and the heel is no longer controlled.

The combination of different materials permanently changes the flexibility of the sole, changes the cushioning effects on the foot, changes the elasticity of the sole, and increases the weight of the shoe. Inserts add to the rigidity of the shoe and interfere with the rocking sequence. Because of the low profile of the last at the heel and in the toe area, a well-fitting shoe may painfully constrain the foot and may compress the toes at the crease. A high insert leads to instability of the hindfoot and promotes a forward sliding of the heel. The semi-rigid insert is compacted in the shoe and produces a "floating" foot if the shoe is slightly too large and the sides are not tightly held. Consequently, the biomechanics of the shoe are disturbed, leading to a loss of performance in competition shoes. In training or running shoes, there will be a definite decrease in comfort.

The high-performance shoe can be fitted individually, can be adapted to individual levels of performance, can be geared to competition, can improve performance, and can incorporate orthopedic corrective measures easily and harmoniously. This cannot be done in mass-produced training and running shoes. The mass-produced shoe is turned over to the orthopedic shoemaker, but only some corrective measures can be applied by him. The mass-produced shoe is not designed for changes, and any external change usually leads to permanent and unpredictable changes in the midsole. The uniform structure of the shoe will be destroyed.

This means that to accomplish desirable changes in the training shoe, all possible corrective measures had to be technically perfect, had to use biomechanically acceptable materials, and had to be kept within financially responsible bounds. The variations had to be fitted into production schedules and had to be economically practical. A joint endeavour between orthopedic shoemakers and an athletic shoe company was able to translate these concepts into reality and produce a series of products.

How are these changes manifested in the training shoe or in athletic shoes? The training shoe built according to orthopedic principles is constructed on a modular basis, so that each module can be changed individually. In making the changes, materials were used that were the same as those used in the shoe. The shape corresponds generally to the well-known training and running shoes, but has five special construction features (Fig 27–2):

1. The last is shaped differently than in the conventional athletic shoe. When a conventional no. 42 last was used, the volume of the shoe was increased by 6%. This means a larger toe box, a 4-mm increase in height at the toe, and a 8-mm increase in the height of the heel counter. This shape permits the use of a space-consuming insert and, if necessary, of a length equalizer.

2. The heel counter is 2 cm larger than before and is extended into the metatarsal area. This provides a tighter hold on the heel with improved control of the hindfoot. It also prevents the displacement of the insert.

3. The insole is entirely level, broad, and stable (in some athletic shoes there is either no insole at all, or if present it is only partial). It rises slightly toward the heel, corresponding to the position of the heel. Correc-

tive and supportive inserts of different materials can be superimposed on the plain insole. Preexisting distortion of the insole can be ignored. The mechanical and physical properties of this insole correspond to those of the routinely used insoles in standard athletic shoes. It is just as stable and has just as much resilience in the heel region.

4. A midsole of medium hard polyurethane is vulcanized onto the insole. This is done so that in case the outer edge of the shoe is raised, or a metatarsal pad is used, the foot does not sink into a very soft sole and thereby undo all the corrective measures. The midsole presents no problems. It can be readily modified and altered and have a variety of different stiffening sheets glued onto it, and so adapted, it can meet any and all requirements.

5. The rubber sole is available with three different contours. After it is heated, it can be readily separated from the midsole. After the midsole has been subjected to orthopedic adjustments, a new rubber sole has to be cut from a large sheet, since the old sole would no longer fit onto the modified midsole. The new sole is attached with a special adhesive—neo-

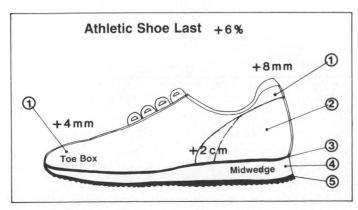

FIG 27–2.
Design concept of the special training shoe (see text).

FIG 27–3.
The insert covers the entire sole. The thickness of the insert is compensated for by the last design.

prene ultra. This is an adhesive that works with both rubber and polyurethane. If desirable, a "ball pivot" can be attached in the forefoot area.

To prepare the insert (Fig 27–3), the entire sole is covered with Frelen, Prix, Tepefom, or HB foam or a combination of the above. All these substances are polyurethanes, but all have different cushioning properties and flexibility. HB-foam is used in smaller and lighter patients. Prix polyurethane is used in heavier patients, since the material is firmer and has better resilience. When Tepefom is used, the insert is cut out, warmed, and placed into the shoe. The patient puts on the shoe while the material is still warm. The insert will then essentially become a mold of the foot under load, but can still be modified subsequently. The forefoot and the midfoot are principally involved in making this pressure mold; the heel is not significantly involved.

In addition to the low-cut training shoe, a boot is also available. Since this has a high shaft, a built-in insert can compensate for a difference in leg length of 2 cm.

The use of similar materials with the same characteristics has the advantage that the changes are not no-

FIG 27–4.
Integrated midfoot rocker.

FIG 27–5.
Patient with leg-length differential and peroneal palsy provided with orthopedic training shoes and an integrated peroneal splint.

ticeable, and the corrective athletic shoe does not look like one. This is obviously of no consequence as far as the correction is concerned, but has a positive psychologic effect.

A simple and effective corrective result is illustrated by the two following examples: Elevation of the external edge of the shoe can be done effectively to correct a genu varum.

Midfoot and forefoot rockers of different heights can also be installed easily, quickly, without any difficulty, and—to a large extent—unnoticeably (Fig 27–4). Even the very difficult to manage, surgically corrected talipes equinus can be corrected without major problems (Fig 27–5). Differences in leg lengths or in the size of the feet can be equalized and a peroneal spring can be built in. A Marquardt-type butterfly rocker can also be incorporated easily.

SUMMARY

Orthopedically modified athletic shoes are indicated for all patients with a variety of foot problems requiring orthopedic assistance. Differences in leg length can be equalized; mild misalignment of the axes and a very large variety of foot deformities can be corrected. The changes are made on prescription by an orthopedic shoemaker. There are usually several models in stock. This trade is limited to the expert orthopedic shoemaker.

Although further conceptual changes are being proposed all the time for the athletic shoe, the currently available series has demonstrated that an athletic shoe with orthopedic modification is a sound idea. The solutions proposed are eminently practical, since they do justice to the most varied demands and can provide adequate assistance even for difficult problem feet.

28 — Athletic Shoes for the Handicapped

K. Wietfeld

Recognition and support of handicapped athletes by governmental agencies will require that a large number of these athletes be provided with orthopedic shoes (Table 28–1). Classification of the degree of severity of damage in handicapped participants in competitive athletics suggests the following indications for orthopedic shoes in Class A (Table 28–2):

- Point 4: Bilateral loss of forefoot.
- Point 5: Unilateral, complete paralysis of the lower leg or unilateral incomplete paralysis, including spastic paralysis of the lower leg.
- Point 10: Bilateral foot deformities that make walking without orthopedic shoes impossible.

In Class C, the following indications exist (see Table 28–2):

- Point 1: Loss of one leg.
- Point 3: Ankylosis or severe restriction of motion in one ankle.
- Point 4: Unilateral foot deformity that makes walking without an orthopedic shoe impossible.
- Point 5: Shortening of one leg by at least 6 cm.

There are several classes among handicapped athletes, who are eligible for the "German Sports Medal" and who will certainly require orthopedic shoes. These include classes M2, M3, M6, and M10 (Table 28–3).

The appliance catalog of the health insurance companies recognizes orthopedic gym shoes as an available item, provided that the insured participates regularly in athletic events for handicapped persons and that the orthopedic athletic shoe is necessary for the particular athletic activity.

Medical indications may exist even for a bathing shoe, if the foot deformities are severe enough, or if the foot cannot tolerate weight bearing even for short distances.

To prescribe orthopedic, "made-to measure" shoes or bathing shoes, it is not sufficient to determine the degree of the handicap; it is also necessary that the proposed athletic activity require such shoes.

THE INDICATIONS FOR MADE-TO-MEASURE ORTHOPEDIC SHOES

The directives for the prescription of made-to-order orthopedic shoes in general, established by W. Marquardt

TABLE 28–1.

Competitive Activities for Handicapped Athletes

Badminton	Prell ball
Basketball	Roll ball
Bowling	Sitting ball
Fist ball	Sitting volley ball
Soccer tennis	Table tennis
Court fist ball	Door ball
Skittles	Volley ball
Fly ball	Water ball (Polo)

TABLE 28–3.

Classification of Handicaps for the "German Sports Medal": Overview of Handicaps From a Functional Point of View

Class	Handicap
M2	Short leg by at least 6 cm compensated by orthopedic shoe (if compensated by other appliance, see condition 4-US)
M3	Loss of forefoot, including Chopart's amputation Loss of all toes on both feet
M6	Loss of both forefeet, including Chopart's amputation
M10	Significant limitation of one foot, including ankylosis Tibial or fibular nerve paralysis

and accepted by the third-party payers, are even more restrictive for the orthopedic athletic shoe (Table 28–4). For instance, the athlete with pes planovalgus will not be able to get orthopedic athletic shoes if he or

TABLE 28–2

Classification of the Various Handicaps for Athletic Activity Purposes

Class A
1. Handicap that allows only sitting or wheelchair games
2. Above knee amputation
3. Below knee amputation, including Pirogoff's amputation
4. Bilateral forefoot loss
5. Unilateral total lower leg paralysis or partial leg paralysis, including spastic paralysis
6. Hip or knee ankylosis
7. Bilateral ankle ankylosis
8. Pseudoarticulation or other injury in thigh or leg, requiring the wearing of a protective orthopedic appliance
9. Unstable knee requiring the use of an orthopedic appliance
10. Bilateral foot deformities making walking without orthopedic shoes impossible

Class C
1. Unilateral forefoot amputation
2. Significant limitation of one knee or hip
3. Ankylosis or significant limitation of one ankle
4. Unilateral foot distortion—walking impossible without orthopedic shoe
5. Short leg by at least 5 cm
6. Significant limitation of shoulder or elbow
7. Loss of one finger and thumb or three fingers
8. Loss of one eye
9. Significant limitation or ankylosis of one foot joint; paralysis of tibial or fibular nerve

she engages only in "sitting" ball games. In persons with differences in leg length without paralysis or foot deformity, athletic shoes will be provided only if the difference exceeds 4 cm. The guidelines are even stricter for patients with foot-length differences, since athletic activities of the handicapped usually occupy only 2 to 3 hours/week.

The made-to-measure orthopedic athletic shoes are made to correspond to the pathology of the handicapped athlete. The material demands are considerable, since under athletic

TABLE 28–4.

Indications for Made-to-Order Orthopedic Shoes*

1. Pes planovalgus
2. Clubfeet
3. Contracted or paralytic pes equinus
4. Talipes
5. Significant ball or claw pes cavus
6. Arthrodesis of the ankle joint
7. Difference in leg length of more than 3 cm
8. Difference in foot length of more than 2 cm
9. Amputation of big toe or more, including entire foot
10. Significant contracture of the toes
11. Trauma or inflammation residuals with deformity

*Modified from *Marquardt, W.*

loads, even non–high performance loads, the pressure and torsion forces are greater than those to which the regular shoes are exposed.

Good cushioning properties of the footbed and the heel, as well as solid control of the shaft are non-negotiable prerequisites for all athletic shoes for the handicapped person. In most cases, the external shape of the shoe conforms to the "fixed rocking shoe" of Rabl. In this shoe, a peroneal rail is built into the extended shaft, and the rotational momentum is increased by a retracted rocker sole and a markedly elevated tip.

Standard athletic shoes can frequently be modified along orthopedic lines (Fig 28–1). The indications for such changes are much broader, since those who are less severely handicapped engage in athletics much more vigorously and thus may be bothered more, by even relatively minor handicaps.

THE INDICATIONS FOR ORTHOPEDIC MODIFICATIONS

According to Baumgartner, the following indications should be considered (Table 28–5):

1. Difference in the length of the legs, up to 3 cm (in athletic shoes this may be increased to 4 cm for the above mentioned reasons): The elevation should be wedge-shaped and should be inserted under the heel and sole.

2. Axis deviation of the foot or knee: Elevation of the inner or outer edge of the shoe is sufficient. When the inner edge is raised, the heel must be extended laterally to prevent supination.

3. Instability of the hindfoot, due to ligamentous insufficiency: This can be stabilized by enlarging the contact surface area of the heel. Optimal stability can be obtained by wearing athletic boots with high shafts and lateral shaft reinforcement.

4. Pain on weight-bearing or motion, e.g., when the lower extremities are affected by arthritic changes: This can be alleviated by buffer heels and heel pads.

5. Functional limitations of the ankle: it is recommended that the tip of the shoe be raised with a metatarsal rocker. In functional limitations of the tarsal or metatarsophalangeal joints, a more ventrally located rocker should be considered for immobilization.

6. Milder foot or toe deformities: These can be relieved by appropriate modifications of the uppers. These modifications may consist of the incorporation of pads or of a widening of the shaft.

For complaints in the area of the sole, i.e., painful splayfoot or pes planus, a butterfly rocker or an arch support can be incorporated, as suggested by Marquardt. When arch supports are built in or when the edge of the shoe is raised on one side, the heel area must be supported with a firm heel counter to prevent displacement of the heel.

The orthopedic modifications of mass-produced shoes, listed and illustrated in Figure 28–1, are reimbursable and are included in the appliance catalog.

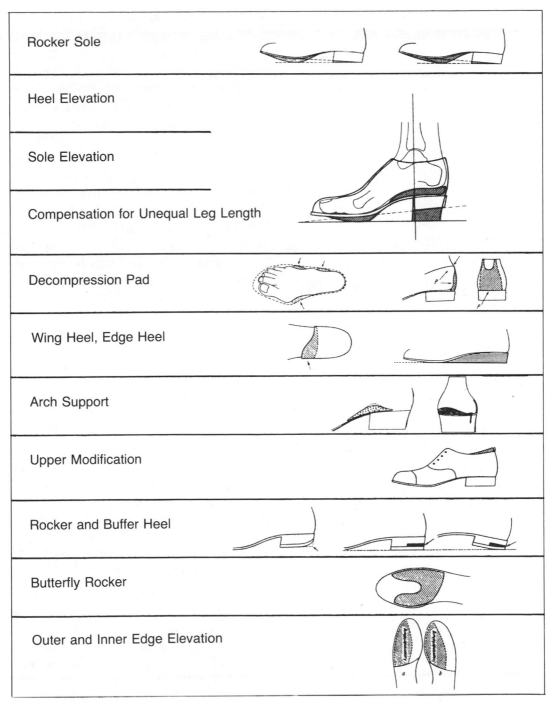

FIG 28–1.
Orthopedic modifications in commercial shoes.

TABLE 28–5.

The Indications for Orthopedic Modifications*

Indication	Modification
1. Leg length difference up to 3 cm	Heel or sole elevation
2. Axis deviation of feet or knees	Elevation of inner or outer edge
3. Hindfoot instability	Increased heel surface
4. Lower extremity pain on load or movement	Buffered heel
5. Loss of function of foot joints	Rocker sole
6. Mild foot or toe deformity	Adjustment of upper

*Modified from Baumgartner.

THE INDICATIONS FOR SHOE LINERS

In some instances, it is possible to avoid the unsightly, made-to-measure orthopedic shoes by providing liners to be worn with standard shoes.

The shoe liners are worn under the socks and in mass-produced shoes. The indications for shoe liners include

1. Flaccid paralysis, e.g., peroneus palsy or polio residuals.
2. Spastic paralysis, e.g., hemiplegia, or infantile cerebral palsy.
3. Mild or moderate foot deformities, e.g., mild clubfoot, "C"-foot, or pes planovalgus.
4. Partial or total amputation of the foot.
5. Differences in leg length in excess of 3 to 4 cm. This group also includes the footdrop contractures in which the contralateral side must also be raised because of a functional extension of the afflicted foot. An additional advantage of the shoe liner is that it can be produced at low cost.

In footdrop without contractures, i.e. peroneal palsy, instead of rigid peroneal devices, a special corrective footdrop sock can be prescribed. If there are no major deformities, this sock can be worn in standard shoes.

The orthopedic shoe trade offers a special athletic shoe, designed for the postsurgical management of ankle ligament or capsule injuries. Lateral shaft reinforcement provides sufficient stability and permits early mobilization of the ankle in the sagittal plane. This shoe is also appropriate in peroneal palsy and can be used after ankle arthrodesis as well, if provided with a rocker sole.

CLINICAL EXAMPLES

The following few clinical examples will serve to illustrate the practical applications of orthopedic modifications or made-to-measure shoes.

Case 1.—A 37-year-old woman with a shortening of the right leg by 6.5 cm as a result of juvenile coxitis. The right shoe was raised by 4 cm. She plays tennis and rides a bicycle.

Case 2.—A 16-year-old girl with a contracted drop foot after injury. For skating, she was provided with a made-to-measure boot with bilateral integrated heel elevation.

Case 3.—A 64-year-old man with battle injuries. A right calf crush injury led to peroneal palsy, contracted footdrop, and claw toes. He was provided with orthopedic athletic shoes with an integrated peroneal splint on the right, bilateral heel, lifts to make up for the footdrop, and a rocker sole. Athletic activities include gymnastics, table tennis, and bowling.

Case 4.—A 63-year-old man with

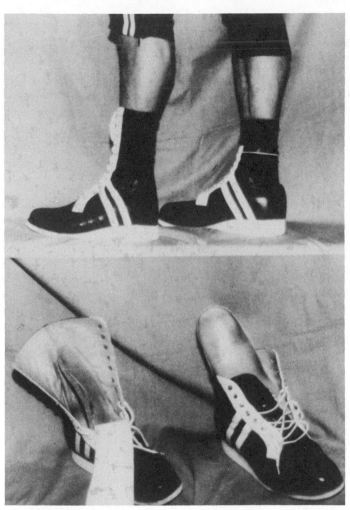

FIG 28–2.
Orthopedic athletic shoes for an athlete with ankylosis on the left hip and partial stiffness of the right hip and right knee. The corrections consist of a built-in peroneal splint and raised shaft on the left and a metatarsal roll.

right-sided sciatic palsy, 2-cm shortening of the right leg, and a left-sided pes planovalgus. He was provided with made-to-measure orthopedic shoes with a medium shaft and a right built-in, so-called Berlin cap, a modification of the small peroneal boot of Kraus. Additionally, he was provided with a heel lift and a right footbed. Athletic activities include fistball, table tennis, and bowling.

Case 5.—A 65-year-old man with battle injuries: ankylosis of the left hip, partial stiffness of the right hip and left knee, left peroneal palsy. He was provided with made-to-order or-thopedic shoes with an integrated peroneal splint on the left, a raised shaft, a metatarsal roll, and a heel wedge. This combination represents the "fixed rocker shoe" of Rabl (Fig 28–2). Athletic activities include fistball, bowling.

SUMMARY

Orthopedic shoes make it possible for disabled persons to become active in athletic events and join the large group of handicapped athletes. This will keep them active and add to their quality of life through contacts with other athletes and through the satisfaction of achievement. They will also strengthen their muscles, so important in compensating for their disability.

The technical opportunities offered by the orthopedic shoe industry should make it possible for a large additional number of disabled persons to engage in athletic activities.

29

Impact Cushioning in Arthritis Patients

D. Gebauer

X. Bonefeld

N. Cziuk

Even normal walking can cause pain in patients who have degenerative arthritic changes in their lower extremity. The therapeutic spectrum ranges from systemic medication and local percutaneous or intra-articular drug therapy, to physical medicine, remedial gymnastics, orthotic appliances, and surgical intervention, e.g., derotation osteotomy, arthrodesis, and total joint replacement.

In almost all stages of arthritis, shock-absorbing shoes represent a simple method of reducing the impact load. The various commercially available models show considerable individual differences and may have impact-cushioning components only in the heel area or in the entire sole and heel. Numerous complaints from wearers of such shoes encouraged us to develop a new shoe in cooperation with industry. It seemed reasonable to compare the essential characteristics of this shoe with commercially available, impact-cushioning shoes and leather-soled street shoes. Only then could the beneficial effects of impact cushioning and its role in arthritic patients be evaluated.

MATERIALS AND METHODS

Ignoring parameters, such as fit, comfort, and appearance, that are controlled by the configuration of the uppers, we compared the remaining characteristics of impact cushioning and slippage prevention. The models that were compared are listed in Table 29–1.

Impact Cushioning

Two methods are used to measure this parameter. In one study, the energy uptake potential of the heels was measured during slow load velocities of 10, 100, and 1,000 mm/minute. This was done in accordance with the Deutsches Institut für Normung (/) protocol 4,842, part 1, and measurements were made with increasing pressure to a maximum of 5 kN. The second study investigated the cushioning potential under severe impact conditions in a special measuring device. In this machine, the shoe was thrust from a given height against a plastic surface by a spring-loaded release mechanism (Fig 29–1). The Kist-

TABLE 29–1.

Shoe Models and Materials Under Study

Shoe No.	Type (and Manufacturer)
I	Brown Slipper
	Ultraflex sole
II	Gray-laced shoe
	Dr. Maertens air-cushion shoe
III	Brown-laced shoe
	Dr. Maertens Softwalkers-Majola
IV	Black shoe with leather heel (30 mm) and leather sole
V	New design

ler plate, placed under the impact surface, recorded the forces generated as a function of time. A comparison of the maximal forces and of the impulse values could determine the relative impact cushioning potential of the different shoes, under extreme conditions.

Slippage Prevention

Slippage prevention must be studied on both dry and wet surfaces. Extreme danger of slippage can be tested after the application of a polyurethane solution such as Pril to the floor. These were the three conditions under which polyvinyl chloride (PVC) floors were tested. The greatest danger of slippage during the walking cycle is in the braking phase, when the heel comes into contact with the floor. This occurs during the first 5% to 14% of the support phase.

In Fig 29–2, the relationship between the initial friction force (F_{RA}), the tangential force (FT_T), and the normal force (F_N) are illustrated. If F_{RA} is smaller than the tangential force, the heel will slip. Extensive studies have shown that the ratio of the initial friction force and the normal force equals the initial friction value, μ_{RA}, which must be greater

than 0.2 and should be greater than 0.4.[3] The loads appearing in walking were generated in a "walk simulator" (Fig 29–3). To measure the friction value μ the rocking motion of the foot was transformed at the onset of the slip into a gliding motion with a slippage device that simulated natural conditions.[1] The ground forces, F_{RA} and F_N, were measured with a Kistler plate. The curves of the friction force and normal force served to calculate the friction value μ at the point of the maximal friction forces. This was then used as the significant value. It must be pointed out that the shoe-ground materials studied do not follow Coulomb's law of friction, but that the friction value is a function of velocity.

In the load simulation study, the physiologic spring cushioning of the shoe-leg system could not be taken into account. For this reason, all "fall-

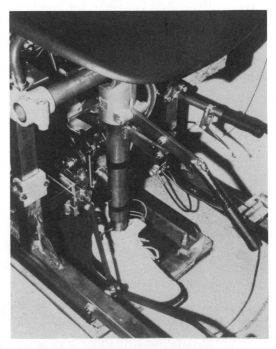

FIG 29–1.
Measurement device for hard shocks.

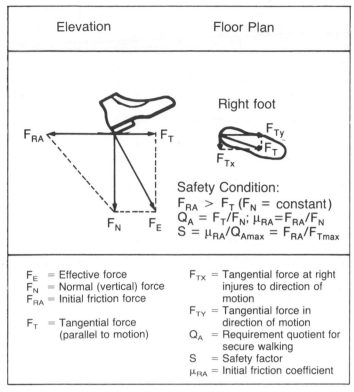

FIG 29–2.
Force relationships on placement of foot on a horizontal surface.

ing" studies were performed from different heights and with the leg as straight as possible. Acceleration at the anterior pelvic crest was measured with a specially designed belt on which the sensors were oriented vertically to capture the acceleration at the hip in the arthritic patient.

Both leather and air-cushion shoes were studied.[2]

RESULTS

In the investigation of impact cushioning during low-velocity loads,

FIG 29–3.
The "Site-Prod-Traveler" to simulate the sliding sequence.

TABLE 29–2.

Maximal Distortion and Energy Uptake Potential in the 50-to 5,000-Newton Interval

Shoe No.	Shoe Type/Manufacturer	Maximum Load (kN)	Load Velocity (mm/min)	Maximum Distortion (mm)	Mean Energy Uptake Potential (Joules)
I	Brown slipper/	5	10	16.2	
	Ultraflex sole	5	100	15.5	23.1
		5	1000	15.8	
II	Gray-laced shoe/Dr.	5	10	14.5	
	Maertens Factory air	5	100	14.4	24.9
	cushion shoe	5	1000	14.4	
III	Brown-laced shoe/Dr.	5	10	17.6	
	Maertens Factory	5	100	17.8	25.7
	Softwalkers-Majola	5	1000	18.7	
IV	Black shoe with leather	5	10	2.7	
	heel and leather sole	5	100	2.8	4.2
		5	1000	2.9	
V	New design	5	10	20.2	
		5	100	19.6	36.0
		5	1000	18.5	

the energy uptake potential, $E = \int F \, ds$, between 50 and 5,000 newtons, was determined from the force (F) vs. change in length (ds) diagram and from maximal distortion. Table 29–2 shows the relatively minor differences observed between the impact-attenuating shoes. As anticipated, the shoe with leather soles showed only minor distortion.

Measurement of the attenuating potential after hard impact also demonstrated quite clearly the differences between the leather shoe and the impact-cushioning shoes. In addition to the differences in maximal force, a smaller impulse was also observed during the first critical 0.125 seconds.

In Table 29–3, the rank order of maximum force and impulse on the linoleum floor are shown.

The studies on slippage prevention in the walk simulator showed divergent trends under the various experimental conditions (Table 29–4). Under dry conditions, e.g., the friction value for the new shoe V is clearly better. Under identical load conditions on a wet PVC floor, the μ value was less favorable. The same was true when the floor was moistened with a Pril solution. It can be seen that a certain shoe may have very good friction characteristics under dry conditions, but compare unfavorably with other shoes on a wet surface.

TABLE 29–3.

Rank Order of the Shoes for Maximal Force and Impulse on a Linoleum Surface

Shoe Type	Rank Order	Maximum Force (kPa)	Impulse (Ns)
I (brown)	1	966	545.0
V (white)	2	1,008	567.5
II (gray)	3	1,242	602.5
IV (leather)	4	1,286	630.0

TABLE 29–4.

The Characteristic Friction Value (μ) of the Individual Shoe Models Under Different Ground Surface Conditions

Shoe No.	Shoe Type	Initial Friction Force (μ)		
		Dry	Water	Pril
I	Ultraflex (brown)	0.64	0.53	0.29
II	Dr. Maertens (gray)	0.80	0.61	0.32
V	New design (white)	1.38	0.44	0.17

In comparative "falling" experiments in which a leather-soled shoe and a Dr. Maertens air-cushion shoe were used, it was evident both subjectively and objectively that there were appreciable differences as far as impact attenuation was concerned. Already in the first experiment—a fall from a stair with a height of 20 cm—there was pain in the hip joint when the leather shoe was worn. This forced us to conduct all subsequent experiments with the patient in a slight knee-bend position. All experiments with the air-cushion shoe could be performed with the leg straight and without pain. Even under these conditions (straight leg vs. slightly bent knee), the air cushion shoe demonstrated for every fall at least a 15% smaller acceleration value in the hip area than that observed with the leather shoe.

SUMMARY

Both the simulation studies with slow and fast impact loads and the physiologic acceleration measurements at the pelvic crest clearly showed the advantages of the impact-cushioning shoes over the standard, leather-soled street shoes. When selecting one of the several available impact-cushioning shoes, one should also pay attention to the slippage-preventing characteristics of the shoe.

To bring the widest range of criteria to bear on the selection of the shoe, the safety features should be evaluated on wet and on polyurethane moistened floors. The final evaluation must be made after the experimental subjects have worn the shoes over a period of several months. Only under such standardized experimental conditions and only under physiologic loads can the technical properties of a shoe be tested.

REFERENCES

1. *Bonefeld, X.*: Die Bestimmung des Gleitverhaltens von Schuhsohlen auf Bodenbelägen. Forschungsbericht der Bundesanstalt für Arbeitsschutz und Unfallvorschung Nr. 265. Wirtschaftsverlag NW, Bremerhaven 1981
2. *Gebauer, D.*: Zur Biomechanik künstlicher Hüftgelenke. Fortschr. Ber. VDI-Z. 17/21 (1984)
3. *Skiba, R., X. Bonefeld, D. Mellwig*: Voraussetzung zur Bestimmung der Gleitsicherheit beim menschlichen Gang. Z. Arb. wiss. 4 (1983), 227–232

30 Computer-Assisted Electromyographic Running Studies of Athletic Shoes With Various Sole Configurations

F. Bodem

R. Volkert

W. Menke

F. Brussatis

The critical mechanical load on the human locomotor system occurs during running in the form of ground reaction forces during the stance phase of the running sequence. The spatial-temporal distribution of these forces can be affected by the sole configuration of the running shoe. Orthopedic patients frequently have some area in their lower extremities that require additional protection, but otherwise they have no contraindication to moderate running training. It is the task of orthopedic technology to use biomechanical principles and to design a sole configuration that will decrease the load on the sensitive structures of the lower extremity. An effort must be made to evaluate these effects and their mechanism from the perspective of qualitative biomechanical understanding of human walking and running sequences.

In fact, a direct qualitative and quantitative assessment of the biomechanical effects of such activity by direct measurement techniques and by comparison with a suitable theoretical model is very difficult indeed and can be performed only at considerable cost. One feature that can be measured qualitatively and, at least as far as trends are concerned, quantitatively is the electromyogram (EMG). This noninvasive technique can measure the recurrent rhythmic activity of the muscles of the lower extremity that participate in the running motions. We have attempted to demonstrate the effects of various sole configurations on the activity of selected muscles during running by using a kinesiologic electromyographic motion analysis system developed in our biomechanical laboratory.

MATERIALS AND METHODS

A Kinesiologic-Electromyographic Measurement System

The structure and function of the measurement system used in our studies is shown schematically in Fig 30–1. The experimental subject performs the test run on a level walkway of 14 m. In developing our measurement system, we preferred a level surface to the treadmill. Preliminary studies had demonstrated that running on the treadmill caused significant changes in the kinesiologic and electromyographic data when compared to the natural running sequence on a level surface. This effect may be due to the difference in the visual orientation of the experimental subject. On the treadmill, the environment is stationary; in a level run the relative relationship of the runner to the environment changes.

During the test run the following measurements were obtained:

1. Electromyographic skin surface potentials on selected lower extremity muscles: In this study, the activity of the rectus femoris, biceps femoris, tibialis anterior, peroneus longus, and soleus muscles was measured. The muscle potentials were measured with Ag/AgCl skin surface electrodes. Immediately proximal to the elec-

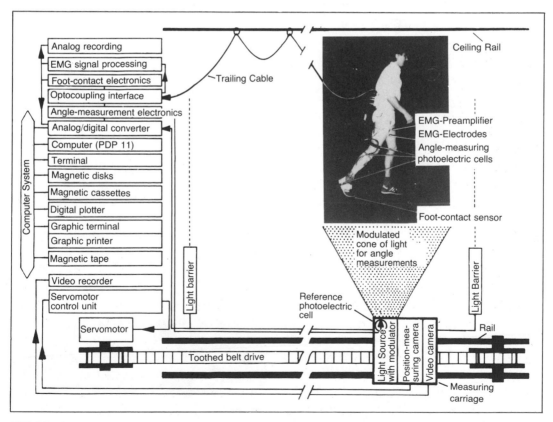

FIG 30–1.
Schematic representation of the kinematic-electromyographic motion analysis system.

trodes, a miniaturized preamplifier was in line to minimize signal distortion due to artifacts and interference during the transmission of the impulses. The EMG signals were transmitted to a distribution box attached to the back of the experimental subject. After additional amplification, the signal was transmitted from the box by an easily tractable trailing cable guided in a ceiling rail to a stationary terminal amplifier and electronic filter. The experimental subjects were protected by an optocoupling interface. All electronic equipment between the subject and the interface were battery activated.[2]

2. Angle displacement of the foot, lower leg, and thigh in the sagittal plane: The angles were measured with an optoelectronic goniometer system (POLGON[3]) that was adapted to the special requirements of our motion analysis system. In this angle measurement system, the experimental subject moves in an intense light cone originating from a projector. The light is modulated optically by a rotating polarizer of predetermined angle frequency. Photoelectric cells with an analyzing filter are attached to those body parts whose angular movements are to be measured. These cells generate amplitude-modified sinusoidal signals in the modulated light cone at twice the angle frequency of the rotating polarizer. Through a special electronic switching system, the signals were compared in their modulated plane with a fixed reference photoelectric cell. From this comparison, a voltage signal that is proportional to its angle from the sagittal plane is generated electronically for each angle-measur-

ing photoelectric cell.

The experimental subject must remain in the cone of light from the modulated light source during the entire measurement period. To accomplish this, the light source is mounted on a carriage that moves on rails parallel to the experimental subject. The carriage is driven by a stationary electric motor via a cogwheel cable. The speed of the carriage is regulated automatically by a signal received from the experimental subject by a special optoelectronic camera mounted on the carriage. This autoregulatory signal keeps the carriage and the modulated cone of light automatically alongside the runner, independently of his speed.[1] Figure 30−2 illustrates the carriage; Figure 30−3 shows the experimental subject equipped with angle-measuring photoelectric cells and EMG electrodes. The carriage is also equipped with a video camera so that the experimental running sequence can be taped by a video recorder from a lateral view.

3. Temporal division of the running motion into stance and swing phases: This study is performed by attaching flat, pressure-sensitive, floor

FIG 30−2.
The measuring carriage of the optoelectronic angle measurement system.

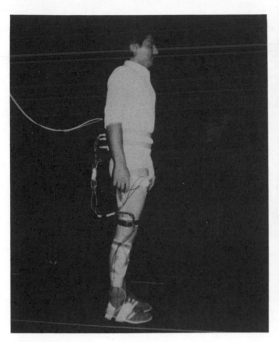

FIG 30–3.
The subject with angle-measuring photoelectric cells and EMG electrodes attached.

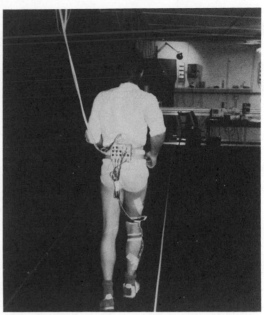

FIG 30–4.
The subject during a measurement period.

contact sensors to the heel and fore-foot of the experimental subject. After processing, all measurement signals are transmitted by cable to an analog/digital converter of a computer. They are then digitalized and stored on a magnetic disk or tape as raw data for future analysis. Fig 30–4 shows a subject during a measurement run. Figure 30–5 shows the computer setup used for the motion studies. It consists of a central computer unit, 2 magnetic disk recorders, 2 magnetic disk drives, 2 magnetic cassette drives, 1 analog/digital interface, 1 terminal, 1 graphic video terminal with a hard copy unit and digital plotter.

Analysis of the Measurement Data

The assessment program separates the measured and digitally stored running sequence into double steps by analyzing the periodicity of the angle changes of the lower leg. As starting and ending points of the double step, the moment is selected when the lower leg crosses a vertical line during the forward swing phase. The double steps of the test run, arrived at in this fashion, show very little temporal variation within the group. They are therefore standardized mathematically to the duration of the shortest step taken during the run. Every measurement taken during the run is arithmetically averaged over the group of the standardized double steps. This process is based on the well-known technique of "signal averaging" of periodically recurring signal sequences having some fluctuations. Regularly recurring characteristics in the measurement sequence of the standardized double steps are enhanced, and the incidental irregularities are

FIG 30−5.
The computer setup of the
measurement system.

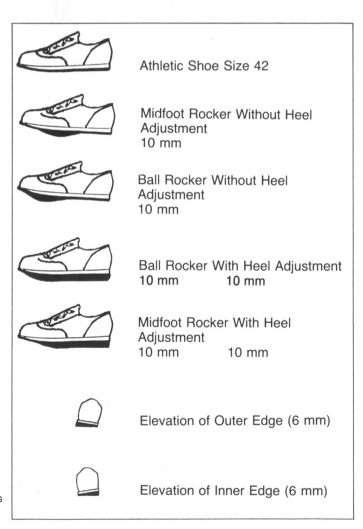

Athletic Shoe Size 42

Midfoot Rocker Without Heel
Adjustment
10 mm

Ball Rocker Without Heel
Adjustment
10 mm

Ball Rocker With Heel Adjustment
10 mm   10 mm

Midfoot Rocker With Heel
Adjustment
10 mm   10 mm

Elevation of Outer Edge (6 mm)

Elevation of Inner Edge (6 mm)

FIG 30−6.
Display of the sole configurations
under study.

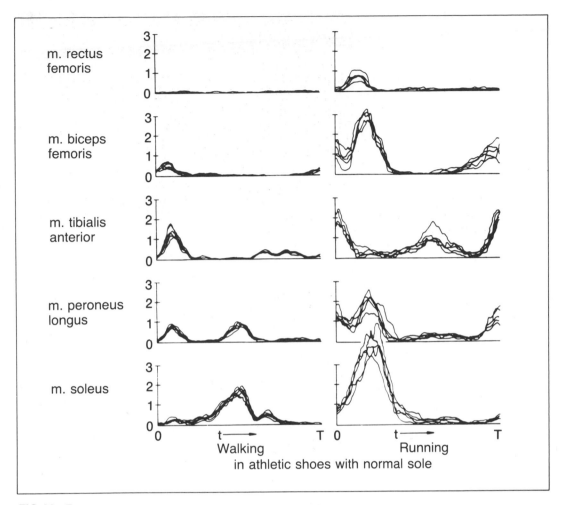

FIG 30–7.
Electromyographic activity of the muscles studied in walking (T = 1.25 seconds) and running (T = 0.77 seconds) in running shoes with normal soles.

suppressed. In this way, characteristic tracings can be obtained of each goniometric and electromyographic measurement point for each gait sequence.

Before averaging, the electromyographic signals were numerically adjusted over the entire standardized double-step ensemble and filtered through a continuous integration interval of 0.1-second duration. This produces a smoother activity curve for the muscles under study and per-

mits much more satisfactory comparisons than the raw EMG. For further analysis, these curves are graphically represented by a computer-controlled digital plotter or by a graphic terminal.

The Sole Configurations Studied

Using the above described electromyographic measurement and assessment system, we studied the running

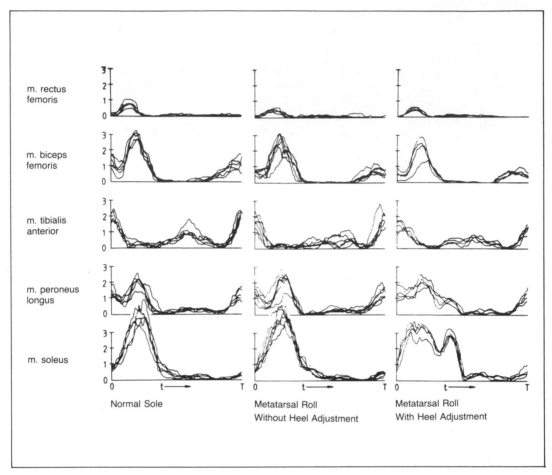

FIG 30–8.
Electromyographic activity of the muscles studied in running (T = 0.77 second with midfoot rocker.

sequences of a 24-year-old test subject, who wore shoes with a variety of sole configurations (Fig 30–6):

1. Normal sole.
2. Midfoot rocker (10 mm) without heel adjustment.
3. Ball rocker (10 mm) without heel adjustment.
4. Ball rocker (10 mm) with heel adjustment.
5. Midfoot rocker (10 mm) with heel adjustment.
6. Outer edge elevation (6 mm).
7. Inner edge elevation (6 mm).

The test runs were synchronized with a metronome so that each double step lasted 0.77 second. The first two double steps were used by the subject to synchronize his steps with the metronome and were not included in the analysis.

PRELIMINARY RESULTS

Figures 30–7 to 30–10 show a graphic representation of six consecutive test runs obtained under identical conditions in which the above de-

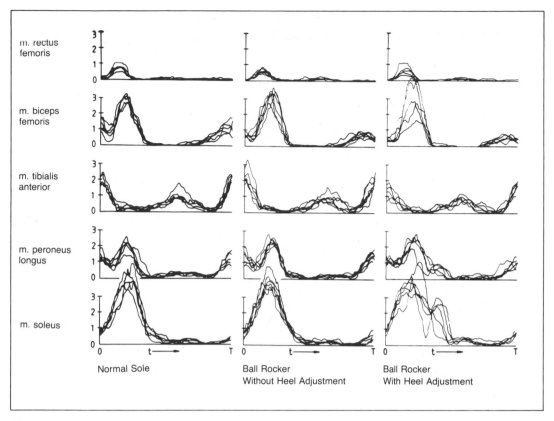

FIG 30–9.
Electromyographic activity of the muscles studied in running (T = 0.77 second) with a rocker under the ball of the foot.

scribed measurement and assessment system was used. They are composites of the electromyographic activity sequences of the muscles under study. The units are arbitrary but identical in all diagrams. The abscissa represents one standardized double step. The beginning (t=0) and the end (t=T) of the double step coincide with the long axis of the lower leg crossing the vertical during the forward swing of that leg.

Even though there are obvious fluctuations in the details of the curves obtained under identical experimental conditions, it is apparent that there is a good reproduceability

of the essential characteristics of the temporal sequence.

To show the order of magnitude of change in the electromyographic activity, Figure 30–7 shows the difference between walking (T=1.25 seconds) and running (T=0.77 second). The ensuing qualitative and quantitative changes in muscle activity are obvious. The shift of the peak activity of the soleus and the peroneus longus muscles in the direction of the beginning of the double step, corresponds to a shift of the stance phase in the same direction.

In Figures 30–8 to 30–10, the electromyographic activity of the mus-

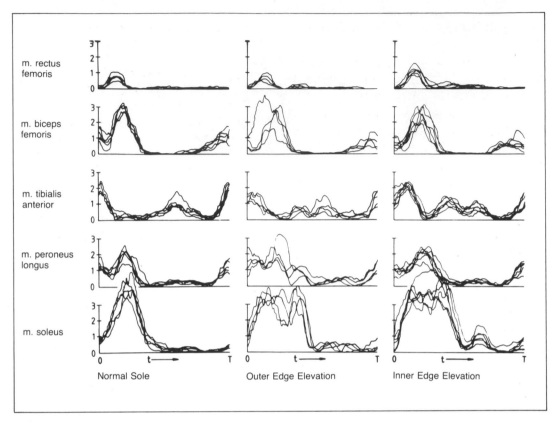

FIG 30–10.
Electromyographic activity of the muscles studied in running (T = 0.77 second) with outer and inner edge elevation of the sole of the shoe.

cles is shown during runs (T=0.77 second) in which the subject is wearing a variety of different sole configurations. These runs are compared to a run with a normal sole.

When the subject runs with a midfoot rocker, evident prolongation of the activity of the soleus and peroneus longus muscles occurs only when there is a simultaneous adjustment of the heel. The other muscles show no change in comparison with the run with normal soles. Similar results are obtained in the run with the metatarsophalangeal rocker.

When either the inner edge or the outer edge was raised, there were clear changes in the activity se-

quence, particularly of the soleus, the peroneus longus, and the tibialis anterior muscles. There was a distinct and not unexpected, spread of the peak activity curve.

SUMMARY

The results of our studies indicate that changes in the configuration of the sole, of a magnitude introduced by us, have definite effects on the electromyographic activity characteristics of the lower extremity while a subject is running. The findings contribute to our understanding of the general biomechanical effects of the configuration of the sole on running. When configuration of the soles are changed less drastically, as, e.g., in trying to optimize the sole configuration for a specific purpose, the electromyographic findings would probably be less obvious than in our studies, when appropriate statistical methodology is used, however, electromyography performed according to our model may still yield valuable results.

REFERENCES

1. *Bodem, F., F. Brussatis, B. Mertin, T. Wunderlich, H. Wagner*: A test-subject-tracking measuring carriage with optoelectronic position-feedback control for the kinematic analysis of the gait of orthopedic patients. Med. Progr. Techn. 8 (1981), 141–147
2. *Bodem, F., F. Brussatis, T. Wunderlich, B. Mertin*: A kinesiologic electromyography system for the computer-controlled analog and digital recording and processing of muscle action potentials of walking subjects. Med. Progr. Techn. 8 (1981), 129–139
3. *Styles, P.R.*: POLGON. An aid to gait analysis. Asian Med. J. 19 (1976), 35

31   Relationships Between Running Injuries and Running Shoes—Results of a Study of 5,000 Participants of a 16-km Run—The May 1984 Berne "Grand Prix"

B. Marti

The jogging scene seems to offer a real paradox: On the one side we have the shoe industry making wonderful promises based on scientific laboratory studies ("like running on clouds"; "cushioning, support, control"; "Model X knows where it's at"); on the other side, we have the running public, confused and insecure, trying to find its way among the enticements of shoe advertisements. Despite the promises, the runner not uncommonly has a rude awakening in the form of injuries that arise during the run. Runners with such injuries frequently wind up in the doctors office.[5, 7] This may be the reason why the medical profession has looked very critically at the jogging craze.[4] The runner frequently associates his troubles with his most important athletic equipment, the running shoe. From a medical point of view, the re- lationship between run-related overload injuries and the running shoe are of both prophylactic and therapeutic interest. Unfortunately, to date, there are very few empirical data.

The etiology of overload manifestations in the locomotor system (hereafter referred to as running injuries) appears to be multifactorial, according to current thinking[8]:

"Endogenous" etiologic factors include

- Biomechanical and coordinational predeterminants (running style).
- Level of training.
- Recuperative powers.

These are different from "exogenous" factors such as

- The range and intensity of training.
- Site of training (surface).

- Running shoes.
- Special conditions for recuperation (massage) or prophylaxis (stretching).

Depending on the point of view of the individual, different values will be assigned to these factors. In view of the great efforts made by the manufacturers to produce the best possible shoe (orthopedically correct, functionally supportive, to some extent therapeutic), the following questions must be asked from a scientific point of view: To what extent do the modern running shoes protect against running injuries? Are there differences between the different brands? What makes a quality shoe? Placed in the context of price, are cheap shoes prone to lead to injury? Do shoes have certain characteristics that the buyer may or may not consider and that do play a significant role? On the basis of the experiences of the 1984 Berne study, we hope to be able to give an answer to these questions.

METHODOLOGY

All runners participating in the 16-km run of the May 1984 "Grand Prix" (GP) of Berne (Switzerland) were given a questionnaire that covered the following subjects:

- Characteristics of their training (during the 16 months before the GP).
- Motivation for running and competing.
- Nature and duration of run-related injuries (in great detail for the last year).
- Number and reason for physician visits (during the year before the GP).
- Demographic information, height, weight, etc.
- Etiologic co-factors of the running injuries: make of the shoe, cost, use of inserts, preferred training terrain.

Age and running time were taken from the official record. All data were stored on magnetic tape and subjected to computerized statistical analysis (SAS program, chi-square significance test).

Of the 6,620 registered Swiss runners (91% male, 9% female), 5,038 participated in the study (76.1% return rate). The average age of the males was 33.0 years (range, 8–75 years); the mean time for the 16-km run was 1:13:20. The runners not participating in the study (23.9%) were younger (by 2.6 years) and slower (1:16:09). No additional information was obtained from this group.

RESULTS

All runners with running injuries that occurred during the 12 months before the GP run in May 1984 were put into one of three groups, which were analyzed separately. Three levels of injury were recognized that required the following:

1. Complete cessation of training (minimum: 3 weeks)
2. Reduction in training
3. Full training, injuries permitting

We also asked for the duration of the injuries, for interruptions in training, for location of the injury, and nature of the injury.

Table 31–1 shows the average incidence and duration of running injuries in the entire Berne GP field (N=5,038). Every fifth runner had to stop training for more than 1 month during the year before the GP competition, and 3 of 10 runners had their training affected by injuries for about 1.5 months. It is obvious that the modern running shoe does not protect absolutely against running injuries.

Causes of Running Injuries

As mentioned above, the causes of the running injuries are manifold. For this reason, it is important to know the factors that significantly affect the rate of incidence of running injuries before the effects of the running shoes are singled out for discussion.

The Berne Study of 1984 can give no information concerning the important, so-called endogenous etiologic factors (e.g., the biomechanics of the running style). Several exogenous causes, however, were considered and analyzed.[7] Two appeared to be significant:

1. Increasing the dimensions of training increases the risks of injury.

This assumption may be open to some doubt: Of the GP runners who ran an average of 500 km in 1983, 16% suffered running injuries, while those who trained three times as much (the 1983 average was 1,500 km) had an incidence of 21%. For significantly increased training (3,000 km/year), the incidence of injuries increased only slightly to 23%.

2. The 15.3% of the runners who had a significant running injury before the study year of 1983 had a significantly increased incidence of injury during the study year; 30.6% had an injury during the study year as compared to 18.5% among the athletes who had no history of previous injury (P<0.001). A "positive history" for injuries increased the risk factor for a recurrent injury during the study year by 74%.

All the other factors had little, if any, effect on the incidence of injury. Surprisingly enough, these factors included GP running time, age, years of active running, relative body weight (expressed as lean body mass index [BMI]), or preferred training terrain. Shoe inserts appear to have a statistically marginally significant preventive effect. This is not easy to prove since inserts are used primarily by runners who are at high risk for inju-

TABLE 31–1.

Frequency and Duration of Running Injuries in 5,038 Participants in the "Grand Prix of Berne," 1984

Runners (Male and Female) With	Frequency (%)	Duration in wk (SD)
Training interruption (2 wk) due to running injury	19.4	4.9 (±4.5)
Reduced training due to injury	29.0	5.1 (±6.5)
Full training despite injury	29.1	7.3 (±8.9)

ries (e.g., very extensive training, positive history for previous injuries).

Comparison of Different Brands of Shoe

These introductory remarks are necessary for a better understanding of the data in Table 31–2, where the different brands of running shoes are compared with each other. In the questionnaire sent to the participants, the question "Which brand of shoe do you prefer?" could be answered in six ways: The four most popular brands in Switzerland were listed individually, one answer was "other," and one answer was "I have no preference."

Table 31–2 shows the frequency of running injuries (and some other data) classified according to the 6 possible answers. Two points must be kept in mind: (1) since a positive history of previous injury significantly affects the "injury-induced interruption of training," this table includes only the runners with a negative history and (2) since the amount of training was also significant, a "corrected incidence of interruption of training" was calculated. This number adjusts the differences in kilometers run in 1983 and thus allows a fairer comparison of the various brands.

The most important parameter, from a prophylactic medicine point of view, was the incidence (frequency) of training interruptions related to running injuries. This showed a definite distribution: One brand (Karhu) showed significantly more running injuries (P<0.05). The relatively large group of runners who

indicate no preference and who presumably switch brands more or less frequently showed a significantly lower incidence of running injuries (P<0.001). The duration of the training interruptions was similar in all six groups.

In the group that reduced training (frequency, duration) because of running injuries, the picture was more uniform, with the exception of the "other-brand" group where the incidence was clearly higher.

In the last group, which "continued full training despite some injury" the situation was also relatively uniform. There was a definite trend, however, that indicates that statistically speaking a decrease in the severity of the running injuries was accompanied by an increase in their duration.

The median running time during the race (adjusted for age in runners over 35 years of age) showed variations that can be explained on the basis of differences in training.[6] The group identified as "other brand" was an exception. Its running time was a good 2 minutes slower, but this could be expected on the basis of its more limited training.

The runners who used particular shoes had no preference for any of the three running surfaces. The "other-brands" group stood apart here as well. Nevertheless, there was no statistical evidence that would link the terrain to the incidence of running injuries.

One in ten wore custom-made inserts. For Karhu, this was one in five. As mentioned before, inserts are worn primarily by persons who are at

TABLE 31–2.

Frequency of Running Injuries and the Preferred Running Shoe in 3,446 "Grand Prix" Runners (Over 16 Years Old With a Negative History for Running Injuries)

Brand of Shoe	Adidas	Nike	Puma	Karhu	Other	No Preference
No. of runners (%)	1,153 (33.5)	782 (22.7)	251 (7.3)	153 (4.4)	161 (4.7)	946 (27.5)
Runner with						
Training interruption due to running injury (%)	19.9	20.1	17.1	26.3	18.0	14.3
Duration (wks)	4.7	4.5	5.0	4.7	3.8	4.5
Training reduction (%)	27.1	30.3	28.0	27.5	38.2	25.0
Duration (wks)	5.8	5.7	4.7	4.4	5.3	5.1
Full training with injuries (%)	26.7	31.0	27.6	34.2	26.8	26.8
Duration (wks)	6.1	7.4	7.8	7.3	7.9	7.7
No. of km run in 1983 (SD)	894 (±877)	1,017 (±904)	803 (±727)	1,296 (±935)	1,245 (±995)	832 (±887)
Frequency of training interruptions corrected for km run*	20.3	20.1	17.9	25.2†	17.0	15.0‡
Running time GP 84 (corrected for age)	1:11:53	1:10:44	1:12:48	1:08:26	1:11:27	1:12:21
Preferred Running Surface (% runners)						
Hard surface, street, etc.	18	20	14	14	32	17
Natural surface, woods, etc.	38	31	37	36	28	36
Mixed surface	44	49	49	50	40	42
Runners using inserts (%)	10.0	10.0	9.6	19.9	11.3	9.6
Cost of shoe (mean of 4 price ranges), $	58.80	75.00	64.00	82.00	70.00	60.00

*The average number of kilometers run in 1983 does not vary markedly between groups. Nevertheless, the differences are sufficiently large to affect the incidence of running injuries/training interruptions. For this reason, a hypothetical "corrected rate" was calculated for all six brands based on 1,000 km/y for 1983. These figures were used in the statistical analysis.
†P<0.05
‡P<0.01

an increased risk for running injuries. Thus, this fits in well with the other observations about Karhu. The cost of the running shoes showed some shoe-specific differences (four price ranges were used).

In summary, the group that had no preference for any one brand of shoe showed the most favorable results (significantly fewer training interruptions). There were neither advantages nor disadvantages among three of the major brands, including the two leaders—Adidas and Nike. The fourth largest brand, Karhu, seems to be associated with an important distinction (significantly more training interruptions). Admittedly the reason for this finding is difficult to interpret.

Such a global look at brands may not do justice to the individual models within the brands. The GP runners were not queried about their specific shoe model, since this would have been statistically impossible.

The only other specific information about the running shoe that was ascertained was cost. It was assumed that cost correlated, at least to some extent, with the quality of the running shoe. How realistic this assumption is remains to be seen.

Comparison on the Basis of Cost

Table 31–3 shows the same variables for the entire GP running group as Table 31–2, but is tabulated according to the four price ranges. No distinction was made on the basis of individual brands.

Several trends become obvious. The most significant is the correlation between higher prices and increased running injuries. It is probably incorrect, however, to interpret this surprising finding to mean that more expensive shoes cause more running injuries and running-related problems.

A statistical correlation, like the one above, can be interpreted in two different ways. In this instance, it may well be that runners with existing injuries buy more expensive shoes than the healthy runner in hopes that the prophylactic and therapeutic virtues attributed to the expensive shoes may be true. At the very least, it must be said that the expensive models show no advantage as far as the incidence of running injuries is concerned. Additional facts that added to the unfavorable image created by this group was that it included a very high proportion of insert users and that the mean running time in this group of runners was 1.5 minutes slower than would have been expected on the basis of their training in 1983.

There is a clear relationship between the cost of the shoe and the age of the runner, which would suggest that the amount of money paid for the running shoe may be a function of income.

The inverse of the hypothesis that expensive running shoes protect from injury would be that inexpensive shoes are "injury prone." The data of the Berne GP race were analyzed on this basis as well. Only 2.7% (N=118; runners over 16 years of age) could be assigned to the group wearing "cheap" shoes. The other 97.3% of the runners either wore one of the name brand shoes, or spent more than $40 for their shoes. Of the 118 runners, 14 (11.9%) had to interrupt

TABLE 31–3.

Running Injuries and the Cost of the Running Shoes in 5,026 "Grand Prix" Runners

Shoe Price Range	<$40	$40–$60	$60–$95	>$95
No. of runners (%)	311 (6.2)	2,145 (42.7)	2,310 (46.0)	260 (5.1)
Age of runners (mean in yrs)	27.9	32.3	35.4	36.9
Runner with				
Training interruptions due to running injury (%)	9.0	16.7	21.9	33.0
Duration (wks)	4.7	4.4	5.1	5.5
Training reduction (%)	20.2	25.1	32.0	36.0
Duration (wks)	4.6	5.7	5.5	6.3
Full training with injuries (%)	18.3	24.3	30.8	34.6
Duration (wks)	5.4	7.2	7.5	8.1
No. of km run in 1983 (SD)	418 (±508)	819 (±847)	1153 (±998)	1237 (±922)
Runners with positive history for injuries (%)	7.2	13.7	21.9	16.0
Frequency of training interruptions corrected for km differences and % of positive history for running injuries	14.3	17.4	20.5	31.9
Running time GP 1984 (Corrected for age)	1:19:21	1:13:57	1:10:33	1:11:32
Preferred running surface (% of runners)				
Hard surface, street, etc.	20	16	18	21
Natural surface, woods, etc.	41	40	35	25
Mixed surface	39	44	47	54
Runners using inserts (%)	4.2	10.6	14.1	21.7

their training during the year under study. Even making adjustments for the low level of training in 1983 (475 km) and the relatively low percentage of runners with a positive injury history (12.0%), the "corrected incidence of running injuries" is 16.1%, which is still below the average for the whole group.

It cannot be demonstrated that cheap running shoes have a negative effect. The comment that the runners using really cheap shoes could not be identified by our research methodology has little merit, since in the entire, large miscellaneous group of more than 5,000 runners, only a small minority, less than 3%, wore potentially injury-prone, mass-produced, cheap running shoes.

It is possible that neither the brand nor the cost of the shoe is important, but that the important issue is the criteria on the basis of which the runner selects his shoes. The Berne GP runners were given eight criteria and were asked how important each of these were in their selection process. A rank order of all shoe selection criteria was calculated for all runners (N=5,038) and is presented in Table 31–4. The "scale of

TABLE 31–4.

Rank Order of the Shoe Selection Criteria

	Scale of Relative Value
1. Orthopedically correct construction of the running shoe	2.71
2. Fit/comfort	2.65
3. Slip-resistance/profile of sole	2.12
4. Durability	1.88
5. Low weight	1.53
6. Cost	1.22
7. Appearance (color/model)	0.55
8. Used by champion runners	0.38

*Scale of relative value is from 0 (not important) to 3 (very important).

relative values" is from 0 to 3. A value of 0.0 means that no runner considered this criterion important; a value of 3.0 means that all runners considered this criterion to be very important. It is gratifying to note that a broad group of recreational runners and hobby joggers consider important the same criteria designated as important by the experts.[1] It is noteworthy how little value was placed on the external appearance of the shoes. In this respect, it may be important that a questionnaire reflect the rational behavior of the respondent rather than not assess his emotional or instinctive response.

A possible hypothesis would suggest that the runners having an increased risk of injury select their shoes by criteria other than the accepted, prophylactically favorable ones. The incidence of running injuries was calculated for four of these "dangerous" selection criteria. These were low value placed on "orthopedically correct construction," high value placed on "low weight," "cost," and "appearance (color, model)." Again adjustments were made on the basis of frequency of training interruptions, which make allowances for the number of kilometers run in 1983 and for a positive history of injuries (Table 31–5).

There are no significant differences in the incidence of running injuries. There is even a trend that suggests that the runners who select their shoes on the bases of unusual criteria may have a lower incidence of injuries. It is impossible to define a typical "risk behavior" in the way the individual selection of running shoes is done.

TABLE 31–5.

Frequency of Training Interruptions Due to Running Injuries and Atypical Shoe Selection Criteria in 4,358 Male "Grand Prix" Runners

Shoe Selection Criteria	GP Runners (%)	Interruptions Due to Injuries (%)	No. of km Run in 1983	Positive History for Injuries (%)	Corrected Frequency (%) of Interruption
Orthopedically correct design "unimportant" or "less important"	4.7	16.2	681	10.6	18.5
Low weight "very important"	11.5	17.9	875	12.1	18.8
Cost "very important"	4.3	18.0	849	12.0	19.0
Appearance (color, model) "important" or "very important"	7.3	18.1	734	12.7	19.7

DISCUSSION

The literature emphasizes the prophylactic, protective virtues of the modern running shoe.[1,2] This claim cannot be supported by extensive data collected from a broadly based, large-scale sampling study on average runners. This may be due to the relatively insensitive research methodology that used a relatively crude screen and picked up only a few criteria. It did not include such potentially very important individual criteria as axis deviations in the locomotor system, hyperpronation tendency of the ankle, and ligamentous insufficiency.[1-3, 8] There are no data from other epidemiologic studies that would allow a comparison of our findings with other runner populations. In the few published studies (e.g., reference 5), the running injuries are always defined and analyzed differently. Whether the incidence of running injuries, described in the Berne study, already incorporates the alleged prophylactic protective effects of the modern running shoe cannot be assessed. Two matters appear to be significant:

1. None of the well-known brands shows any advantages as far as running injuries are concerned. The results are unfavorable for one brand (Karhu).
2. Runners who indicate no brand preference and thus, presumably, change brands more frequently are much less frequently put on the sidelines by running injuries.

This finding is contrary to the recommendations of the literature[1] but reminds us of the old runner's rule, according to which using two or more different pairs of running shoes during training was good for the locomotor system. This dictum—even if heard—is unlikely to induce the manufacturers of running shoes to reduce their research and promotional activities to any significant degree.

SUMMARY

The incidence and duration of running injuries observed in more than 5,000 average runners, who participated in May 1984 in a 16-km street race, were described and analyzed as to their possible relationship to the running shoes used. A comparison of the individual brands showed no particular advantages. For one brand the results were unfavorable (more running injuries with a significance of $P<0.05$). Cheaper running shoes were not more conducive to injuries. Expensive shoes have no discernible advantages and appear to be associated with a higher incidence of injury. This relationship should not be taken at face value. In general, the average runner seems to select his shoes on the basis of commendable criteria, but even those who deviate from these criteria have no higher incidence of running injuries.

Acknowledgment

The author wishes to thank R. Rehmann, Ch. E. Minder, and Ch. Liniger for their help with the computer and the word processor.

REFERENCES

1. *Brody, D.H.:* Running injuries. Ciba clin. Symp. 32 (1980), 1–36
2. *Clement, D.B., J.E. Taunton:* A guide to the prevention of running injuries. Aust. Fam. Physician 10 (1981), 154–164
3. *Drez, D.:* Running footwear. Am. J. Sports med. 8 (Symposium) (1980), 140–141
4. *Grant, H.:* Joggitis, Marathonitis and Marathon mania (letter). S. Afr. med. J. 59 (1981), 849–850
5. *Koplan, J.P., K.E. Powell, R.K. Sikes* et al.: An epidemiologic study of the benefits and risks of running. JAMA 238 (1982), 3118–3121
6. *Marti, B., T. Abelin, C.E. Minder:* Relationship of training and life-style to 16 km running time of 4000 joggers (the '84 Berne "Grand-Prix" Study). Submitted
7. *Marti, B., T. Abelin, O. Schoch:* Zur Epidemiologie laufbedingter Beschwerden bei Joggern (Berner Läuferstudie '84). Schweiz. med. Wschr. 116 (1986), 603–608
8. *Segesser, B.:* Ätiologie von Sportverletzungen und Sportschäden. Schweiz. Rdsch. Med. (Praxis) 72 (1983), 1539–1543

Index